Louise FitzGerald is Lecturer in Screen Studies at the University of Brighton.

Melanie Williams is Lecturer in Film Studies at the University of East Anglia. She is co-editor of *British Women's Cinema* (2009).

Exploring a Cultural Phenomenon

Mamma Mia!
The Movie

Edited by **Louise FitzGerald**
and **Melanie Williams**

I.B. TAURIS
LONDON · NEW YORK

Published in 2013 by I.B.Tauris & Co Ltd
6 Salem Road, London W2 4BU
175 Fifth Avenue, New York NY 10010
www.ibtauris.com

Copyright Editorial Selection © 2013 Louise FitzGerald and Melanie Williams
Copyright Individual Chapters © 2013 Caroline Bainbridge, Kate Egan, Louise FitzGerald, Sarah Godfrey, Georges-Claude Guilbert, Sue Harper, Ceri Hovland, I. Q. Hunter, Claire Jenkins, Betty Kaklamanidou, Kerstin Leder Mackley, Deborah Mellamphy, Melanie Williams, Malcolm Womack

The right of Louise FitzGerald and Melanie Williams to be identified as the authors of this work has been asserted by the authors in accordance with the Copyright, Designs and Patent Act 1988.

All rights reserved. Except for brief quotations in a review, this book, or any part thereof, may not be reproduced, stored in or introduced into a retrieval system, or transmitted, in any form or by any means, electronic, mechanical, photocopying, recording or otherwise, without the prior written permission of the publisher.

ISBN   978 1 84885 942 5
eISBN 978 0 75569 866 0
ePDF 978 0 75569 867 7

A full CIP record for this book is available from the British Library
A full CIP record for this book is available from the Library of Congress

Library of Congress catalog card: available

Typeset by Newgen Knowledge Works, Chennai

Contents

Contributors vii
Acknowledgements xi

1. Facing our Waterloo: evaluating *Mamma Mia! The Movie* 1
   Louise FitzGerald and Melanie Williams

2. Everyone listens when I start to sing: gender and
   ventriloquism in the songs of *Mamma Mia!* on
   stage and screen 20
   Malcolm Womack

3. *Mamma Mia!*'s female authorship 37
   Melanie Williams

4. 'See that girl, watch that scene': notes on the star
   persona and presence of Meryl Streep in *Mamma Mia!* 60
   Deborah Mellamphy

5. 'Knowing Me, Knowing You': reading *Mamma Mia!*
   as feminine object 76
   Caroline Bainbridge

6. The power of sisterhood: *Mamma Mia!* as
   female friendship film 94
   Betty Kaklamanidou

7. Embracing the embarrassment: *Mamma Mia!* and
   the pleasures of socially unrestrained performance 109
   Ceri Hovland

8. The same old song? Exploring conceptions of
   the 'feelgood' film in the talk of
   Mamma Mia!'s older viewers 127
   Kate Egan and Kerstin Leder Mackley

9. My, my, how did I resist you? 145
   I. Q. Hunter

10. Not too old for sex? *Mamma Mia!* and
    the 'older bird' chick flick   163
    Claire Jenkins

11. Dancing queens indeed: when gay subtext is
    gayer than gay text   177
    Georges-Claude Guilbert

12. The hero of my dreams: framing fatherhood in
    Mamma Mia!   189
    Sarah Godfrey

13. What does your mother know?
    Mamma Mia!'s mediation of lone motherhood   205
    Louise FitzGerald

14. Afterword: when all is said and done   223
    Sue Harper

Bibliography   228
Index   241

Contributors

Caroline Bainbridge is Reader in Visual Culture at Roehampton University, UK. She is the author of *A Feminine Cinematics: Luce Irigaray, Women and Film* (Palgrave Macmillan, 2008) and *The Cinema of Lars von Trier: Authenticity and Artifice* (Wallflower Press, 2007) as well as co-editor of *Culture and the Unconscious* (Palgrave Macmillan, 2007). She has also published a number of journal articles and book chapters, most commonly on aspects of cinema and gender. She is Director of the Arts and Humanities Research Council (AHRC) Media and the Inner World Research Network (www.miwnet.org).

Kate Egan is Lecturer in Film Studies at Aberystwyth University, UK, and her primary research interests are in the areas of British cinema, horror and genre cinema, cult cinema, film censorship and audience and reception studies. She is the author of *Trash or Treasure?: Censorship and the Changing Meanings of the Video Nasties* (Manchester University Press, 2007) and *The Evil Dead* (Wallflower Press, 2011), and is currently preparing an edited collection (with Sarah Thomas) on cult film stars, entitled *Cult Film Stardom: Offbeat Attractions and Processes of 'Cultification'* (Palgrave Macmillan).

Louise FitzGerald is Lecturer in Screen Studies at the University of Brighton, UK. Her primary research interests are the politics of representation, cultural and race theory, and children in popular culture and she has written articles on these topics. Her PhD, 'Negotiating Lone Motherhood: Gender, Politics and Family Values in Contemporary Popular Cinema', is being prepared for publication.

Sarah Godfrey is Lecturer in Film and Media Studies at the University of East Anglia and City College Norwich, UK. She has articles forthcoming on the resurgent paternalism of American action film and television (co-authored with Hannah Hamad) and is co-editing a book about British film maker Shane Meadows.

Georges-Claude Guilbert is Professor of American Studies at the Université François Rabelais, Tours, France. He is the author of *Carson McCullers: Amours décalées* (1999), *Madonna as Postmodern Myth* (2002), *C'est pour un garçon ou pour une fille?: La Dictature du genre* (2004), and *Après Hanoi: Les Mémoires brouillés d'une princesse vietnamienne* (2011). He is the editor of *Literary Readings of Billy Wilder* (2007) and has published many Gender Studies/Cultural Studies articles. These days he is particularly busy supervising PhD theses on American television series.

Sue Harper is Emeritus Professor of Film History at the University of Portsmouth, UK. She has published widely on British cinema, and her publications include *Picturing the Past: The Rise and Fall of the British Costume Film* (1994), *Women in British Cinema: Mad, Bad and Dangerous to Know* (2000), *British Cinema of the 1950s: The Decline of Deference* (2003, with Vincent Porter), *The New Film History* (2007, with James Chapman and Mark Glancy), and *British Culture and Society in the 1970s: The Lost Decade* (2010, with Laurel Forster). She has also written a range of articles on audience taste. Sue was Principal Investigator of a major AHRC research project on British cinema of the 1970s (www.1970sproject.co.uk), which resulted in her co-authored book with Justin Smith, *British Film Culture of the 1970s: The Boundaries of Pleasure* (2011).

Ceri Hovland is a PhD student at the University of Reading, UK, where she has also taught as a sessional lecturer. Her thesis, 'Analysing Performance in Hollywood Film: Close Analysis and

Epistemological Framing', was funded by a studentship from the Graduate School of Arts and Humanities, University of Reading, and has just been submitted. Her published work includes an article on *The Virgin Suicides,* performance and point of view for the *Journal of Adaptation in Film and Performance* and a chapter on mimesis and narration in *Acting in Moving-Image Culture* (Transaction, 2012).

I. Q. Hunter is Reader in Film Studies and Director of the Centre for Adaptations at De Montfort University, Leicester, UK. He has published widely on British cinema, cult films and adaptation and is currently writing *British Trash Cinema* for the BFI/Palgrave.

Claire Jenkins is Lecturer in Film and Media Communications at Bath Spa University. She was awarded her PhD for her thesis entitled 'Family Entertainment: Representations of the American Family in Contemporary Hollywood Cinema' in 2009. Her research interests include gender, sexuality and the American family, superheroes, and masculinity in *Doctor Who.*

Betty Kaklamanidou is Lecturer in Film History and Theory in the Film Studies Department at the Aristotle University of Thessaloniki, Greece. She is the author of two books in Greek (*When Film Met Literature,* 2006, and *Introduction to the Hollywood Romantic Comedy,* 2007) and she has participated in various international conferences. Her fields of study include film and politics, adaptation theory, genre and gender, and contemporary Greek cinema. In March 2011, she was awarded a Fulbright scholarship to conduct research in the USA during the academic year 2011–12.

Kerstin Leder Mackley is a Research Associate on the interdisciplinary Low Effort Energy Demand Reduction project in the Department of Social Sciences, Loughborough University, UK. She previously contributed as a Research Fellow to the Research Councils UK funded Tales of Things and Electronic

Memory project, School of Engineering and Design, Brunel University. Her general research background lies in audience and reception studies, with a particular focus on people's emotional engagements with the media. Kerstin is a member of the editorial board of *Participations: Journal of Audience and Reception Studies*.

Deborah Mellamphy is a PhD graduate in Film Studies in the School of English, University College Cork (UCC), Ireland. Her thesis is entitled 'Hollyweird: Gender Transgression in the Collaborations of Tim Burton and Johnny Depp'. Her research interests include stardom, performance and gender in Hollywood cinema, television studies and video game studies. She currently teaches several film and literature courses at UCC and is co-editor of the online graduate and early-career researcher journal *Alphaville: Journal of Film and Media Studies*.

Melanie Williams is Lecturer in Film Studies at the University of East Anglia, UK. She has published on British cinema in *Screen, Cinema Journal, Feminist Media Studies, Quarterly Review of Film and Video, Sight and Sound, Film Quarterly* and *Journal of Gender Studies* as well as several edited collections. She is the co-editor of *British Women's Cinema* (Routledge, 2009).

Malcolm Womack is a PhD candidate in the School of Drama at the University of Washington, USA, where he is currently completing his dissertation on Harlem's Cotton Club. He has written for the *Journal of Popular Culture* and *Studies in Musical Theatre*, and has provided entries for *Scribner's Encyclopedia of American Lives* and the *African American National Biography*.

Acknowledgements

Over the last year, a new verb, 'mamma-mia-ing' (def. working on the *Mamma Mia!* book), has unwittingly entered the vocabulary of our families, friends and colleagues. We would like to apologise to all those people who have found themselves adopting this fraudulent verb and thank them for their support during our work on this project. We would also like to thank wholeheartedly all the contributors to the book for their efforts and endeavours, often to very tight deadlines, and the staff at I.B.Tauris for their efficient work in moving this book from initial idea to completed publication. Special thanks also go to Karina Aveyard for providing intriguing information about the Australian reception of the film, of which only a tiny amount could make it into the book, and Eylem Atakav for the customised coffee cups.

The idea to write about *Mamma Mia!* was inspired by many conversations with students, colleagues and friends, most notably with the students from Louise FitzGerald's Media and Cultural Theory seminars and with her PhD supervisior, Professor Diane Negra. Louise would like to thank them all for their insights and encouragement. Most importantly, she wishes to thank her children, Holly, Tim and Millie, for their love, for their continued support, and for the music.

Melanie Williams would like to thank Matthew Bailey for his love, support and childcare beyond the call of duty, and her dad Neil Williams for playing the *ABBA Greatest Hits* (with the intriguing gatefold sleeve), *Super Trouper* and *The Visitors* LPs a lot when she was a kid and getting her hooked on the original music of ABBA. And given the maternal focus of the film under discussion in this book, it seems fitting to take this opportunity to thank her mother and her daughter once again for their love and inspiration.

Finally, we would both like to thank ABBA for the music, and the makers and audiences of *Mamma Mia! The Movie* for giving it to us in new and sometimes surprising ways.

Chapter 2 by Malcolm Womack reworks material that first appeared in "Thank You for the Music": Catherine Johnson's feminist re-voicings in *Mamma Mia!*, *Studies in Musical Theatre*, Vol. 3, Issue 2 (November 2009).

1

Facing our Waterloo: evaluating *Mamma Mia! The Movie*

Louise FitzGerald and Melanie Williams

'Mamma Mia! is not like other films.'[1]

As the remark from critic Ian Nathan quoted above suggests, there appears to be something rather exceptional about *Mamma Mia! The Movie* (Lloyd, 2008). Even those with extensive experience of cinema exhibition recognised the film as something special. In 2011, looking back over a career of nearly 70 years, Bridgewater-based film projectionist Ray Mascord placed *Mamma Mia!* in the illustrious company of classic Hollywood musicals such as *Seven Brides for Seven Brothers* (Donen, 1954), *Oklahoma!* (Zinnemann, 1955) and *Carousel* (King, 1956) as one of a number of the most unforgettable films he had shown. Even in his notably long career, its screening stands out in his memory: 'They sang with the film. I took out the porthole glass and listened to them during the film. At the end, they all applauded.'[2] This rather touching description of this special night out at the pictures in a small British town, culminating in spontaneous applause, manages to evoke something of the atmosphere of the film and the cultural excitement surrounding it. The purpose of this collection of essays is to explore this special-ness in greater depth; precisely how and why *Mamma Mia!* is '*not* like other films'.

Mamma Mia! was exceptional not only in the warm participatory response it elicited from audiences and its enormous commercial success (detailed below), but also in the fascinating variety of reactions, positive and negative, it drew from different commentators and reviewers, many of whom noted the film's distinctive politics of representation and the fact that it gave significant narrative space to characters more frequently marginalised in mainstream cinema. For all these reasons, the film is culturally significant and worthy of serious scholarly attention within Film and Cultural Studies. However, we ought to state at the outset that our desire to examine this film in depth is not motivated purely by glacially objective academic enquiry. This is a film that we have both enjoyed and participated in (at the tops of our voices) and cried at. And this was after having both been distinctly unimpressed by aspects of it on our initial viewing: the amateurish and cringeworthy first 15 minutes; ABBA's wonderful music being covered by over-emoting, less-than-adequate singers; the saccharine nonsense about a girl needing her father to achieve emotional maturity; the marginalisation of Greek characters in a film set in Greece. However, something happened to change our minds, and our shared wish to get to the bottom of this U-turn in our appreciation of *Mamma Mia!* underpins this project.

With hindsight it seems strange, but at the beginning of 2008 the trade press's predicted prospects for *Mamma Mia! The Movie* were not outstanding. It wasn't listed in *Screen International* as one of the 'tentpole' films of its year (those productions that keep the industry's fortunes aloft), unlike *The Dark Knight* (Nolan, 2008), *Hancock* (Berg, 2008) and *10,000 BC* (Emmerich, 2008).[3] When the same publication came to review *Mamma Mia!* in July it anticipated that the film would 'generate revenues for Universal but maybe not "money, money, money"'.[4] Similarly, *Variety* recognised its solid bankability on the strength of being a pre-sold property (an already phenomenally successful stage musical) but predicted a respectable rather than outstanding profit margin (and used the same hackneyed ABBA-related pun to express it): 'Universal should reap reasonable "money, money, money" in all territories'.[5] However, by the end of the year, it was a different story. *Mamma Mia! The Movie* outstripped these modest expectations and the film went on to become the fifth highest grossing film of 2008 worldwide.[6] *Screen International* was forced to eat its words and did a piece on it as one the 'mega-hits' of its year, the top box-office attraction 'in about 15 markets, from Iceland to Germany to South Africa' and also doing well in the Asian markets of Japan and South Korea.[7] In Australia, a country with an honourable heritage of ABBA appreciation, *Mamma Mia!* was the second highest grossing film of its year, earning 31.7 million Australian dollars,[8] but in the UK, *Mamma Mia!* broke domestic box-office records, becoming the highest grossing film ever screened in British cinemas up to that date.[9]

Stories abounded in the trade press about the film's exceptional box-office clout, screenings of it managing to save the oldest cinema in Wales from closure[10] as well as playing a major role in boosting revenues for the British cinema chain Cineworld by 4.4 per cent in 2008.[11] The *Guardian* also made the point that this UK/US co-production was the most profitable British film ever, having earned '£66,995,224 in the UK, knocking *Harry Potter and the Philosopher's Stone* off its perch as the most financially successful British film. *Casino Royale* moves down a place to number three and the top 10 is completed by the other Harry Potter films, *The Full Monty*, *Bridget Jones's Diary* and *Love Actually*.'[12] Even in the USA, traditionally resistant to the charms of ABBA's unique brand of Europop, *Mamma Mia!* still put in a strong showing, ranking as the thirteenth most commercially successful film of 2008, actually beating several of the films that had been regarded as tentpole productions, including *The Chronicles of Narnia: Prince Caspian* (Adamson, 2008), *Valkyrie* (Singer, 2008) and Emmerich's *10,000 BC*.[13] Having netted over US$570 million worldwide by the close of 2008, it had become 'one of Universal's top grossing and most profitable movies ever'.[14] In Britain at least, its success in cinemas has been more than matched by its success in the home entertainment market, where it became the fastest selling DVD ever, again beating *Titanic*'s record, and, by January 2009, it had sold over 5 million copies, meaning a copy was owned by an estimated one in four UK households.[15]

Even considered purely in financial terms, *Mamma Mia!* is a remarkable film, all the more so because it departs significantly from the usual template in recent years for blockbuster success, particularly the appeal to a young, male consumer. Like another surprise mega-hit of 2008, *Sex and the City: The Movie* (King, 2008), *Mamma Mia!* ignored the usual demographic to whom major films are encouraged to address themselves and pitched itself instead at the perpetually overlooked female audience, converting the niche appeal of the 'chick flick' into a new mode of female-centred blockbuster.[16] By contrast, *The Dark Knight*, released in the very same week as *Mamma Mia!*, fitted much more comfortably into the accepted model of male-orientated action narrative, and hence its success was altogether more predictable (and heralded by its strong opening weekend, whereas *Mamma Mia!*'s exhibition and marketing strategy was much more focused on longevity[17]). However, Nolan's film was also endowed with significant cultural capital due to its socio-political critique, auteurist kudos and highly regarded male lead performances; for *Variety*, it was a 'bold, bracing, and altogether heroic reinvention of the iconic franchise. An ambitious, full-bodied crime epic of gratifying scope and moral complexity, this is seriously brainy pop entertainment.'[18] This very positive review actually shared the same page in *Variety* as the rather less effusive review of *Mamma Mia!* ('the storyline plays out more like an oversized ABBA promotional vehicle than a fully dramatic piece'[19]), the two films being the two major releases for that week. But their juxtaposition on the page also provides a wonderful synecdoche for their opposing positions within contemporary popular culture. The illustrative images speak eloquently of their differences, with brooding, noir-ish images of Christian Bale and Heath Ledger in blasted cityscapes on one side of the page juxtaposed with Meryl Streep joyously leading her brigade of dancing queens through a sunny Greek taverna on the other. Obviously, the content of each film determines the content of the publicity stills used to illustrate it, but what seems remarkable about the layout of this one page is its feeling of division: between masculine and feminine; dramatic weight and musical fluff; dark engagement with contemporary reality and ephemeral escape from the same condition; perhaps also critical approval and critical dismissal.

Despite their obvious differences, the two films had something in common: they were based on well-known 'pre-sold' properties, in the case of *The Dark Knight* the comic book hero Batman and with *Mamma Mia!* the phenomenally successful 'jukebox musical' using ABBA's songs, seen by an estimated 45 million theatregoers worldwide since opening in London in 1999.[20] The decision to make a film based on a stage musical fits in with a key trend in contemporary cinema, following in the footsteps of stage-to-screen transfers such as *Phantom of the Opera* (Schumacher, 2004), *Dreamgirls* (Condon, 2006), *Sweeney Todd* (Burton, 2007), *The Producers* (Stroman, 2005) and *Hairspray* (Shankman, 2007), the latter two actually being films-turned-musicals-turned-films-again, indicative of the importance of cross-media flow. *Mamma Mia!* takes its place alongside these films as powerful evidence for the 'return of the Hollywood musical', the genre renaissance spearheaded by the hits *Moulin Rouge!* (Luhrmann, 2001) and *Chicago* (Marshall, 2002), and further consolidated by the global popularity of *High School Musical* (Ortega, 2006) and its sequels and the television series *Glee* (Ryan Murphy/Fox, 2009–).

Various reasons have been suggested for the prominence of the musical during certain periods, with its success in the 1930s inextricably linked with that decade's economic depression. Similarly, the recent revival in the genre's fortunes might be linked to socio-economic conditions, not least millennial financial crisis and the anxieties of the post-9/11 world. According to its director, Phyllida

Lloyd, the stage musical *Mamma Mia!* provided exactly the kind of escapist balm required by those bruised by financial misfortune:

> I met a woman the other day whose business was going belly-up, it was her birthday, she was bursting into tears – and her sister rushed in and said, 'What can we do?' This woman cried out, 'Just take me to Mamma Mia!'[21]

The idea of the musical as tonic, as temporary escape, is a well-worn one, but it applies especially well to the US reception of this Mediterranean fantasy in the immediate wake of 9/11, with the opening of its New York production occurring only a few days after the terrorist attack. Producer Judy Craymer indicates the sense of pride felt by the production team and performers in providing entertainment for the beleaguered city:

> At the opening night were some of the firemen who had been to hell and back. It was wonderful to see all these Irish-American firemen enjoying themselves. One of them turned to me and said 'This is the first time since 9/11 that I've seen my wife smile.'[22]

This same production elicited a fan letter from Meryl Streep after she had seen it with her children, a document treasured by the production team and which would subsequently accrue further significance when the show was finally adapted for the screen with Streep in the central role of Donna. The ramifications of this casting decision, juxtaposing highbrow dramatic kudos and light-hearted physical exuberance (as one critic noted, *Mamma Mia!* 'had Silkwood do the splits'[23]), are discussed in Deborah Mellamphy's chapter in this collection.

However, the positive dimension of feelgood frivolity was not always recognised by reviewers of *Mamma Mia! The Movie* (it was certainly recognised by fans of the film though, as Kate Egan and Kerstin Leder Mackley's chapter in this collection illustrates). Looking at its reception in the UK, there is clear evidence of a critical split, often along the fault line of gender. The *Guardian* reviewer Peter Bradshaw's response to the film, entitled 'Super pooper', remodelled the lyrics to the film's theme song accordingly: 'How on earth could it not – be – shit? One more smirk, and then I knew it would bomb, One more scene and I'd a great need to vom, Oh-woah....'[24] *The Independent*'s Robert Hanks, also indulging in scatological metaphors, thought 'it looked like absolute cack'.[25] Just how far the critical antipathy towards the film might be mapped onto a wider antipathy towards the feminine is indicated by James Christopher's review in *The Times*, in which he refers to Christine Baranski's Tanya as a 'beanpole' and a 'sex-starved sophisticate who munches young men for breakfast' while the 'Dancing Queen' sequence is described in deeply misogynist language as 'a Greek congo of local scrubbers on a barefoot bounce: The sight of these women vamping to *Dancing Queen* on a wobbly wooden pier is a truly terrifying spectacle'.[26] Writing in the same paper a few days later, Melanie Reid offered an entirely different response to the film, praising it as 'an uninhibited, fun, cheesy, hugely tongue-in-cheek women's film'.[27] Her response to the 'Dancing Queen' scene that had revolted and terrified James Christopher was quite different: 'And there was me thinking what fun it would be if I was part of it.' The film was already proving an indisputable popular success, but, according to Reid, a lethal cocktail of snobbery and misogyny prevented many reviewers – especially men – from seeing its worth: 'Never have the posh male critics been marooned higher or drier. They have missed the joke, you see. Almost everyone else in the world it seems – especially women – got it.'[28] This idea is echoed in Caroline Bainbridge's chapter in this collection, in which she discusses *Mamma Mia!* in terms of female communicative exchange.

This feminist-inflected reclamation of *Mamma Mia!* continued in the *Guardian*, home of Bradshaw's scathing 'Super pooper' review, where again it was noted that the film 'got totally panned by male critics, but they just didn't understand it'.[29] In a feature on the film's popularity with female viewers, the opinions of several female public figures were also sought, with often surprising results. Feminist writer and activist Julie Bindel described it as 'a breath of fresh air', which while it was not a feminist text was nonetheless definitely 'a women's film' and 'much better than the way women are usually portrayed'.[30] This was echoed in novelist Jeanette Winterson's response to the film: 'There are so many films where women are sidelined and marginalised, just to turn that around is in itself a political act.'[31] Many of the women interviewed made a direct link between the progressive politics they perceived in the film and the fact that it was written, produced and directed by women. This is an authorial situation still very rare in contemporary cinema, and Melanie Williams' chapter looks at issues of gendered authorship in more detail. However, this kind of feminist 'cheerleading' for the film also came in for some criticism from journalist Catherine Bennet:

> If there really is to be a Mamma Mia! sequel, may we expect one or two small parts for feminists? They have surely earned it. After five months in which it has become the most profitable, most sung-along to, most life-enhancing, generally most record-breaking film and DVD event in British history, it would be understandable if the makers of Mamma Mia! considered additional support from some high-profile feminists to be of little moment. But praise from this unexpected quarter has attracted a fresh audience of the type that never goes to see a critically panned, feel-good musical surpassing silliness performed, exclusively, by people who can't sing, unless a respected feminist has reported that it made her feel happy for the first time ever.[32]

Bennet indicates how the film had become, momentarily at least, a token of exchange in larger debates about feminism, post-feminism and female culture, with feminists seeking to find a point of alignment with 'the common woman' in their shared appreciation of *Mamma Mia!* (and perhaps there is also the worrying suggestion here that the film had to be 'validated' by feminism, and made safe for consumption among the intelligentsia).

But one of the reasons why several female commentators wanted to defend this film in the face of a 'hate-filled' masculine critique undoubtedly has something to do with its unusual prioritising of older women, and Claire Jenkins's chapter in this collection addresses this topic.[33] The pleasure of on-screen recognition might also be seen as the core reason for its appeal to that demographic group; after all, women who are 'north of middle age', in the words of producer Judy Craymer, do not often have films made about them or aimed at them.[34] The juvenile leads Sophie and Sky, played by Amanda Seyfried and Dominic Cooper, are certainly important in the film but more narrative weighting is given to the emotional trajectory of the ingénue's mother, Donna, a role given further dramatic significance by being played by venerated actress Meryl Streep. The romantic resolution that tops off the feelgood film is *her* wedding rather than her daughter's. Sky and Sophie have their love duet 'Lay All Your Love on Me', but most of the musical numbers prioritise the feelings and experiences of the film's mature women. These range from their reawakened sexual desire ('Mamma Mia!', 'Take a Chance on Me'), to their camaraderie and mutual support ('Chiquitita' and 'Dancing Queen') – and the film's evocation of female friendship is the topic of Betty Kaklamanidou's chapter – to the moving expression of the experience of motherhood in 'Slipping through My Fingers' ('Get ready to cry now,' said one woman to her friends when this song began at the screening we attended, clearly already familiar with its emotive power). The connection between *Mamma Mia!* and motherhood – the focus of Louise FitzGerald's chapter – transcended its on-screen representation, with the film being strongly marketed as a 'mum text', especially in relation to the DVD's promotion as the ideal Christmas present or

Mother's Day gift (another sound explanation for its exceptionally large sales figures). *Empire* magazine even sent the mothers of its usual team of critics along to review it, acknowledging that 'what their mothers know' might be a more meaningful barometer of 'the Mia effect' than their own critical appraisal.[35]

However, it is important that the notion of *Mamma Mia!* as feminine text should not become overdetermined. It is worth remembering the significance of the male characters in the film, played by prominent contemporary stars including Pierce Brosnan and Colin Firth, and also that questions surrounding paternity drive the film's narrative, as Sarah Godfrey discusses in her chapter. Also, one must state, male viewers *have* enjoyed this film (see Egan and Leder Mackley's chapter, in which more than one of the self-identifying fans of the film is male). Indeed, one of the obituaries for Pete Postlethwaite recorded that when asked when he had been happiest, the actor answered, 'Last Sunday night in front of the fire, watching Mamma Mia!' with his family.[36] Another dimension of male appreciation of *Mamma Mia!* is evoked in Georges-Claude Guilbert's fascinating account in this collection of his own investment in ABBA's songbook and *Mamma Mia!* as formative queer texts.

In the fervent wish Melanie Reid expressed to be up on the screen joining in with the 'Dancing Queen' parade, she indicated how far *Mamma Mia!* is about not just enjoying the watching of a film but wanting to be part of it in some way. *Mamma Mia! The Movie*, like its theatrical antecedent, offered a wonderful platform for audience participation, especially singing and sometimes dancing along with the ABBA hits liberally sprinkled throughout. As Jane Fryer noted, in her jokily quasi-anthropological investigation into the success of *Mamma Mia! The Movie*, screenings of this film flouted the usual decorum of 'going to the cinema to sit quietly and "Shush!" loudly at anyone rattling sweet wrappers too noisily' and replaced it with the unusual but 'incredibly moving' situation of 'belting out Abba songs with a bunch of strange women and the occasional startled man'.[37] As one 38-year-old female cinemagoer 'almost buried under two great vats of popcorn' testified, joining in was 'the whole point. You become part of it — you're in the chorus, you're on the island, you're at the wedding, you're finding true love... but most of all, you're having a great time.'[38] And this could be expanded into participatory events as vast as the series of 'epic screenings' at the O2 Arena, marketed as 'one of the most uplifting experiences you can imagine'.[39] As I. Q. Hunter notes in his chapter, repeat viewings and audience participation are hallmarks of cult film appreciation and *Mamma Mia!* presents an interesting challenge to 'the masculinity of cult', enforcing a broadening of its horizons to take account of a film that in many ways is an absolute anathema to its macho maverick ethos. The pilgrimage to movie locations that characterises cult film practices is also in evidence in relation to *Mamma Mia!*, with some viewers taking their participatory activity to the next level by modelling their weddings on the one featured in the film.[40]

Any critical account of *Mamma Mia!*'s invitation to participate must recognise the indispensible role played by not only the songbook of ABBA but also the group's wider position in popular culture. *Mamma Mia!* may have been the most successful cinematic outing for ABBA's music to date but it was by no means the Swedish supergroup's first foray into film. In their 1970s heyday they had appeared in their own film, *ABBA: The Movie* (Hallström, 1977), based around their record-breaking Australian concert tour. ABBA's unparalleled popularity in Australia has been explained via a shared position on the periphery of global pop culture; as Björn Ulvaeus noted, both Sweden and Australia were 'way off the main map'.[41] Significantly, Australia would also be the site of ABBA's renaissance in the 1990s as the place of origin for the tribute band Björn Again as well as a number of films such as *The Adventures of Priscilla, Queen of the Desert* (Elliott, 1994), with its ABBA-fixated drag artists, and *Muriel's Wedding* (Hogan, 1994), the first film to use 'I Do I Do I Do' as an unconventional wedding march and to notice the strange symbiosis between the music of Benny and Björn and blushing brides – or blushing grooms in the case of *I Now Pronounce You Chuck and Larry* (Dugan, 2007). In *Muriel's Wedding*, the music of ABBA is used to soundtrack the heroine's initial isolation, sitting alone in her bedroom quietly miming the lyrics of 'Dancing Queen'. But it is also ABBA's music that underpins her ultimate liberation, as she teams up with new best friend Rhonda to deliver a barnstorming performance of 'Waterloo', transcending the bitchy coterie that she had previously tried to fit in with, and finally realising that the vehicle for true happiness is not a lavish wedding but lasting friendship. ABBA provides the perfect theme music for the uncool misfit who eventually triumphs.

Priscilla, *Muriel* and the group Björn Again all share a sense of ABBA as the acme of 1970s kitsch (especially sartorially) while simultaneously sincerely appreciating and celebrating the glorious transcendent quality of their music, which manages to combine unstoppable catchiness with unsuspected musical complexity. Sincere appreciation was also the keynote of the group's Scandinavian cinematic homecoming, with their hit 'SOS' being chosen by Swedish director Lukas Moodysson to conclude his film *Tillsammans/ Together* (Moodysson, 2000). As one of the group's biographers, Karl French, notes, ABBA have undergone 'a dramatic shift in perception, journeying through levels of appreciation – pre-ironic, ironic, post-ironic' until finally becoming 'simply beloved'.[42] However, even back in the 1970s a few early adopters were prepared to take them seriously; at the height of his angry young man stardom Elvis Costello included a cover of 'Knowing Me, Knowing You' in his live sets. In later years ABBA's music has been covered or sampled by artists as diverse as Sinead O'Connor, The Fugees, Westlife and Madonna. There certainly seems to have been a shift in recent years, in Britain at least, from using ABBA as shorthand for 1970s naffness to granting them an elevated position in the pantheon of great pop music. Back in the mid-1990s, Steve Coogan's characterisation of the hopelessly unfashionable television personality Alan Partridge made much of the character's fondness for ABBA, even borrowing one of their song titles for his deliberately dreadful chat show *Knowing Me, Knowing You with Alan Partridge* (BBC, 1994–5). But by the time Coogan came to play a lightly fictionalised version of himself in *The Trip* (BBC, 2010), there was no ironic edge to his love for ABBA, and instead 'Steve Coogan' was full of sincere praise for the dramatic intensity of 'The Winner Takes It All', even unashamedly belting it out while driving along the motorway. This provides a neat illustration of how ABBA songs have been retooled for different purposes at different times and in different texts, the topic addressed by Malcolm Womack's chapter, in which he discusses *Mamma Mia!* writer Catherine Johnson's appropriation of ABBA's music.

As we have already seen, certain quarters of the critical establishment were quick to dismiss the film as cinematic ordure, while others advocated it as latent female liberation. However, there was a third way of approaching the film, characterised by expressions of bemusement and confusion, as with Ian Nathan's dumbfounded enquiry 'What strange alchemy is this? The shoddier it gets, the more appealing it becomes.'[43] The idea that *Mamma Mia!* was capable of enacting a surprising turnaround in critical priorities is also suggested in Jenny McCarthy's review for the *Sunday Telegraph*:

> Just as a mean little scowl was beginning to knit my brows, however, the music kicked in, and Noel Coward was right about the potency of cheap music. In fact, its potency powers the entire film off the ground... what a super trouper Streep is, one suddenly thinks, belting out the hits in a tight, flared satin catsuit; and what a

decent old chap Pierce Brosnan is, with his faltering sincere voice. And there's that thoroughly jolly woman, Julie Walters...creeping up on Stellan Skarsgård with that jerky little comic walk that older people use when approaching the disco floor. The film, eventually, succeeds in its aim of turning the viewer into the equivalent of a benignly uncritical drunk at a big family wedding.[44]

This idea of the film as a special case, not to be approached using the usual critical armoury, recurs in several reviews, often drawing parallels with informal public events that require the kind of 'benignly uncritical' stance recommended by McCarthy, such as a wedding disco, karaoke singalong, 'summery pantomime'[45] or 'playschool nativity performance'.[46] This third category of critical response, hinging not on warm embrace or outright dismissal of the film but on something in between the two, enacts an internal division, at times almost verging on self-destruction. For instance, Mark Kermode's webcast of his review of *Mamma Mia!* sees the critic wrestling, sometimes even appearing to do this physically, with his contradictory reactions to the film. Fully conscious of its many failings ('drunken karaoke'), he nonetheless finds himself enjoying it enormously, and not just in a hackneyed 'so bad it's good' fashion but rather in a way that drastically reorientates his critical priorities and sees him talking about the world being temporarily flipped over, and reaching towards explanatory models from philosophy: 'It's like Cartesian theory!'[47]

Actually, the idea of the film as Cartesian works remarkably well, not least in its grounding in a dualism of mind and body. Intellectually, the viewer may know the film is of questionable quality, but viscerally the reaction is quite different. This is often spoken of in terms of a seduction, with several critics evoking the question in the lyrics of the film's theme song, 'How can I resist you?' (which also provide the starting point of I. Q. Hunter's compelling account of his own changing response to the film).

This idea of *Mamma Mia!* being a film that appeals despite the viewer's better judgement is one that fascinates us, perhaps because the film also seems to have worked its strange magic on us, and this goes beyond glibly wanting to celebrate a guilty pleasure. What is also interesting is how far, having been seduced by the film, there is still a residue of embarrassment about this process having taken place. As Simon Mayo said in response to Mark Kermode's effusive celebration of the film's weird appeal: 'If you love *Mamma Mia!* you have to prove how intelligent you are.' Indeed, that may be why we're working on this book. For the *Mamma Mia!*-refusers, too, embarrassment seems to be the keynote of their response and grounds for its rejection, and of course the film's narrative makes much of the embarrassment faced by Meryl Streep's character when she is forced to confront what she regards as her shameful sexual past. A musical populated by actors with little or no previous singing or dancing experience is almost certain to provide ample grounds for an uncomfortable experience for performer and viewer alike. Indeed, as Stellan Skarsgård states, 'this film is very much about embarrassment',[48] the subject at the heart of Ceri Hovland's chapter in this collection. The willingness to risk humiliation and give it your all may well constitute the source of the film's power, as director Phyllida Lloyd suggests when she speaks of 'the Mamma Mia! spirit' as 'a sort of chaotic roughness. A state of imperfection where anything can happen: you might fall on your arse, or you might jump in the air and do the splits.'[49]

As several contributors to this book discuss, one of the most memorable moments in *Mamma Mia!* is its valedictory coda that sees its main cast members throwing off the shackles of embarrassment and going full tilt at their group rendition of 'Waterloo'; we wanted this collection of essays about the film to have a similarly triumphant send-off, which it does in the shape of Sue Harper's afterword. It's telling that 'Waterloo' should be the song chosen for this jubilant cast farewell, with its lyrics hinging on surrender, both military and romantic, and acceptance of one's fate. 'Let the joy wash over you,' urges the film's publicity campaign, encouraging unquestioning acceptance of its pleasures, and we are aware that in compiling this book in which the diverse components of the film are carefully interrogated we are contravening that basic instruction on how to read this text, namely not to 'read' it at all. Nonetheless, as we suggest in the title of this introduction, *Mamma Mia!* represented a kind of critical Waterloo that needed facing (finally): an immensely popular cultural text that had given rise to an extraordinary variety of personal and critical responses, including our own changing and often contradictory views. What we hope to achieve in this collection of essays is a detailed scholarly investigation of *Mamma Mia! The Movie* that maintains an awareness of the ultimate elusiveness of the text under discussion, and has no desire to shut down debate (or indeed to kill pleasure). Instead we hope to stay true to the ethos of the film, as expounded by Phyllida Lloyd, of applying ourselves to the task in hand with 'maximum seriousness' while always bearing in mind that the un-intellectualised bliss of 'maximum silliness'[50] is just as vital to the film's astonishing appeal.

Notes

1. Nathan, Ian, 'Yo mamma!' *Empire*, January 2009, p. 158.
2. Barkham, Patrick, 'Oh, what a beautiful life in cinema', *Guardian* (G2), 16 February 2011, pp. 2–3.
3. Lodderhose, Diana, 'Hitting the high notes', *Screen International*, 4 January 2008, pp. 22–3.
4. Goodridge, Mike, '*Mamma Mia! The Movie*', *Screen International*, 4 July 2008, p. 21.
5. Mintzer, Jordan, '*Mamma Mia!*', *Variety*, 14 July 2008, p. 36.
6. http://boxofficemojo.com/yearly/chart/?view2=worldwide&yr=2008&p=.htm (accessed 11 April 2011).
7. Mitchell, Wendy, 'Making a mega-hit: the key ingredients', *Screen International*, 7 November 2008, pp. 6–7. A later report confirmed it as 'the number one film of the year in 15 countries including Austria, Germany, the Netherlands, New Zealand, Greece, Hungary, Norway, Portugal, South Africa, Spain, Cyprus, Iceland, Slovenia and Sweden.' Ward, Audrey, '*Mamma Mia!* overtakes *Titanic* as UK's

highest grossing movie', *Screen International*, 16 December 2008, p. 5.
8. *Screen Australia* 2008 box-office data. Thanks to Karina Aveyard for providing this information.
9. Anon., '*Mamma Mia!* rules UK', *Screen International*, 19 December 2008, p. 5. It beat the record set by *Titanic* (Cameron, 1997) but would soon be toppled from that pinnacle by the same director's *Avatar* (Cameron, 2009).
10. Anon., '*Mamma Mia!* saves Welsh cinema', *Cinema Business*, October 2008, p. 7.
11. Anon., 'Cineworld revenues up by 4.4%', *Cinema Business*, January 2009, p. 4.
12. Brown, Mick, '*Mamma Mia!* movie spells money, money, money', *Guardian*, 30 October 2008, p. 12.
13. http://boxofficemojo.com/yearly/chart/?yr=2008&p=.htm (accessed 11 April 2011).
14. Anon., '*Mamma Mia!* rules UK', p. 5.
15. By comparison, the DVD of tentpole film *The Dark Knight* had sold only 1.5 million copies in Britain by the same point. Anon., '*Mamma Mia!* becomes the biggest selling DVD ever!', *What DVD.net*, 1 January 2009. http://www.whatdvd.net/mamma-mia-becomes-the-biggest-selling-dvd-ever-dvd-review-296.html (accessed 11 April 2011).
16. York, Ashley Elaine, 'From chick flicks to millennial blockbusters: spinning female-driven narratives into franchises', *Journal of Popular Culture*, Vol. 43, No. 1, 2010, pp. 3–25.
17. Gant, Charles, 'ABBA hit top note', *Sight and Sound*, September 2008, p. 9.
18. Chang, Justin, 'A "Knight" to remember', *Variety*, 14 July 2008, p. 36.
19. Mintzer, '*Mamma Mia!*', p. 36.
20. The *Mamma Mia!* official website. http://www.mamma-mia.com (accessed 11 April 2011).
21. Hattersley, Giles, 'Mamma mia, there's a fire within Judy Craymer's soul', *Sunday Times* (News Review), 23 November 2008, p. 2.
22. Craymer quoted in Andersson, Benny, Ulvaeus, Björn and Craymer, Judy, *Mamma Mia! How Can I Resist You? The Inside Story of Mamma Mia! and the Songs of ABBA*, London: Phoenix, 2008, p. 220.
23. Nathan, 'Yo mamma!', p. 158.
24. Bradshaw, Peter, 'Super pooper', *Guardian* (Film and Music), 11 July 2008, p. 7.
25. Hanks, Robert, 'Streep meets her Waterloo', *Independent* (Arts and Books Review), 11 July 2008, pp. 8–9.
26. Christopher, James, 'Here we go again', *The Times* (T2), 10 July 2008, p. 16.

27. Reid, Melanie, 'These dancing queens can be high art too', *The Times*, 14 July 2008, p. 22.
28. Ibid., although male critics don't come posher than Derek Malcolm and he rather liked 'the sheer good-natured energy of it all'. 'My, my, how can you resist?', *Evening Standard*, 10 July 2008, p. 41.
29. Naomi Alderman quoted in Cochrane, Kira, 'The mother of all musicals', *Guardian* (G2), 27 November 2008, p. 8.
30. Julie Bindel quoted in Cochrane, 'The mother of all musicals', p. 8.
31. Jeanette Winterson quoted in Cochrane, 'The mother of all musicals', p. 8.
32. Bennet, Catherine, 'My, my, how can I resist you?', *Observer*, 7 December 2008, p. 17.
33. Reid, 'These dancing queens can be high art too', p. 22.
34. Cochrane, 'The mother of all movies', p. 7.
35. Nathan, 'Yo mamma!', p. 159.
36. Bergen, Ronald, 'Obituary: Pete Postlethwaite', *Guardian*, 3 January 2011, p. 32.
37. Fryer, Jane, 'Mamma mania!', *Daily Mail*, 26 December 2008, p. 12. http://www.dailymail.co.uk/femail/article-1101958/Mamma-mania-We-join-chorus-line-phenomenally-popular-film.html#ixzz1MG2dAGRT (accessed 13 April 2011).
38. Ibid.
39. 'Calling all dancing queens to join the biggest party in town: mega Screening of *Mamma Mia! The Movie*.' http://www.theo2.co.uk/general/mega-screening-of-mamma-mia-the-movie.html (accessed 12 April 2011).
40. One report noted how 'Fans of the ABBA inspired film are flocking to book their own marriage on the island of Skopelos.' Campbell, Matthew, 'The *Mamma Mia!* weddings in Greece', *Sunday Times*, 9 August 2009, p. 13. Moreover, a recent British television series, *Nice Day for a Greek Wedding*, has taken this nuptial exodus as its topic: 'In the hope of capturing some of the *Mamma Mia!* magic, some 50,000 Brits lug their fancy threads to Greece every year to marry, and in this new series we'll follow a few of those who want to marry within reach of an ouzo.' http://tv.sky.com/nice-day-for-a-greek-wedding (accessed 25 April 2011). More general tourism to Skopelos, the main location in the film, has also seen a meteoric increase. See Smith, Helena, 'Money, money, money for Greek island as *Mamma Mia!* draws tourist hordes', *Guardian*, 20 December 2008, p. 3.
41. Björn Ulvaeus quoted in Andersson, Ulvaeus, and Craymer, Judy, *Mamma Mia! How Can I Resist You?*, p. 39.
42. French, Karl, *ABBA Unplugged*, London: Portrait, 2004, p. x.

43. Nathan, 'Yo mamma!', p. 158.
44. McCarthy, Jenny, 'Thank god for the music', *Sunday Telegraph* (Seven), 13 July 2008, p. 30.
45. Malcolm, 'My, my, how can you resist?', p. 41.
46. O'Hara, Helen, 'Mamma Mia!', *Empire*, December 2008, p. 32.
47. Kermode's BBC Radio 5 Live review is available via YouTube. http://www.youtube.com/watch?v=61UolzFTVPI (accessed 11 April 2011).
48. Pavia, Will, 'Actors' singing experience? Mostly in the bath', *The Times*, 1 July 2008, p. 4.
49. Nathan, 'Yo mamma!', p. 158.
50. Ibid., p. 159.

2

Everyone listens when I start to sing: gender and ventriloquism in the songs of *Mamma Mia!* on stage and screen

Malcolm Womack

The 1977 film *ABBA: The Movie*, directed by the man responsible for ABBA's music videos, and future Academy Award nominee, Lasse Hallström, follows the Swedish pop group on their phenomenally successful Australian tour. Throughout, the concert and backstage footage of the band is intercut with the fictional storyline of an Australian disc jockey trying vainly to get an interview with the members of ABBA, chasing them across the country and witnessing manic ABBA fandom firsthand. The band is pictured everywhere, always together, with the faces of Agnetha, Benny, Björn and Frida on concert posters, television programmes and a wide range of merchandise, including T-shirts, lunchboxes, pillows and knee socks. There are two moments in the film, though, that make it plain that ABBA is not a wholly equal collective as first presented, and that the women of the group are treated quite differently than the men. At the band's first Australian press conference, Benny and Björn talk on the rigours of touring, the creative process and the Swedish tax code, and yet when Agnetha is asked a question it is to address a recent magazine poll that voted her the star 'with the sexiest bottom'.

Although her stilted English response is good-humoured ('How can I answer to that?' she laughs. 'I haven't seen it.'), it is clear that the apparently all-male press corps sees the men of ABBA as artists and businessmen, but sees the women quite differently. More telling, though, is an expositional moment later in the film when the disc jockey researches the group, sketching out the band's history in voice-over while the film cuts between still photos of the band members and aerial footage of Sweden. 'They live in Stockholm, they have summer houses on the islands,' he says, before discussing their creative process. 'Most songs written together in a small cottage by jamming together,' he adds and the camera swoops over Swedish woods to a small cottage, where through the window we see Benny and Björn sitting at a piano and working on a song – Agnetha and Frida are nowhere to be seen.

Although the women's image is everywhere on the barrage of marketing and merchandise, and they are certainly showcased during concert performances, it is the two men in ABBA – Agnetha and Frida's band mates, then lovers, then spouses and finally ex-husbands – who are responsible for the music, the meticulously crafted pop songs about their partners' complicated romantic journeys. These men, Benny and Björn, had written songs for their wives to sing about what it was like to be a woman, and more significantly, what it was like to be a woman in love with Benny and Björn. In using these songs for the musical *Mamma Mia!* however, and placing these lyrics in the mouths of dramatic characters as constructed by the playwright rather than well-known pop stars as constructed by their audience, librettist Catherine Johnson has often subverted their original lyrical meanings. In popular music the lyrics are frequently of secondary importance to the music and the experience of audiences when they confront these lyrics in the theatre, when the words come from new voices and take on a new significance, when the familiar is made strange. An audience encountering this music in the theatre rather than on the radio brings an entirely different set of expectations to the songs, and Johnson's dramatic strategies of re-gendering the singers and placing the songs in a narrative context profoundly changes how these songs are received and understood. The music of ABBA was written by men to be sung by women, a ventriloquial undertaking that is fundamentally changed when the songs are repurposed by a woman, sometimes to be sung by men. This act of Brechtian alienation from the familiar – in the case of the ABBA songbook, the incredibly familiar – lets the audience that remembers the Swedish supergroup fondly, and that ascribed to their songs a level of authenticity based on the band's well-known personal history, revaluate the lyrics and question the gender constructs inherent in the music and images of the popular band. By looking at how the music of ABBA was received by listeners during the height of the band's popularity, and how the music has been repurposed for the stage, we can see that Johnson and the creative team of *Mamma Mia!* have done more than trade on a kitschy image and catchy music to create a blockbuster jukebox musical; they have fundamentally re-imagined the lyrical content of the ABBA songbook, reconstructing some questionable songs and subverting ABBA's ideas of gender in order to create a surprisingly feminist piece of theatre.

Popular music scholar Simon Frith uses the texts of popular songs to ask the important postmodern question of authorship and ownership: whose 'voice' is there and who is talking?[1] For those few who read the music sheet, clearly the authorial voice belongs to the songwriter. Far more common, however, are those who encounter popular music in its intended mode, by listening to the songs, and then the authorial voice changes. 'Whose voice do we hear now? Again there's an obvious answer: the singer's, stupid! And what I argue,' he concludes, 'is that this is, in fact, the stupid answer.'[2] Stupid or not, it is the answer that most listeners immediately jump to, as the performer's musical skills and emotive ability and the indefinable interplay between the singer's body, the text of the song and the interpretation of the material create a direct communicative experience between singer and listener, with the songwriter seemingly absent. And, when the private life of the celebrity singer mirrors (at least in the public imagination) the lyrical content of the song, the idea that the song is direct communication from the honest voice of the performer gains traction. Frank Sinatra's anthemic 'My Way' is such a case, an assertive statement of self, and any listener even slightly familiar with Sinatra's life can easily read an authentic address into the lyrics about personal triumph over public disapprobation. The fact that 'My Way' was written by Paul Anka, and has been performed by singers as diverse as Elvis Presley and Sid Vicious, is irrelevant to fans of Sinatra – to them, 'My Way' is Frank's song; his is the authorial voice. Frith writes,

> In pop, biography is used less to explain composition (the writing of the song) than expression (its performance): it is in real, material singing voices that the 'real' person is to be heard, not in scored stylistic or formulaic devices.
> ... it is the performing rather than the composing voice that is to be taken as the key to character.[3]

The argument that the listener ascribes elements of biography to the singer rather than to the songwriter is particularly relevant with the musical canon, and personal biographies, of ABBA. ABBA was formed by two sets of couples, Agnetha Fältskog and Benny Andersson, and Björn Ulvaeus and Anna-Frid "Frida" Lingstad (the band name ABBA being an acronym of their first names). This idea of a foursome with matching romantic relationships was a significant part of how the band represented itself – their personal commitments to one another were part of their wholesome image (*ABBA: The Movie* features a number of older Australians who praise the band for being 'clean') and one of the books from the 1970s that was quickly published in the wake of this highly marketable pop phenomenon was titled *ABBA: The Lovers Whose Music Conquered the World*. Their merchandise featured either the band's logo or all four of their faces, their videos emphasised group togetherness (whether walking in the woods, lounging at a picturesque Swedish cabin or pretending to be gradeschoolers taking classes together) and their wardrobe onstage and in photographs was garishly unified.

Although the merchandising treated them equally, the women were more prominent than the men in the public imagination. They sang the lead on most of the band's songs, creating the immediate relationship with listeners that comes from direct linguistic communication with charismatic lead singers, and with the sole exception of 'Does Your Mother Know', which charted at number 4 in the UK and featured Björn's only solo vocals, all of the 19 ABBA singles that broke into the top ten in the US or UK charts were sung by the women. They were also easily distinguishable from one another, in both physical appearance and temperament – tall, brunette, flamboyant Frida and the smaller, blond, reclusive Agnetha – as opposed to the less distinctive men – Björn, who had a beard, and Benny, who didn't (although he would grow one himself after a few years, rendering the men even more indistinguishable). With a band like ABBA, which had such a definite visual style, appearances mattered. For some, Agnetha and Frida were ABBA. In numerous ABBA parodies, such as those by the men of the sketch show *Little Britain* or the comedy team of French and Saunders, it is the women who are most easily impersonated and take prominence, and in the queer synthpop band Erasure's drag homage for their album *ABBA-esque*, there are no stand-ins for Benny and Björn at all. But even though the women are the most immediately recognisable members of ABBA, during the height of the band's popularity they never broke free from the group entirely. In 1974, Agnetha began making a solo album as, unlike Frida, she was a songwriter herself, although only one of her songs was ever recorded by ABBA ('Disillusion', from their first album). Her project, 'Elva Kvinnor I et Hus' ('Eleven Women in One House'), was an ambitious undertaking. Each song on the album was meant to be from the perspective of a different woman, and the album was planned to have a fold-out cover that gave brief biographies of each of these fictional women alongside the lyrics. Her collaborator, Swedish writer Bosse Carlgren, greatly enjoyed the process of writing with the pop star. 'When she sang as a young teenager it was so heartfelt,' he said in an interview. 'You could say it was not the highest quality lyrics maybe, but the girl's heart and soul was in it.'[4] Agnetha's original plan of writing various women's songs in various women's voices was scuttled by her producers, however, who understandably wanted her to capitalise on the success of ABBA and convinced her to open the album with a Swedish-language version of the ABBA hit 'SOS'. Although she would later record ABBA's 'That's Me' as a solo artist, at this point in her career, according to Carlgren, Agnetha 'wanted it to be her own music through and through'; however, the financially sensible addition of a proven ABBA hit for the opening track put an end to her original thematic concept.[5] Carlgren remembered a deflated Agnetha finishing the project without her earlier enthusiasm, busy with endless publicity and recording new songs with ABBA, as she returned to singing the songs that her husband wrote for her.

As the marriages within the band failed, any lyrical content about heartache and separation was understood by listeners through the kind of autobiographical lens outlined by Frith. This ascribed a personal authenticity to these songs that was absent from others. There were other musical acts made up of romantic partnerships whose histories followed through unions and break-ups, but in both practice and public understanding they were quite different from ABBA. The tumultuous relationships inside Fleetwood Mac, for example, or the seminal punk band X were chronicled in their music, and the followers of both bands were inclined to interpret the songs through their understandings of the personalities within the groups. Although it is hard to imagine two more different singers, in terms both of style and of presence, than the ethereal gypsy-skirted Stevie Nicks and the earthy, tattooed Exene Cervenka, both women positioned themselves and were understood by their fans very differently than the women of ABBA. Cervenka and Nicks (as well as Nicks' band mate Christine McVie, also undergoing well-publicised romances and separations) were songwriters themselves, with control over their music and how they chose to express love, loss and womanhood. These bands had their own followers tracking the personal lives of the band members, and they were aware which songs were written by whom (especially as these bands shared lead vocals between their male and female members far more often than ABBA). Agnetha and Frida had no such control. Both of those other bands, as well, were amalgamations of disparate personalities and styles, while ABBA was again a more homogeneous collective, four wholesome Swedes in ridiculous matching outfits. Listeners understandably believed that Agnetha and Frida's melancholy songs of failed love were their authentic feelings, rather than the lyrical constructions of their ex-husbands.

'Everyone danced to Abba,' wrote Judy Craymer, the producer of *Mamma Mia!*, 'but no one really listened to the lyrics.'[6] This is understandable, given both Benny and Björn's mastery at crafting pop music and their lack of interest in writing lyrics for female singers in their second language. Björn told an interviewer, 'In the beginning, the lyrics didn't have much meaning for us. They were just a few clichés put back to back to give the girls something to sing.'[7] Benny disagreed, praising the insight and gender sensitivity of his writing partner, saying, 'Björn has written a lot of lyrics that fit really well with women. It's like he has a sense of what it is like being a woman. And I hear this from women as well.'[8] Popular music traditionally does strive to capture universal feelings of romance and separation, and while the trope of pining for love is common in pop music, in ABBA it is taken to an extreme, with the women positioned as desperate and powerless without their men. Their breakout hit was, after all, a song comparing falling in love with literal military surrender. The women of the ABBA songbook, as written by Benny and Björn, performed by Agnetha and Frida and understood as authentic expressions of self by their audiences, were, behind the glamour of pop stardom, somewhat pathetic creatures. They were often infantilised, as in the fairy tale references of 'I Have a Dream', the schoolgirl imagery of 'When I Kissed the Teacher' and lyrics such as 'I'm a bashful child beginning to grow' from 'The Name of the Game'. They were drudges, singing 'I'm nothing special / In fact, I'm a bit of a bore' in 'Thank You for the Music', and cataloguing the miserable banalities of single life in 'The Day before You Came'. They were desperate for a man in 'Gimme Gimme Gimme (A Man after Midnight)', desperate in the face of losing a man in 'SOS' and ridiculously ecstatic when they finally have him in 'I Do, I Do, I Do, I Do, I Do'. Indeed, the most empowered female character comes from arguably their most famous song, 'Dancing Queen', and her power comes from her ability to 'leave them burning' with her teenage sexuality. She is also described entirely in the second person, which is flattering to the listener but heightens the fact that when strong women appear in ABBA's lyrics, they tend to be someone the singers can only describe and never truly become. The female singer is frequently positioned as unexceptional at best and pathetic at worst, incapable of action or self-improvement, and only given purpose by the intervention of a benevolent man.

Staging the songs

Mamma Mia! turns that dynamic on its head by telling the story of a mother who takes men on her own terms and a daughter who learns to do the same, and subverting the audience's relationship with the music of ABBA to emphasise the point. *Mamma Mia!* is a jukebox musical, and the inherent pleasures of this sub-genre remain for theatre-goers — realising the depth of a particular artist's songbook, hearing half-forgotten numbers from lesser albums, and experiencing that moment when the opening bars or opening lyrics are recognised by an audience, immediately followed by murmurs of acknowledgement and surprise throughout the theatre, which in turn is followed by the audience's laughing at the recognition of their shared experience. But unlike the spate of jukebox musicals that preceded and followed it, *Mamma Mia!* fundamentally reinterprets the musical songbook of the featured artist. By placing these songs in the mouths of dramatic characters rather than the publically constructed personalities of Agnetha and Frida, and in a dramatic narrative rather than the self-containment of the songs themselves, these songs communicate with the audience quite differently. *Mamma Mia!*'s opening number, 'I Have a Dream', doesn't change all that much; it is a fairy tale of a song, staged like a fairy tale as a young woman literally wishes on the stars. But having it sung by the ingénue, Sophie, rather than the celebrity, Agnetha, changes everything. Sophie is a young woman seeking to define herself by men (an absent father and a fiancé seemingly straight from a romance novel — Sky, the young financial executive who has left his successful career in the city to rediscover himself in the waters of the Mediterranean), and this song comes at the start of her journey of self-discovery. Rather than a song that infantilises the then-29-year-old international celebrity Agnetha, it becomes one that heightens the youth and immaturity of the sheltered 20-year-old ingénue Sophie.

'Thank You for the Music' is Benny and Björn's ultimate song of vertriloquial self-congratulation, and perhaps the most problematic song in ABBA's canon. The first lines in this song written by a husband for his wife talk about being 'nothing special' and 'a bit of a bore', an embarrassing diminishment that leads into the chorus that has her proclaim her gratitude for the songs assigned to her. It is a swelling anthem, what Benny described as a song where 'you can easily imagine Vera Lynn leading a sing-along of "Thank You for the Music" during the London blitz'.[9] ABBA closed out their live performances with this song in a fashion more reminiscent of a theatrical curtain call than a rock show encore, standing with all their backup musicians in a line at the stage apron and singing out to the audience. It is easy to imagine the audience flattered into thinking that it was they whom the pop superstars were thanking, perhaps for somehow inspiring the band's music. ABBA, though, was notoriously uninterested in live performance, despite the massive audience turnout. In a 2009 article for the *Sunday Times*, Björn wrote, 'I remember well the time Benny Andersson and I found we were no longer forced to go on tour and play to often uninterested audiences to pay the rent.'[10] It isn't the audiences that Benny and Björn are having their wives thank; it is themselves. Johnson repurposes 'Thank You for the Music' into a statement of gratitude from daughter to mother. Using the early lyric 'Mother says I was a dancer before I could walk / She says I began to sing long before I could talk', and with the play's central dramatic conflict being the relationship between Sophie and her mother, Johnson re-appropriates a text of self-gratitude into one of maternal gratitude, changing the surface meaning of the song from nebulous to specific, and the authorial meaning of the song from patriarchal and ventriloquial to matriarchal and sincere.

Donna's songs are more straightforward, with this character's worldly wisdom playing the foil to her daughter's naivety. They mostly take ABBA's lyrics at face value, whether expressing financial woes ('Money Money Money'), surprise ('Mamma Mia!') or melancholy about lost love ('The Winner Takes It All'). She has one song, though, 'Super Trouper', that receives a matriarchal intervention from the playwright. About this number, essentially a love song to a lighting fixture, Björn says simply, 'to write a song about a spotlight was not easy'.[11] Johnson stages the song at Sophie's bachelorette party, as Donna and her friends Rosie and

Tanya recreate their pop band, Donna and the Dynamos. The band is clearly meant to evoke ABBA through their ridiculous ABBA-esque outfits and, of course, by singing one of ABBA's songs, but unlike the Swedish group, Donna's band is apparently composed entirely of the three women. Although creating characters who were in a band seems like an obvious choice for the writer of a jukebox musical and an easy way to justify the performance of certain expected songs, this is the only performance within the world of the play, the only time characters sing on a stage within the stage. The inherent ridiculousness of the song is played up in this moment, with the onstage audience enjoying the song ironically, serving as a hint to those beyond the footlights that they should as well. This is the moment in *Mamma Mia!* that informs the audience that they are under no obligation to take the music of ABBA seriously and that the musical is a reinterpretation, not a straight-faced attempt to imbue the audience with a newfound appreciation of or reverence for their source material.

ABBA's lyrics for 'Super Trouper' tell of the gruelling life of a travelling pop star and how much she looks forward to her tour ending, but tonight she is re-energised, knowing that her man is in the audience: 'somewhere in the crowd there's you'. When repurposed for *Mamma Mia!*, the 'you' seems altered. The object of the song is no longer a concert-going lover whom the singer is overjoyed to see (a staple of female pop songs, and always a flattering fantasy for male fans in the audience); rather, within the context of the play, this is a song from mother to daughter. Silly though this song is, in the hen party context of the play Donna literally sings this song to Sophie, embuing it with an implication of happy days in Sophie's infancy when the stress of touring was mitigated by maternal love, changing the sole joy in the singer's dreary life from a relationship with her man to a relationship with her daughter.

The greatest transformations of the ABBA songbook occur when Catherine Johnson changes the gender of the singers. In much popular music, lyrics are often seen as relatively unimportant when compared with the style and structure of the music itself, and something to be careful of if, like ABBA, you are hoping to attract an international audience.[12] Indeed, Elisabeth Vincentelli argues that 'one of the reasons ABBA was popular everywhere was that its lyrics were as plain as its melodies were complex. ... They were immediately accessible for anyone to whom English is a second language.'[13] Lyrics may have been a secondary concern for Benny and Björn, particularly in the early days of ABBA when their goal was to craft pop hits in a second language, but in musical theatre lyrics carry a great deal of weight. They serve as inner monologues, they advance the plot and they provide a direct communication between character and audience. A musical theatre audience tends to pay greater attention to the lyrics in the songs, while a popular music listener might ultimately be more interested in a song's rhythm, melody and beat. The songs of ABBA may be quite familiar to the audience, but seated in the theatre, experiencing them in a new format, the audience is receiving them in a wholly different way, one that forces them to engage with the text differently and to pay closer attention. This process is heightened in *Mamma Mia!* when a male voice sings a recognisable woman's song. Lyrics sung in close harmony by Agnetha and Frida in songs heard by the audience countless times before, songs that they have come to associate with a certain degree of female authenticity, become something unfamiliar when sung by a lone baritone. This process forces the audience to experience something of a Brechtian distanciation, a *Verfremdungseffekt*. This word has been variously translated and understood, but essentially refers to the performative effect of making the familiar strange in order to cause an audience to re-evaluate their assumptions about what they took for granted. Brechtian scholar Sarah Bryant-Bertail offers the useful addendum that 'this does not mean simply erasing old modes and inventing new ones, but rendering even old ones newly apparent'.[14] In this case, it is the well-known hits of ABBA that are rendered strange and different, and the assumptions the audience is positioned to confront are the way gender is constructed through the lyrics, both in the world onstage and in the older mode of the 1970s, and the familiar hit songs of ABBA.

'SOS' was ABBA's first hit single after winning the Eurovision Song Contest with 'Waterloo', and even though Björn admits that 'the lyric perhaps is still not the best' it fits nicely into the recurring theme of Agnetha and Frida as powerless, confused and reliant on the love of a man.[15] They are literally women in distress, hopeless without love and despairingly asking 'when you're gone how can I even try to go on?', and the song builds to the titular distress signal of the chorus. Re-imagined as a duet between a man and a woman, the uncertainty and panicked desperation is diffused and shared: it is no longer just a woman spiralling out of control; it is a shared gender-neutral experience. Likewise, ABBA's sophisticated 'Knowing Me, Knowing You' (excised from the film) is now sung by a man, and expressions of loss that are in keeping with the usual sorts of lyrics Benny and Björn wrote for their wives ('Walking through an empty house, tears in my eyes') are transformed by having an onstage baritone rather than the melancholy Agnetha express them.

'Lay All Your Love on Me', as the title suggests, follows many of the tropes of a pop love song, although the singer's sexual obsession is certainly unhealthy. The declaration to her lover that 'everything is you' feels like a harmless exaggeration, but when she follows it by talking about her fear when her man isn't near, her lack of pride and her overweening jealousy, she is positioned as co-dependent and absolutely irrational. This is part and parcel of how Agnetha and Frida are represented in the music of ABBA, but by re-gendering the song into a declaration from Sky to his fiancée these sentiments are called into question. They may be interpreted by the audience as a statement of unqualified love and support, much in keeping with Sky's role as a storybook hero whose life revolves around his beloved. Throughout it all, though, Sky is undercut onstage by the sight of the backup singers, a chorus line of dancing scuba divers, making his protestations of love wildly joyful but also tremendously immature, and ultimately ridiculous.

Screening the songs

In the film, 'Lay All Your Love on Me' becomes a duet, swapping the desperation of ABBA and the masculine reversal of Sky in favour of a song where beautiful young people affirm their love, with a shirtless and muscular Sky (Dominic Cooper) and a swimsuit-clad Sophie (Amanda Seyfried) crawling towards him on all fours. The dancing snorkellers appear briefly, and have a few moments of posing and comedic dancing, but the camera then quickly cuts to shots of the well-toned Sky jet-skiing. The impact onstage is greatly different. In film, the director by necessity controls an audience's gaze, in this case from the lovers to the clowns, who are quickly dismissed in favour of the lovers at a romantic sunset, whereas the theatrical audience chooses where to focus, aware that the young couple protesting exuberant love are literally being upstaged by the mocking dancers. The film audience is given only one image at a time, whereas the audience for a theatrical production is given several disparate images, causing them to shift focus and read the elements of the scene in communication with one another. The *Verfremdungseffekt* in moments like these is negated on film, something director Phyllida Lloyd makes explicit in the DVD commentary with her half-joking references to 'movie magic' as her explanation for the construction of a seamless filmic world where the audience is left with an image that has been provided of the attractive young lovers at sunset, rather than allowing them to decipher the staged spectacle of young lovers and ridiculous chorus boys. Other moments of gender reversal and lyrical re-appropriation are changed for the movie. 'Thank You for the Music' is played over the closing credits, signalling a return to ABBA's self-congratulation as a now disembodied Sophie sings her gratitude as the names of the cast and crew scroll by. Donna (Meryl Streep) is no longer being thanked; the Universal production team is. The song 'When All Is Said and Done' is added to the film, and although it works to position Sam (Pierce Brosnan), who stands at the head of the wedding table, leading the company in song, in something of a patriarchal role, ABBA's original female-voiced acceptance of a relationship's end here changes temporality as well as gender, as Sam now sings it as a reflection on his past with Donna rather than a statement about current romantic dissolution.

Mamma Mia!'s gender swapping also works in the other direction, with a woman taking one of the few men's songs from the ABBA canon. When Benny or Björn took lead vocals, it was usually in songs about sexual control, where the man is positioned as an object of desire rather than an object desperate to be desired and where the sexual come-ons are assertive rather than desperate. For a band not often associated with machismo, 'Rock Me' hits all the common rock and roll tropes of a man promising to 'teach you how to rock all night'. 'Honey Honey' has the men responding to the women's enthusiastic praise of their sexual prowess by warning them not to get too attached, and 'Does Your Mother Know' portrays the male singer as an object of teenage lust – in a way, the flip side of 'Dancing Queen' – where the man is the object of the advances of a sexually adventurous young girl who, despite being 'so hot', must be rebuffed. It is 'Does Your Mother Know' that gets repurposed for *Mamma Mia!,* with Donna's middle-aged friend Tanya (Christine Baranski) singing it as a dismissal of an unimpressive would-be Lothario. While Pepper (Michael Philip), a comic figure in the play, makes aggressive passes at her, Tanya uses her confidence and sexual power roundly to mock him, both through choreography (by mimicking and exaggerating his dance moves) and through a re-gendered understanding of the lyrics. 'Does your mother know that you're out?' was intended as a playful question when a man asked it, a flirtation, but when a woman asks the same question it becomes simply emasculating. Giving this song to a woman, and an older woman at that, changes the dynamic of the relationship between the singer and the object, and the unfamiliarity the audience experiences by having a woman's voice singing a man's song calls into question the sexual politics of the original. Rather than the flip side of 'Dancing Queen', the female singer Tanya, who herself has 'left them burning' before ultimately rejecting her potential paramour, has done what Agnetha and Frida were unable to do and become the Dancing Queen herself.

Ultimately, *Mamma Mia!*'s greatest cultural impact may be that it has given a new generation a completely different way to listen to the music of ABBA. This is no small accomplishment. Much as ABBA was a global success in the 1970s and 1980s, with numerous hit singles and album sales that rank fourth all-time (only surpassed by the Beatles, Elvis Presley and Michael Jackson), *Mamma Mia!* on both stage and screen has been massively popular in the 1990s and 2000s. The stage musical has been translated into well over a dozen languages, it has broken box office records in several countries and, as of writing this in 2011, there are seven professional productions of *Mamma Mia!* staged every day throughout the world. While older viewers of the show re-engaged with ABBA's songs in a new way, the immense popularity – indeed the ubiquity – of *Mamma Mia!* ensures that, for younger listeners, these songs, among the most popular in the world, have been distanced from Agnetha and Frida and are now bound to Donna and Sophie.

Notes

1. Frith, Simon, *Performing Rites: On the Value of Popular Music*, Cambridge, MA: Harvard University Press, 1996, pp. 183–4.
2. Ibid.
3. Ibid., p. 185.

4. De Hart, Jeffrey, 'Interview with Bosse Carlgren', *Agnetha Fältskog Worldwide Fan Club*, 12 February 1998. http://www.carlgrens.info/htmlfiles/lyricsfiles/jefffey4th.html (accessed 5 January 2011).
5. Ibid.
6. Backcover of Andersson, Benny, Ulvaeus, Björn and Craymer, Judy, *Mamma Mia! How Can I Resist You? The Inside Story of Mamma Mia! and the Songs of ABBA*, London: Phoenix, 2008.
7. Potiez, Jean-Marie, *ABBA: The Book*, London: Aurum Press, 2003, p. 232.
8. Ibid., p. 112.
9. Ibid., p. 64.
10. Ulvaeus, Björn, 'Filesharing is defended by gigging performers, but who pays the songwriter?', *Sunday Times*, 12 September 2009, p. 12.
11. Andersson, Ulvaeus and Craymer, *Mamma Mia! How Can I Resist You?*, p. 98.
12. Hesmondhalgh, Damian, 'Cultural imperialism', in *Continuum Encyclopedia of Popular Music of the World. Volume 1, Media, Industry and Society*, New York: Continuum, 2003, p. 197.
13. Vincentelli, Elisabeth, *ABBA Gold*, New York: Continuum, 2004, pp. 89–90.
14. Bryant-Bertail, Sarah, *Space and Time in Epic Theater: The Brechtian Legacy*, Rochester, NY: Camden House, 2000, p. 15.
15. Andersson, Ulvaeus and Craymer, *Mamma Mia! How Can I Resist You?*, p. 28.

3

Mamma Mia!'s female authorship

Melanie Williams

With the victory of Kathryn Bigelow in the category of Best Director, the 2010 Academy Awards ceremony witnessed the long-awaited dismantling of one of the last remaining symbolic barriers to women's full participation in the film industry. It seemed entirely fitting that it should have been Bigelow who finally broke the all-male lineage, given her prominent position in discussions of female film authorship, both inside and outside academia. For Deborah Jermyn and Sean Redmond, she is a 'Hollywood transgressor', defying expectations about suitable projects for women film-makers, focusing instead on male-dominated drama replete with taut action sequences, as in her Oscar-winning *The Hurt Locker* (2008).[1] However, other critics have suggested that Bigelow's unusual specialism in traditionally masculine genres may be less progressive than it initially appears. For Martha P. Nochimson, the high critical esteem in which Bigelow is held stems precisely from her eschewal of feminine modes in a climate that denigrates cultural production aimed at and associated with women: 'Looks to me like she's masquerading as the baddest boy on the block to win the respect of an industry still so hobbled by gender-specific tunnel vision that it has trouble admiring anything but film-making soaked in a reduced notion of masculinity.'[2] Hence Bigelow's work is far more easily recuperated within a phallocentric film establishment than the work of some her female peers whose films may enjoy greater commercial success but whose chosen genres, commonly perceived as feminine ones, rank much lower in an unspoken hierarchy of taste. As Nochimson argues:

> the outsize admiration for [Bigelow's] masterly technique and the summary dismissal ... of directors like Nora Ephron and Nancy Meyers reveal an untenable assumption that the muscular filmmaking appropriate for the fragmented, death-saturated situations of war films is innately superior to the technique appropriate to the organic, life-affirming situations of romantic comedy ... why the general opinion that Ephron and Meyers aren't up to much because they don't use hand-held cameras and flashy cuts?[3]

Many female directors are perceived as figures of lesser importance not only because of their chosen cinematic style but also because they fail to fulfil the requirements of being a marketable auteur, crucial within contemporary cinema culture. Thinking of this new emphasis on the director-as-celebrity, both Pam Cook and Yvonne Tasker have used Kathryn Bigelow as a case study for examining how the female film director, still the exception to the general rule, is represented visually and figuratively. Tasker notes a tension between different kinds of visibility afforded to Bigelow as a hard-boiled action director but one of atypical gender: 'If her films are "unladylike", portraits that parade a sultry if not aggressive "femininity" invariably accompany profiles of the filmmaker.'[4] Meanwhile Cook describes the balancing of androgyny and femininity in a widely circulated publicity image of Bigelow from the 1990s depicting the director 'wearing a dark jacket over a white shirt, leaning back slightly, with hands in pockets, looking coolly into camera, almost as if this were a fashion shot. A camera eyepiece is worn as a necklace – a touch of irony which comments on both her gender and her professional status.'[5] Even when Bigelow finally enjoyed her Oscar victory, significant attention was paid to her sartorial choices on the night as well as the fact she triumphed against her ex-husband, James Cameron.

As both Cook and Tasker suggest, the presentation of the persona of the director resonates in particular ways if the director in question is a woman, and in such promotional discourses we can discern what Tasker calls the 'distinct articulation of the (still atypical) agency of women filmmakers with respect to discourses of femininity and creativity'.[6] Whereas the model of the maverick auteur beloved by film buffs actually maps onto Bigelow's career and persona fairly neatly, it proves far harder to apply to many other women directors, to the obvious detriment of their visibility and status.

Kathryn Bigelow's Oscar win may just have been the most publicly prominent expression of burgeoning female power in Hollywood – although it is vital to remember that there is still a lot of ground to cover before anything even resembling parity is achieved. In 2008, the year of *The Hurt Locker*'s first release, other female directors enjoyed prominent success: Catherine Hardwick's franchise-founding *Twilight* ranked as the seventh highest-grossing film of the year in the USA, while Anne Fletcher's romcom *27 Dresses* was also a notable hit.[7] As a gothic teenpic and a light-hearted romance respectively, Hardwick's and Fletcher's films fit much more readily into expectations about women's 'natural' cinematic talents than the machismo and auteurism of Bigelow's vision. This might also be said of *Mamma Mia! The Movie*, another hugely successful film of that year, which boasted not only a female director in Phyllida Lloyd but also a female screenwriter (Catherine Johnson) and female producer (Judy Craymer), providing strong evidence for the growing eminence of women in contemporary film-making. In Judy Craymer's words, she, Johnson and Lloyd were 'the tribe of women'[8] who had overseen the enormously successful stage musical and, despite their lack of feature film experience, were essential for its successful translation to the screen. This close-knit female group would also prove essential to the marketing of the film, with a strong link forged between the on-screen group of three female friends and their behind-the-scenes equivalents, as Craymer suggests: 'The studio was promoting the three of us as this trio. They saw us as the women and it was, for me, nearly 20 years of my life. That was the story to tell.'[9] It was as a triumvirate that Lloyd, Craymer and Johnson won their ITV Achievement of the Year prize at the 2008 UK Women in Film and Television awards, a less prominent win than Bigelow's perhaps but still worthy of note. Indeed, one of the most striking things about *Mamma Mia*'s authorship is the way it is repeatedly represented as a tripartite structure, going beyond the usual straightforward equation of authorship solely with the director.

In this chapter, I wish to apply to *Mamma Mia! The Movie* some of the ideas that have circulated historically and continue to circulate around gender and film authorship and how female film-makers are envisioned and evaluated. This film problematises traditional notions of film authorship not only because it is female-directed but also because it is clearly assigned to a creative conglomerate rather than an individual. Using publicity material, press coverage and ancillary DVD documentaries and commentaries (those notable 'auteur machines' of contemporary film culture, to adopt Catherine Grant's apt phrase[10]), this chapter will examine how Craymer, Johnson and Lloyd have been characterised both as individuals and as participants in an all-female creative team, using them as an intriguing case study for addressing what Yvonne Tasker calls the 'crucial question of the *visibility* of women filmmakers' in modern cinema.[11]

Representing the producer and the writer, and the problem of where to put the songwriters

Those trying to look beyond the commonplace collapsing of film authorship into film direction have often alighted upon the producer and the screenwriter as viable alternative auteurs. This has also had a particular resonance in feminist attempts to re-envisage authorship, with, for instance, Judith Mayne's suggestion that 'consideration of the often-forgotten, often-female screenwriter' might offer a more fruitful avenue of investigation for those looking for 'a female imprint on the film text' than continually fixating on the director as primary author.[12]

If any one woman is 'first among equals' in *Mamma Mia!*'s tripartite female authorship, it is probably not the director or the writer but the producer, Judy Craymer. She is frequently referred to as the mastermind behind first the stage show and all its manifold productions and then its film adaptation, *Mamma Mia!*'s 'originator, producer and self-styled gatekeeper'.[13] It was Craymer who first conceived the idea of a musical based on the songs of ABBA, after having worked with the group's composers, Benny Andersson and Björn Ulvaeus, on their first venture in musical theatre, *Chess*, in the mid-1980s. Her personal connection to them, and her tenacity in pursuing the idea and finally persuading them to grant permission for it to go ahead, are frequently presented as key factors in her success story. Craymer herself suggests that 'for a long time, the story of *Mamma Mia* was the story of Judy Craymer and two blokes with beards who kept saying no'.[14] This hint of an adversarial dynamic within the authorship of *Mamma Mia!* is intriguing, and potentially ruptures the vision of the text as 'the most thoroughly brought-to-you-by-women package', to adopt Colin Firth's phrase.[15] The importance of Benny Andersson and Björn Ulvaeus as the composers of the songs that form *Mamma Mia!*'s narrative bedrock and its core attraction is undeniable. Moreover, as Malcolm Womack notes elsewhere in this collection, there is also a tension within ABBA between male and female authorship, with competing claims of composition and interpretation in 'authoring' the songs, which adds a further layer of complexity to the issue of authorship even in *Mamma Mia!*'s source material.[16] Craymer is at pains to make clear how much depended on the approval of Andersson and Ulvaeus, who could have withdrawn permission at any stage of the production's development; hence she was 'always treading on eggshells' around them.[17] Given the already prominent position of ABBA in popular culture, it is not surprising that the female creative team seem to have often conceptualised themselves less as original creators and more as self-effacing 'handmaidens' to Benny and Björn's vision, facilitating something that was already latent in the songs and just needed bringing out: 'This was the musical Benny and Björn didn't realise they'd written,' says Lloyd.[18] It is interesting to note that both men also enjoy a 'Hitchcockian cameo'[19] in the film, an authorial privilege not enjoyed (to my knowledge) by any of the 'tribe of women'.

Profiles of the producer, Judy Craymer, inevitably frame her story in terms of a triumph against adversity, prevailing not only against Benny and Björn's objections but also against considerable financial difficulties. In order to accentuate the 'rags to riches' narrative, much emphasis is placed on Craymer's previously lowly position in the theatrical hierarchy: she 'spent her early career lugging scenery and answering the phones'[20] and then 'barely had two brass farthings to rub together having sold her flat to bankroll her vision'.[21] Some descriptions even de-skill her and situate her as an inexperienced 'average woman' to make the juxtaposition between past and present more dramatic: 'She was just a middle-aged Abba fan with a dream – but Judy Craymer defied the odds to turn her favourite group's songs into a musical. Now she's a £90m dancing queen.'[22] The pay-off for her tenacity is her current affluent lifestyle, and lots of attention is lavished upon this in profiles of the producer, with detailed descriptions of her appearance and her home littered with expensive brand names:

> [Craymer] lives in a fabulous penthouse flat in Knightsbridge, where Diptyque candles burn in every room and ranks of silver photograph frames march

across the surface of the grand piano. An attractive blonde in a black dress and a black leather jacket, with a white Chanel watch, she has an immaculate manicure and immaculate bare, brown legs. She is, in fact, well camouflaged among the tasteful Kelly Hoppen-ish black, white and taupe décor.[23]

Other articles mention her high-end consumerism ('Judy likes to shop'[24]) or provide a litany of the pricey accoutrements that have been the rewards for her success: 'chauffeur-driven BMW ... enormous Hermes shopping bag in hand ... immaculate blonde dye job ... Chanel jacket'.[25] This very post-feminist image of female success, dominated by high-end consumerism, is something that Craymer simultaneously embodies but also shies away from, requesting of a journalist, 'Please don't write about the fancy car or the shopping. People will think I'm so superficial.'[26]

There sometimes seems to be a marked uncertainty about how to interpret Craymer in publicity and press material. Her single-mindedness in hanging onto *Mamma Mia!*'s film rights despite the blandishments of Hollywood is often read positively as an indicator of her doughty determination: 'there was no way I was going to sell the rights and have someone else do it their way ... she told a roomful of suits bamboozling her with massive seven-figure deals: "I will not be swayed."'[27] Likewise her insistence on keeping the original creative team intact speaks of female solidarity on her part: 'Judy Craymer looks after her own.'[28] But on the other hand, some articles speak of her 'tight creative control over every aspect of every production, all over the world'[29] in slightly ambivalent terms, edging towards the diagnosis of 'control-freakery' that Giles Hattersley reaches, and that Craymer herself partly concurs with: 'False bottoms, platforms, 80-year-old extras, wedding cakes, tapas. You name it, I approved it.'[30]

Certain corners of the British press also make a point of noting the absence of traditional markers of feminine achievement in Craymer's life: 'She's single and childless. ... She doesn't have children because she always thought she wasn't old enough.'[31] This provides an interesting contrast with her collaborator, writer Catherine Johnson, who is most often written about in terms of being a mother. The press coverage of Johnson uses a similar 'rags to riches' narrative as that applied to Craymer, but now with a maternal twist. The *Mail on Sunday*'s headline on Johnson when the stage show first took off was '*Mamma Mia!* I'm a £6M Single Mother',[32] while the *Daily Express* provided this concise summary of the writer's meteoric rise: 'It's all a bit overwhelming for a 44-year-old single mother of two who has spent much of her writing life in damp basement flats on the dole, dreaming of money, money, money.'[33] Whereas Craymer's previous financial instability was defined by her having to remortgage her flat to back her show, Johnson's is defined by being 'barely able to afford nappies'[34] for her infant children. Johnson is also singled out as a lone mother, a maternal identity that has frequently been the subject of vilification, often internalised by the mothers themselves, to which Johnson poignantly testifies:

> I felt I had let them down. The ideal lifestyle I had in mind for them did not materialise. We were told this was the only way to bring up kids if they were not going to become scourges of society and I felt I had cheated them somehow.[35]

A desire to write back against this damaging establishment stereotype of the single mother as failed mother, drawing on her own personal experience, undoubtedly informs Johnson's work, including *Mamma Mia!* For instance, she says of the inclusion of the 'Money Money Money' number in the show,

> Straight away the audience knows who Donna is – a single parent skivvying away, not a gold digger. … I was always moaning about how much I had to work, and when Donna says 'I need a break, I need a holiday', it's all me in there.[36]

However, motherhood doesn't just provide thematic inspiration; it also seems to have acted as the galvanising force of Johnson's development as a writer: 'I had always had this vague sense that one day I would be a writer, one day. But now I had this little chap running around who I felt deserved a bit more out of life.'[37] Maternity has frequently featured as one of the dominant metaphors of women's creativity, and this has also been true in film-making. For example, Yvonne Tasker has noted how 'an emphasis on maternity feeds the picture of a strong, maverick woman' in the depiction of US indie director Allison Anders.[38] It's hardly surprising that the female-directed, matrilineal-entitled *Mamma Mia!* is no exception, with one section in the 'making of' DVD documentary even being entitled 'Birthing *Mamma Mia!*' However, it is important to note that not all the metaphors applied to *Mamma Mia!*'s creative process are oestrogen-inspired; Meryl Streep praises Lloyd for her 'cohones' in taking on the direction of the film,[39] and Craymer uses the traditional image of forthcoming paternity to describe her plans for a screen adaptation of the stage show: 'The film has always been a twinkle in our eye.'[40]

Whereas 'immaculate' is the word harped on in the evocation of Craymer's world, Catherine Johnson is presented as an image of unkempt flawed consumerism with the same kind of high-end brand names placed within an entirely different context:

> Johnson is not, by nature, a high maintenance woman. Escada and Guess bags sit like trophies in her study but are used as rubbish bins. Fluffy designer towels hang in the bathroom, mottled with mascara stains. Her smart new jeep is remorselessly trashed inside, banana skins stuffed into ashtrays, Abba Gold CD sticky with fingerprints.[41]

However, this refusal of high-maintenance femininity also indicates a refreshingly 'down-to-earth'[42] sensibility that is one of the other recurrent motifs of press commentary on Johnson, inextricably linked with her delinquent past, having been expelled from school for wearing a skimpy halter-neck top and arguing with the head teacher.[43] Just as Donna has a slightly racy past but eventually settles down into conjugal respectability and professionalism, her creator Catherine Johnson is seen to follow a similar path, and had to adjust her self-image to accommodate her new success: 'I had a mental image of myself as someone who wasn't that successful. It was a warped view. ... One year into the run I thought, I can't do this anymore. I can't keep up this pretence to myself of being slightly shabby, a loser.'[44] This nervous tic of self-deprecation is a commonplace motif of post-feminism, exemplified by Bridget Jones's constant self-surveillance and self-denigration for not living up to an impossible feminine ideal.[45] In fact, much of the framing of Johnson and Craymer's creative collaboration is presented in these charmingly chaotic and self-deprecating terms, with the original idea for the story linking the musical numbers apparently being hatched during a chat over egg sandwiches, and a working holiday in Madeira to refine the screenplay lapsing into 'lounging around in the sun and only talk[ing] about it for an hour on the plane back'.[46] This is partly to evoke the light-heartedness and camaraderie of their artistic collaboration, making a point of never taking itself too seriously, but one wonders whether it might not also indicate a certain reticence about being seen to be overly hard-nosed or ambitious, maintaining instead an artlessly girly and unthreatening outward image.

Directorial dynamo: Phyllida Lloyd

Whereas Craymer and Johnson have tended to be characterised in larger-than-life terms as a 'ballsy blonde ... with a big laugh and big hands'[47] and a former 'teenage tearaway' who wanted to write 'about people like me, living real, messy lives',[48] the presentation of Phyllida Lloyd, the third member of the 'tribe of women', strikes a different note. Instead she is presented as the 'notoriously calm, methodical director'[49] whose previous theatrical work is loaded with cultural capital: 'Before Abba changed her fortunes, Lloyd was a hugely successful helmer of everything except musicals. With Shakespeare at the National Theatre, Russian comedies at the Royal Shakespeare Company and new plays at the Royal Court.'[50] Her decision to take on such an unashamedly frivolous project is presented as surprising given her highbrow pedigree, not unlike the calumny that greeted the casting of Meryl Streep as Donna (see Chapter 4). However, the slightly unruly edge present in her fellow Dynamos is not entirely absent from Lloyd's identity, with the director describing the aftermath of a particularly convivial night out in Sweden and a 9 a.m. meeting the following morning thus: 'We were offered whiskey when we arrived and Catherine and I both nearly chundered into the wastepaper baskets.'[51] She also admits that she got through the task of directing the film version of *Mamma Mia!* 'by taking up sleeping pills, intravenous caffeine and a certain amount of vodka'.[52] If this suggests quite a high-octane chemically driven approach to film direction, then the evidence provided by the *Mamma Mia!* DVD extras suggests a quite different *modus operandi*. Two of its male stars testify to her cool, unflappable approach to direction, with Dominic Cooper suggesting 'how trustworthy she is, [she's] thought it all out', while Stellan Skarsgård says Lloyd 'never gets upset, [there's] no drama' and instead she works 'slowly and methodically'.[53] Of course, this might be seen as rather uncharismatic, the kind of journeyman plodding style of direction that doesn't get you labelled an auteur (compare it with the anecdotal evidence of the highly charged atmosphere on set during the making of a film by one of Skarsgård's previous directors, the quixotic Lars Von Trier, who *is* seen as an auteur), but it might also be seen as a refutation of the shadow criticism that stalks women directors that they are potential hysterics, unable to withstand the pressure of being captain of the ship.

Another aspersion frequently cast on women directors is that they are uncomfortable with the spectacular, being better suited to low-key intimate drama, but Lloyd seems free from these kinds of criticisms, perhaps due to her considerable expertise in the epic musical pageantry of opera.[54] As Lloyd recounts, at Opera North she 'was working on a much bigger scale, collaborating with conductors, choreographers and chorus masters, learning the architecture of operas, how to move large groups of people around a stage'.[55] Rather, the criticism that has been made of her film direction tends to focus more on her inexperience as a novice director of films with a background in theatre, trying to cover up her lack of 'cinematic prowess' by using a style that ended up feeling 'over-shot and over-cut'.[56]

In her DVD director's commentary and in publicity interviews, Lloyd readily admits her fears on embarking on her first feature film direction job (her only experience akin to it was a filmed version of her production of Britten's *Gloriana* in 2000), coupled with her sense of delight: 'I thought "I'm in movies. I'm directing a mega blockbuster Hollywood movie!"'[57] According to Lloyd, her first moment of relaxation on the picture came during the filming of the complex 'Voulez Vous' sequence when the 'terror' began to recede and she realised – while 'on a crane fifty feet up' – that 'this is fun'.[58] During her DVD director's commentary, she confesses an inclination towards introspection, to 'keep things close to my chest', especially when uncertain of what to do. But she was also sufficiently emboldened to insist upon difficult last-minute crane shots in order to enliven the 'Does Your Mother Know?' number, something she also mentions in an interview reproduced in the film's production notes: 'I was determined that the camera language was going to be different for every song not just for the sake of it, but so that it would do something different for the audience – according to what the plot required at the moment.'[59]

While maintaining her own vision of what the film should be, it is clear that Lloyd's tricky traversal from theatre to film has been made possible by the 'top flight team' she worked with, and she takes care to give them all full credit for their creative input.[60] This includes her fellow Dynamos Craymer and Johnson but also the film's choreographer, Anthony Van Laast, another carry-over from the stage show – 'an absolute rock throughout' – and production designer Maria Djurkovic, whom Lloyd hails as 'another personality whose stamp on this production is going to be remarkable'.[61] On Lloyd's DVD director's commentary, one of her first mentions goes to Director of Photography Haris Zambarloukos, and later on she emphasises the integral importance of editor Lesley Walker and costume designer Ann Roth.[62] In her emphasis on the collaborative and the co-operative aspects of film production, Lloyd not only shrugs off some of the extremes of auteurism but also embodies the commonplace (if unproven) assumption that women have a different way of working that forgoes the egotism and glory-grabbing individualism more readily associated with a masculine working culture. Indeed, as if to consolidate this impression, Lloyd's style of direction is revealed to be gentle and consensual in the DVD's behind-the-scenes look at the filming of the 'Lay All Your Love on Me' number, with the director being not only solicitous of Amanda Seyfried's knees as she crawls across the rough shingle beach location (director as mother/caregiver?) but also very happy to take on board the suggestions of the young actress for how a particular moment could be staged.[63]

Feminist film scholars have been wary of making overly utopian claims 'about finding female subjectivity in films auteured by women',[64] while also recognising the obvious reasons why 'female-authored films may be more open to representations of women reworked to feminist or woman-identified ends'.[65] More populist modes of film criticism have been much happier to assert that the gender of a film-maker inevitably informs on-screen content, and we can see this in responses to *Mamma Mia!* In a piece in the *Guardian* about the film's popularity with women, writer Noorjehan Barmania cites its female production team as one of the key reasons 'why women respond to it',[66] and for novelist Naomi Alderman, the film offered a rare instance of a female gaze in operation, citing the costuming of Amanda Seyfried in a one-piece swimsuit rather than a skimpy bikini as evidence: 'She looks like a young girl really would look on a beach in Greece. It makes you feel relaxed, as a woman watching.'[67] Phyllida Lloyd's DVD director's commentary would seem to concur with this idea of the female director possessing special intimate female knowledge that a male director would not necessarily be party to, and which can then be conveyed onto the screen. She says of the moment when Sophie cuts her leg shaving during 'Slipping through My Fingers' that 'girls would understand the trauma of that on their wedding day'. Although it's not the same, there does seem to be a kinship with an anecdote Samantha Morton recounted about the filming of *Morvern Callar* (2002), directed by Lynne Ramsay:

> I was doing that sex scene and I was on my period, and me and Lynne were both like, well, what are we going to do, because my Tampax string was showing. And in the end she just stopped the camera, leaned over and cut it off. And for all sorts of reasons, I can't imagine a man doing that.[68]

Both suggest the special interior knowledge of the female experience in the women directors that enables them to approach their work in a different way from a male director. Obviously, this is quite distinct from the ideal of the androgyne female director, pace Bigelow, who refuses to be defined by gender and by the (potentially imprisoning) notion of a unique female filmic sensibility, and as Catherine Grant has detailed in her historical overview of how feminist film theory has approached female authorship, the pendulum has periodically swung back and forth in favour of one ideal (transcendence of gender identity) then the other (embodiment of gender identity).[69]

A final point on Phyllida Lloyd: the structuring absence in the marketing of her directorial persona may be sexuality. Although she has been listed fifty-sixth most influential gay figure in modern Britain in the *Independent*'s 'Pink List'[70] and described as 'openly gay' in an interview in *Playbill* magazine,[71] with gay website *Pink News* hailing her inclusion in the 2010 New Year's Honours List (she was made a CBE),[72] this is not mentioned at all in promotional material related to the film. This could be because Lloyd's sexual orientation is seen as unworthy of remarking upon, and entirely irrelevant to the business of successfully helming a major film. Interestingly, this echoes Judith Mayne's observations about the critical reputation of pioneering woman director (and out lesbian) Dorothy Arzner. The initial feminist reclamation of her work in the 1970s prioritised gender over sexuality as the defining feature of her authorial sensibility, despite the strong gay coding of Arzner's image in publicity portraits, not to mention the implications of her focus on female communities: 'if relationships between and among women account for much more narrative and visual momentum than do the relations between men and women in Arzner's work', Mayne argues, then it might be worth taking account of sexual identity as a key component in 'the perspective that informs these preoccupations'.[73] Many decades later with *Mamma Mia!*, another gay woman director made a film predicated on close female friendship, but the idea of it as lesbian cinema remains absent from the majority of critical discussions.

A triumvirate of female authorship

Although Phyllida Lloyd is granted the exclusive communicative channel of her own DVD director's commentary, in it she alludes continually to her working relationship and personal friendship with Judy Craymer and Catherine Johnson, frequently aligning them with the trio of female band mates and friends in the film. Over the semi-improvised scenes featuring Donna's reunion with

Rosie and Tanya, Lloyd speaks more specifically about which behind-the-scenes woman corresponds with which on-screen woman, something dwelt on in interviews by the other women too. Craymer suggests, 'Catherine's the slightly chaotic single mum, I'm high maintenance and Phyllida's the pragmatic one' (although Lloyd suggests in her commentary that all three of them have become more significantly high maintenance since the show's box-office success and the resultant financial remuneration, which is repeated by Johnson and Craymer in the 'making of' documentary on the DVD).[74] During the first part of the film's 'Dancing Queen' number, Lloyd's commentary reiterates the connection between the characters' backstory and the creative team's, saying 'this is what me, Catherine and Judy did in our bedrooms'.[75] Those same bed-bouncing, singing-into-hairbrushes moments are featured in the DVD's 'making of' documentary, and we see them interspersed with images of Craymer, Johnson and Lloyd carrying out similarly bouncy dance movements with the scene perfectly match-cut so that they seem to pick up the song from where Tanya, Donna and Rosie leave it. In many ways, this sequence seems to encapsulate the parallels between female creative agency and on-screen representation – three women off-screen, three women on-screen – while also implying that the film is straightforward autobiography, simply a matter of putting a friendship on the screen rather than the creative challenge of inventing dramatic personae.

These images on the DVD documentary are inaugurated by an interview with Benny Andersson in which he praises 'those three gals', vocabulary that recalls Sadie Wearing's work on the 'girling' of older women within post-feminist culture, simultaneously attempting to celebrate mature vitality while, to a certain extent, infantilising it.[76] Nonetheless, Craymer, Lloyd and Johnson's late but triumphant entry into films might be read as an empowering parable of female achievement in middle age akin to that espoused in their film, as Craymer suggests in an interview: 'It goes to show you can do it at any age. Beat *The*

Mamma Mia!'s female authorship

Lord of the Rings! Harry Potter pushed out the way! Let's have some Martinis!'[77] Moreover, just as the three female friends at the heart of *Mamma Mia!*, Donna, Rosie and Tanya, represent different modes of femininity, so the three Dynamos behind the film suggest the potential power of an alliance between diverse (albeit all white, born in the same year and approximately middle-class) but complementary forms of femininity.

Feminist film theory has eulogised the moment in Dorothy Arzner's *Dance Girl Dance* (1940) in which young dancer Judy (Maureen O'Hara) answers back to an unappreciative audience, telling them exactly what she thinks of them and questioning their right to gaze at her. For Claire Johnston, it was a 'tour de force, cracking open the entire fabric of the film … directly challenging the entire notion of woman as spectacle'.[78] Nearly 70 years later, the female-directed *Mamma Mia!* concludes with another scene breaking the fourth wall, as Donna/Meryl Streep directly addresses the spectator. But now the tone is not confrontational but inclusive, assuming a joyous and appreciative audience who will respond positively to her frame-breaking question about wanting more. Claire Johnston's important early piece of work on women's cinema made two key polemical points. First, in studying female-authored cinema, it was equally, if not more, 'instructive to look at films made by women within the Hollywood system' than at those from art cinema traditions. These mainstream productions were more likely to offer useful models of how 'to bring about a dislocation between sexist ideology and the text of the film'.[79] Second, collective and collaborative work undertaken by women filmmakers should be prioritised, argued Johnston, as a major step forward; as a means of acquiring and sharing skills, it constitutes a formidable challenge to male privilege in the film industry; as an expression of sisterhood, it suggests a viable alternative to the rigid hierarchical structures of male-dominated cinema.[80]

Mamma Mia! may be firmly located within the purview of post-feminist culture rather than the activist feminist culture championed by Claire Johnston, but it nonetheless triumphantly fulfils the two criteria listed above. It is mainstream but also offers an oblique critique of the customary images of older women, placing them at the centre of the film instead of in their usual position in the margins; as Jeanette Winterson has suggested, this in itself is a political act.[81] In its *laissez-faire* approach to Donna's youthful sexual immodesty and its celebration of her strong lone motherhood, the film certainly fulfils Geetha Ramanathan's observations about feminist cinema 'contesting the culture's most sacred ideals' about women.[82] But, more importantly, the film's achievement is not predicated on a single female auteur, the lone visionary of traditional auteurism albeit with a gender switch (as with Bigelow). Instead, equal status and credence are given to three women, and the importance of it being a collaborative female enterprise is continually reiterated. As Catherine Johnson suggests, all three women had to fight to keep the film true to their original vision of 'real older women who are overweight, over-stressed, drunk and needing each other'.[83] They also had to fight to retain that post-credits coda which includes the direct address to the audience, going against the guidance of the studio, which strongly advised dropping it. Maintaining the same 'tribe of women' from stage to screen appears to have been an invaluable strategy in keeping control over the material as it made the transition from one medium to another, a confident statement about understanding the property and its appeal better than anyone else (being the 'keepers of the flame'), but also an eloquent expression of female solidarity and collaborative authorship in contemporary cinema culture.[84]

Notes

1. Jermyn, Deborah and Redmond, Sean (Eds), *The Cinema of Kathryn Bigelow: Hollywood Transgressor*, London: Wallflower, 2003.
2. Nochimson, Martha P., 'Kathryn Bigelow: feminist pioneer or tough guy in drag?', *Salon.com*, 24 February 2010. http://www.salon.com/

entertainment/movies/film_salon/2010/02/24/bigelow (accessed 25 March 2011).
3. Ibid.
4. Tasker, Yvonne, 'Vision and visibility: women filmmakers, contemporary authorship and feminist film studies', in Vicki Callahan (Ed.), *Reclaiming the Archive: Feminism and Film History*, Detroit, MI Wayne State University Press, 2010, p. 219.
5. Cook, Pam, *Screening the Past: Memory and Nostalgia in Cinema*, London: Routledge, 2005, p. 230.
6. Tasker, 'Vision and visibility', pp. 214–15.
7. http://www.boxofficemojo.com/yearly/chart/?yr=2008&p=.htm (accessed 11 April 2011).
8. Hattersley, Giles, 'Mamma mia, there's a fire within Judy Craymer's soul', *Sunday Times*, 23 November 2008, p. 2.
9. Ibid.
10. Grant, Catherine, 'Auteur machines? Auteurism and the DVD', in James Bennett and Tom Brown (Eds), *Film and Television after DVD*, London: Routledge, 2008.
11. Tasker, 'Vision and visibility', p. 214.
12. Mayne, Judith, 'Female authorship reconsidered (the case of Dorothy Arzner)', in Barry Keith Grant (Ed.), *Auteurs and Authorship: A Film Reader*, Oxford: Blackwell, 2008 p. 266. Mayne's suggestion has been brilliantly elaborated by Lizzie Francke in her book *Script Girls: Women Screenwriters in Hollywood*, London: BFI, 1994.
13. Rose, Hilary, 'How *Mamma Mia!* producer Judy Craymer cracked Hollywood', *The Times*, 28 June 2008, p. 5.
14. Anon., 'How *Mamma Mia's* Judy Craymer became the £90m dancing queen', *Daily Mail* (Femail), 3 April 2009, p. 11.
15. 'The making of *Mamma Mia!*' documentary, *Mamma Mia! The Movie* DVD, Universal, 2009.
16. For example, the song that lies at the core of the film's moving treatment of the mother–daughter bond, 'Slipping through My Fingers', was originally written from the point of view of the father, as Benny reveals: 'It's really about a father and a daughter, about Björn and his daughter, although it's sung through Agnetha's lips.' Andersson, Benny, Ulvaeus, Björn and Craymer, Judy, *Mamma Mia! How Can I Resist You? The Inside Story of Mamma Mia! and the Songs of ABBA*, London: Phoenix, 2008, p. 112.
17. Ibid., p. 160.
18. *Mamma Mia!* production notes, BFI Library.

19. Andersson, Ulvaeus and Craymer, *Mamma Mia! How Can I Resist You?*, p. 253.
20. Hattersley, 'Mamma mia, there's a fire within Judy Craymer's soul'.
21. Anon., 'How *Mamma Mia*'s Judy Craymer became the £90m dancing queen'.
22. Ibid.
23. Rose, 'How *Mamma Mia!* producer Judy Craymer cracked Hollywood'.
24. Anon., 'How *Mamma Mia*'s Judy Craymer became the £90m dancing queen'.
25. Hattersley, 'Mamma mia, there's a fire within Judy Craymer's soul'. If further indication were needed of Craymer's successful attainment of the polished mature femininity required by post-feminist hegemony, she even features on the website Beautifulhairstyles.com as an immaculately coiffured 'fifty-plus' model for women to emulate. http://www.beautifulhairstyles.com/mature/over50/judycraymer.html (accessed 11 April, 2011).
26. Hattersley, 'Mamma mia, there's a fire within Judy Craymer's soul'.
27. Ibid.
28. Spencer, Charles, 'A mamma of a movie', *Daily Telegraph*, 28 December 2007, p. 33.
29. Rose, 'How *Mamma Mia!* producer Judy Craymer cracked Hollywood'.
30. Hattersley, 'Mamma mia, there's a fire within Judy Craymer's soul'. Craymer also talks about her love of party planning down to the last detail, to the extent that 'the creative staff now always say, if I'm not around at rehearsals or at note sessions, "Oh, Judy's at a pineapple chunk summit meeting."' Andersson, Ulvaeus and Craymer, *Mamma Mia! How Can I Resist You?*, p. 189.
31. Rose, 'How *Mamma Mia!* producer Judy Craymer cracked Hollywood'.
32. Brook, Danae, '*Mamma Mia!* I'm a £6M single mother', *Mail on Sunday*, 12 September 1999, p. 37.
33. Boase, Tessa, 'Every night 10,000 people around the world sing along to the ABBA musical', *Daily Express*, 1 June 2002, p. 45.
34. Gardner, Lyn, 'Here I go again: Catherine Johnson on life after *Mamma Mia!*', *Guardian* (G2), 26 February 2009, p. 24.
35. Ibid.
36. Andersson, Ulvaeus and Craymer, *Mamma Mia! How Can I Resist You?*, p. 196.
37. Gardner, 'Here I go again: Catherine Johnson on life after *Mamma Mia!*'
38. Tasker, 'Vision and visibility', p. 226.

39. 'The making of *Mamma Mia!*' documentary, *Mamma Mia! The Movie* DVD.
40. Smith, Alistair, '*Mamma Mia!* strikes big screen deal', *The Stage*, 21 April 2006. http://www.thestage.co.uk/news/newsstory.php/12334/mamma-mia-strikes-big-screen-deal (accessed 11 April 2011).
41. Boase, 'Every night 10,000 people around the world sing along to the ABBA musical'. It is interesting that both Craymer and Johnson are interviewed at home rather than in a work setting, suggesting something of the unease within post-feminism in representing the professional woman, and the frequent mitigation of perceived careerism through an emphasis on the domestic sphere.
42. Gardner, 'Here I go again: Catherine Johnson on life after *Mamma Mia!*'
43. Billen, Andrew, 'Catherine Johnson on *Mamma Mia!* and new play *Suspension*', *The Times*, 21 February 2009, p. 20.
44. Boase, 'Every night 10,000 people around the world sing along to the ABBA musical'.
45. See McRobbie, Angela, 'Postfeminism and popular culture: Bridget Jones and the new gender regime', in Yvonne Tasker and Diane Negra (Eds), *Interrogating Postfeminism: Gender and the Politics of Popular Culture*, Durham, NC: Duke University Press, 2007.
46. Andersson, Ulvaeus and Craymer, *Mamma Mia! How Can I Resist You?*, p. 246.
47. Anon., 'How *Mamma Mia*'s Judy Craymer became the £90m dancing queen'.
48. Gardner, 'Here I go again: Catherine Johnson on life after *Mamma Mia!*'
49. *Mamma Mia!* production notes, BFI Library.
50. Benedict, David, 'Phyllida Lloyd has best of both worlds', *Variety*, 6 April 2009, p. 4.
51. Andersson, Ulvaeus and Craymer, *Mamma Mia! How Can I Resist You?*, p. 154.
52. Spencer, 'A mamma of a movie'.
53. 'The making of *Mamma Mia!*' documentary, *Mamma Mia! The Movie* DVD.
54. See Williams, Rachel, '"It's like painting toys blue and pink": marketing and the female-directed hollywood film', *Scope: An Online Journal of Film Studies*, December 2000. http://www.scope.nottingham.ac.uk/article.php?issue=dec2000&id=291&section=article (accessed 11 April 2011).
55. Andersson, Ulvaeus and Craymer, *Mamma Mia! How Can I Resist You?*, p. 151.

56. Mintzer, Jordan, 'Mamma Mia!', *Variety*, 14 July 2008, p. 38. Lloyd's directorial ineptitude is mercilessly mocked in the French and Saunders 2009 Comic Relief film parody sketch where director Chlamydia Lloyd (Miranda Hart) advises her actors: 'So, can everybody stay where they can see the camera please? That's the first rule of film, apparently. Um, stay in the middle of the photograph and bend down if you're tall.'
57. Andersson, Ulvaeus and Craymer, *Mamma Mia! How Can I Resist You?*, p. 252.
58. Director's commentary, *Mamma Mia! The Movie* DVD.
59. *Mamma Mia!* production notes, BFI Library.
60. Heuring, David, '*Mamma Mia!* makes the leap to the big screen', *British Cinematographer*, July 2008, p. 24.
61. 'The making of *Mamma Mia!*' documentary, *Mamma Mia! The Movie* DVD.
62. Zambarloukos says of his work with Lloyd: 'I think it helped that I had worked with Roger Michell (*Venus*, *Enduring Love*) and Kenneth Branagh (*Sleuth*) [because] I could interpret staging and other concerns to a cinematic form quite easily, based on a common language and aesthetics.' Heuring, '*Mamma Mia!* makes the leap to the big screen', p. 24.
63. This is perhaps a legacy of her working practices in the theatre, as Johnson observed: 'The process was very inclusive. There was no feeling of "OK, Catherine writes the scripts, that's her job ..." We were all there and chipping in. I loved the fact that there was no demarcation, and that Phyllida invited ideas.' Andersson, Ulvaeus and Craymer, *Mamma Mia! How Can I Resist You?*, p. 172.
64. Ramanathan, Geetha, *Feminist Auteurs: Reading Women's Film*, London: Wallflower, 2006, p. 5.
65. Tarr, Carrie, *Diane Kurys*, Manchester: Manchester University Press, 1999, p. 5. For a concise summary of the academic debates around female film authorship, see Grant, Catherine, 'Secret agents: feminist theories of women's film authorship', *Feminist Theory*, Vol. 2, No. 1, April 2001, pp. 113–30.
66. Quoted in Cochrane, Kira, 'The mother of all musicals', *Guardian* (G2), 27 November 2008, p. 8.
67. Ibid., p. 7.
68. Leigh, Danny, 'About a girl', *Guardian* (Weekend), 5 October 2002, p. 26.
69. Grant, 'Secret agents'.
70. 'Gay power: the pink list', *Independent*, 2 July 2006. http://www.independent.co.uk/news/uk/this-britain/gay-power-the-pink-list-406297.html (accessed 11 April, 2011).

71. Buckley, Michael, 'Stage to screen: Phyllida Lloyd and Dominic Cooper talk about "*Mamma Mia!*" movie', *Playbill*, 29 June 2008. http://www.playbill.com/features/article/119022-STAGE-TO-SCREENS-Phyllida-Lloyd-and-Dominic-Cooper-Talk-About-Mamma-Mia-Movie (accessed 11 April 2011).
72. Anon., 'Maggi Hambling and Phyllida Lloyd honoured', *Pink News*, 5 January 2010. http://www.pinknews.co.uk/2010/01/05/maggi-hambling-and-phyllida-lloyd-honoured (accessed 11 April 2011).
73. Mayne, 'Female authorship reconsidered', p. 273.
74. Andersson, Ulvaeus and Craymer, *Mamma Mia! How Can I Resist You?*, p. 155.
75. Spencer, 'A mamma of a movie'.
76. Wearing, Sadie, 'Subjects of rejuvenation: aging in postfeminist culture', in Tasker and Negra (Eds), *Interrogating Postfeminism*, pp. 277–310.
77. Hattersley, 'Mamma mia, there's a fire within Judy Craymer's soul'.
78. Johnston, Claire, 'Women's cinema as counter-cinema', in Grant (Ed.), *Auteurs and Authorship*, p. 125.
79. Ibid.
80. Ibid., p. 126.
81. Cochrane, 'The mother of all movies', p. 7.
82. Ramanathan, *Feminist Auteurs*, p. 205.
83. Gardner, 'Here I go again: Catherine Johnson on life after *Mamma Mia!*' Given the slenderness of all three female principals – even Walters with her prosthetic bottom – one might query the idea of it being about 'overweight' women.
84. 'The making of *Mamma Mia!*' documentary, *Mamma Mia! The Movie* DVD.

4

'See that girl, watch that scene': notes on the star persona and presence of Meryl Streep in *Mamma Mia!*

Deborah Mellamphy

In October 1981, Annie Leibovitz's photograph of Meryl Streep graced the front cover of *Rolling Stone* magazine as part of the publicity programme for the release of *The French Lieutenant's Woman* (Reisz, 1981), a film that would consolidate Streep's status as one of Hollywood's most protean actors. Leibovitz is well known for her intimate and unconventional portraits of the famous and she captured a paradoxical mixture of vulnerability and hostility in her photograph of Streep, an uneasy atmosphere that is exacerbated by the fact that Streep's face is covered in white stage makeup. This is not a traditional publicity shot; instead Streep tugs on either side of her face in an exaggerated attempt to pull off the white mask, which, Leibovitz claims, was Meryl's idea to use. In her book *At Work*, Leibovitz explains that Streep was very uncomfortable with all the attention she was receiving in the publicity rounds for Reisz's film. Recalling Streep's disquiet at taking part in the photo-shoot, Leibovitz says Streep

> talked about how she didn't want to be anyone, she was nobody, just an actress. I suggested that she didn't have to be anybody in particular and maybe she would

like to put on white face ... to be a mime. This put her at ease. She had a role to play.[1]

Such imagery of Streep simultaneously hiding behind and trying to escape from the mask is symbolic of the discourses surrounding this 14 times Oscar-nominated actress.

While Meryl Streep is considered one of the most accomplished actors in Hollywood, she is also known as one of the most fiercely private stars. Indeed, one persistent myth that surrounds Streep is that she is an 'anti-celebrity'.[2] Such labelling has resulted in a difficult relationship with audience and press alike, and much of the discourse about her career focuses on how her roles either cast her as emotionally cold and inaccessible or reposition her star persona in an attempt to strengthen her box-office appeal. In fact, James Kaplan, in his article 'Nobody does it better', notes further benefits for Streep in her move from more highbrow drama to comedy films in the 1980s. Kaplan avers that comedy has provided the cultural space where Streep gets to show a different side of her persona. 'It's almost', says Kaplan, 'as if, because she has been taken so seriously for so long, she needs to work (or play) extra hard to focus on her humanity.'[3] This process of repositioning, or 'rebooting',[4] has not been without controversy; indeed her move towards comedy was seen as audience manipulation and capitulation to mainstream mediocrity. However, her more recent appearance in the musical romantic comedy *Mamma Mia!* seems to have afforded the cultural vehicle via which she has succeeded in increasing her box-office appeal. Underpinned by Richard Dyer's idea of the 'always-already-signifying nature of star images', this chapter will focus on Meryl Streep's star image and persona within the past decade and the significance of *Mamma Mia!* as a fulcrum in her career.[5]

Queen of drama or drama queen?

According to Richard Dyer, in his seminal analysis of the social meaning of film stars, the star is constructed according to a system of 'structured polysemy, that is, the finite multiplicity of meanings and affects they embody and the attempts to structure them so that some meanings and affects are foregrounded and others are masked or displaced'.[6] The personae of stars such as Marilyn Monroe and John Wayne negotiate and resolve potential contradictions and become clear and legible images, encouraging audience identification. Yet the same cannot be said of Streep; the contradictions of her persona remain unresolved, which makes it difficult to understand who Streep really is, a point nicely reiterated in Rupert Christiansen's article 'Meltdown', in which he describes Streep as 'the supreme chameleon, possessed of a virtuoso's acting technique which allows her to slither through an incredible variety of incarnations without leaving her audience any very clear idea of who the person behind them might be'.[7] The idea posited here, that Streep's extraordinarily protean performances function as the very obstacle to her being fully embraced by audiences as a star, is reinforced by theatre producer and director Joseph Papp, who described the difficulties faced by Hollywood in constructing the Streep persona: 'she has too many variables—you can't stamp out cookies with Meryl'.[8] Indeed, as Molly Haskell argues, while stars such as Bette Davis and Katharine Hepburn might have played different character types, they embodied a familiar and constant presence due to their distinct and recognisable voices and expressions.[9] In contrast, Streep's constant adoption of different accents and her drive to play different and often controversial female protagonists resulted in a complex and contradictory star persona that appeared to distance her not only from her peers but also from the audience.

Streep began her film acting career at the age of 28, which, according to Elizabeth Vincentelli, might be one of the reasons she has encountered an apathetic reception from audiences. Vincentelli writes:

> We never got to meet her [Streep] as a sexy kid, and in the modern era there's no doubt that public affection

owes a lot to the way in which a young audience desires someone their own age in the launching of a career. So Streep never looked raw or wild; she seemed grown up and sad to say, that is no longer the most admired attribute (in a woman, or in anyone) in this culture.[10]

While Streep's age might have stymied her appeal, her starring roles in films in the late 1970s such as *The Deer Hunter* (Cimino, 1978), *Kramer versus Kramer* (Benton, 1979), *Sophie's Choice* (Pakula, 1982) and *Silkwood* (Nichols, 1983) and her appearance in the early 1980s in the television series *Holocaust* (Titus Productions, NBC, 1978) established her as a 'serious' dramatic actor, creating the blueprint for her subsequent career. The thematic concerns of these films were avowedly serious: the Vietnam war, the Holocaust, nuclear threat, conspiracy, as well as personal traumas such as divorce, maternal loss, bereavement and suicide, led to the portrayal of often uncompromising women. Streep's talent for high drama was developed in high school, where she played several leading roles, and as a result she won a scholarship to Vassar College to study English and Drama in 1967. Her drama teacher, Clinton Atkinson, praised her acting ability: 'I don't think anyone ever taught Meryl acting, she really taught herself,' a sentiment that codes Meryl's talent for acting as inherent – something from within.[11] Streep graduated from Vassar in 1971 and was awarded a place on the Honours Exchange Program at Dartford College, where she studied play writing and set and costume design, whilst performing at the Cubiculo Theatre in New York and in repertory theatre, where she was involved in over 30 stage productions. Later, Streep earned a Master's in Fine Arts at Yale University in 1975, after which she joined the Public Theatre, which led to her being cast in her first on-screen role, in *Julia* (Zinnemann, 1977). However, *Sophie's Choice* arguably remains her quintessential early dramatic role, and one integral to her star persona, as she won her only Best Actress Academy Award and one of her seven Golden Globe awards for her portrayal of Sophie Zawistowski, a survivor of Auschwitz who has travelled to post-war America after her husband and children have been murdered during the Second World War. In this role, Streep delivers an incredibly emotional performance, embodying female suffering and fragility and culminating in Sophie's suicide. It was in this film that Streep's ability to imitate accents with such verisimilitude became integral to her star persona.

No one appears to doubt Streep's dedication to her profession and her technical expertise, but while Streep's dramatic performances have been widely acclaimed, they have not been the object of universal admiration, being too self-conscious and cerebral for some. Most famously, critic Pauline Kael caustically dubbed her 'Our Lady of the Accents', accusing her of acting only 'from the neck up', and Katharine Hepburn claimed that she could not bear the 'click, click, click' of the wheels turning in Streep's head when she watched her perform.[12] Streep even recalls her fiancé John Cazale describing her as a 'delicious robot' because she 'acted perfectly but without the least feeling'.[13] Co-actor Dustin Hoffman labelled her an 'obsessed' and 'selfish' actor after working with her in *Kramer versus Kramer*. That she is a successful, intelligent and independent woman who rejects 'stardom' in favour of professionalism and chooses to play independent and oftentimes unsympathetic female characters who cause consternation might well be indicative of a type of misogyny that sees women like Streep as objectionable. It's worth noting here that actors such as Robert De Niro do not attract the same sort of criticism of their professionalism, privacy and performative skills. Streep is all too aware of the 'special venom that society reserves for powerful women';[14] talking to Kevin West from *W Magazine* in 2006, Streep says, 'The culture wants to cast them as cold, as if somehow they've lost their maternal bearings, their essential womanhood.'[15]

That Streep should make a connection to cultural fears about strong women losing their 'maternal bearings' is interesting given the recurrent significance of the maternal in Streep's roles and in her personal life. Streep is known as fiercely protective of her children, portraying a 'steely wariness at the first intrusion into family matters', and attacking a press photographer who tried to photograph her children in July 1988.[16] However, many of her roles abandon the traditional Hollywood image of mother as nurturer and caregiver, becoming instead the villain of the film. In her key early film *Kramer versus Kramer*, Streep plays the mother who feels unfulfilled in her domestic role, favours her career over her child and abandons her son and husband, only to return and set running a bitter custody battle. Streep is also cast as a problematic mother figure in *A Cry in the Dark* (Schepisi, 1988), as her character Lindy Chamberlain appears to be extremely emotionless after her baby has been killed by a dingo in the Australian outback, particularly in the courtroom scene, where she remains passive during descriptions of the 'murder scene'. According to Molly Haskell, Streep perfectly replicated 'the chilling reserve of the woman who was convicted of murder because the Australian public simply couldn't stand her'.[17] Even though her character was based on a real person, this performance inevitably came to be bound up with the Streep persona as it was difficult for audiences to sympathise with such a 'cold' and 'unfeminine' woman whose deficit of maternal sympathy consolidated her distance from ideals of femininity.

This disconnect between star and audience is apparent not only in her on-screen performances but also in her off-screen persona. The title of Diana Maychick's biography, *Meryl Streep: The Reluctant Superstar* (1984), perfectly captures Streep's uneasy relationship with her own star persona, and the author opens her book with an anecdote that illustrates how the actress 'hates to be recognized'.[18] Streep is one of many major stars who resist the frivolities of their Hollywood persona in an attempt to emphasise and embrace the art of acting. Her performances, with their plethora of award nominations, clearly connect her star persona with 'high art', making them culturally valuable. This is compounded by the fact that her early career was based on often risky low-budget and independent 'quality' dramas rather than on big-budget blockbusters. Virginia Luzón-Aguado argues that Streep (among others) 'excel[s] in performance rather than at the box office … which means that [she] can risk a number of flops without much dent being made in [her] prestige'.[19] Luzón-Aguado continues that 'by foregrounding and vindicating their work as serious performing artists … these actors seek to legitimate and maintain their standing in the overcrowded world of contemporary fame'.[20]

Streep's 'serious' and reserved persona is also compounded by the fact that she is a strongly outspoken political figure and is regularly motivated to accept roles due to her political concerns. As a strong opponent of nuclear power, she was prompted to star in *Silkwood,* and she accepted the role of Roberta Guaspan-Tzavaras in *Music of the Heart* (Craven, 1999) because it was based on the true story of a teacher who fought the Board of Education to teach music to underprivileged children in Harlem. Streep also spoke out against George Bush's ban on gay marriage, vigorously opposed the invasion of Iraq and protested against the pollution of the Hudson River. Her commitment to liberal activism over Hollywood tinsel has culminated in a persona defined by intelligence, independence and reserve that is sometimes negatively characterised as 'stiffness'. This quality adds to the difficulty that critics and audiences seem to have experienced in interpreting and reading her image.

The sunny side of the Streep

Yet, within the last decade, Meryl Streep's persona has been greeted with warmth by critics and audiences alike. Crucially,

Ty Burr argues that Streep only became a 'star' as a result of her more recent, lighter roles in films such as *Mamma Mia!* and *The Devil Wears Prada* (Frankel, 2006), which have imbued her persona with a likeability and populist dimension that did not exist previously when she was known solely as a 'great actress'. A. O. Scott also observes:

> An eminent and admired actress for three decades, she has emerged in the last few years, perhaps surprisingly, as a box office draw. "The Devil Wears Prada", "Mamma Mia!", "Julie & Julia" and "It's Complicated" were all hits, and it is fair to say that her participation in them was not a correlative of their success, but a cause. Esteemed for as long as most moviegoers can remember, she now finds herself beloved.[21]

In fact, her role in *The Devil Wears Prada* could be read as a metaphor for the actress's changing persona. She plays the role of Miranda Priestly, a ruthless, powerful and sophisticated fashion magazine editor whose hard-nosed attitude terrifies her staff, especially her naive, just-graduated assistant, Andrea Sachs (Anne Hathaway). Miranda's professionalism and cold-blooded attitude seem to reflect the ways in which Streep's star persona has been constructed; indeed, Miranda is referred to as a legend and her conversations with Andrea about career choices hark back to some of Streep's own comments about her acting career. As the film continues, the two women begin to warm to one another; Andrea, while nervous of Miranda, is keen to impress her and sees Miranda as a role model, and Miranda begins to recognise Andrea's potential and becomes a surrogate mother figure, nurturing the younger woman and enabling her to fulfil her potential. In so doing, Miranda's behaviour changes and we get to see the once cold-hearted woman turn into a warm and caring maternal figure, a transformation that Andrew Anthony suggests has had a very positive effect on the public's appreciation of Streep. He writes:

> Though Streep is ... one of those actresses who disappears into a role leaving little trace of herself, the role of Priestly [in *The Devil Wears Prada*] none the less shifted perceptions of her. The notion that there was warmth and a beating heart under the porcelain exterior extended beyond the character to the intensely private Streep. The critics loved it and, a little more unusually, so did the public.[22]

While *The Devil Wears Prada* represents a turning point in the ways in which audiences and critics have responded to Streep, *Mamma Mia!* signifies the greatest divergence from the films that defined her early career and persona. As Mick Brown summarises:

> One could argue that Streep hasn't always looked carefully enough – that she is a brilliant actress who has sometimes given better performances than the films have deserved. *Mamma Mia!* is the anomaly, perhaps aberration is a better word – a ghastly schmaltz-fest that ironically more than any of Streep's films seems to have inspired feelings of endearment as well as admiration in her audience.[23]

Streep's choice to do a musical reflects her love of singing, which is well documented. Indeed she was trained to sing professionally and has regularly sung in films such as *The Deer Hunter*, *Sophie's Choice*, *Silkwood*, *Postcards from the Edge* (Nichols, 1990), *Dancing at Lughnasa* (O'Connor, 1998) and *A Prairie Home Companion* (Altman, 2006). None of these films are musicals; in fact many of the songs she sings are performed for dramatic and sentimental purposes. In *Silkwood*, Streep's character's low, lamenting rendition of 'Amazing Grace' provides the audio for the film's closing scene, in which she is killed in a car crash. In addition, Streep's character, Linda, in The Deer Hunter, sings 'God Bless America' following the funeral of Nick (Christopher Walken). Each of these roles hints at Streep's voice training and experience in musical theatre, which, combined with her vast acting experience, became the motivator behind asking her to play the role of Donna in Mamma Mia! Director Phyllida Lloyd revealed:

> We dreamt of asking Meryl to play Donna. We knew she sang; we knew she wanted to do a musical. She combines everything that is required. She's one of those unique actors who can laugh the world's laughs and cry the world's tears. That's what Mamma Mia! needed, and we have it in her.[24]

Despite her obvious qualifications for playing the role, her decision to do so caused disquiet among critics, including Anthony Lane of The New Yorker, who lamented, 'How, we want to know, did the French Lieutenant's Woman wind up jumping off the dock of the bay?'[25]

That Lane should see Streep's role as Donna in Mamma Mia! as the very antithesis of her role as Anna/Sarah in The French Lieutenant's Woman highlights some of the difficulties that arise when an actor moves away from their more traditional roles. Indeed, a role in a light-hearted musical is not what you might immediately envisage for a woman customarily regarded as the world's greatest actress, whose enigmatic presentation of Anna/Sarah, as she stands alone, cloaked in black at the end of the jetty, became such an iconic image for quality drama. This image, characterised by her stasis and her dangerous proximity to the stormy sea, contrasts markedly with the more recent image of Streep in Mamma Mia! where once again she takes her place on a jetty but this time in the company of a large group of women as she ecstatically sings, dances and plays air guitar before plunging into the warm inviting water. This image is notable for its physical movement and air of happiness. These two iconic cultural moments work to illustrate the transformation and progressive lightening in tone, not only of the types of roles Streep plays, but also of the way in which her persona is read by critics and audiences. Indeed, after seeing *Mamma Mia!* Mick La Salle of the *San Francisco Chronicle* challenged the traditional framing of Streep's acting: 'Meryl Streep', he writes 'is a delight, a good singer, a wonderfully spontaneous comedian. What's all the nonsense about Streep's iron-clad technique?'[26] Roger Ebert also conceded that while *Mamma Mia!* was not his 'type' of film, 'Streep's sunshine carries a lot of charm' in the film.[27]

In an interview with John Hiscock, Streep revealed that she was motivated to accept the part of Donna after seeing the Broadway production with her ten-year-old daughter and a group of friends in 2001, shortly after 9/11. She praised the musical's cathartic ability to distract the audience from the tragedy:

> We left floating on air. We were so elated. It couldn't have been a better tonic for the city and I wrote the cast a note thanking them for the music and what they gave to us because it was something that meant a lot at the point. It was a gift not just to my little girl and her dispirited friends but it was a gift to the whole city.[28]

Yet even Streep recognised that the film didn't necessarily fit in with the rest of her career. Talking about when she discovered that she had been cast, Streep says she was elated: 'I just about died. I kept saying, "Are you sure you want me, because I'm not the likeliest choice you know." But I was thrilled because I love the music and it meant a lot to me.'[29] Streep's foray into the musical is significant in adding a further layer to her contradictory persona because it is seen as the film in which she is 'softened'.

Much of Streep's career is located in films whose settings are coded as real and believable and which are often based on real characters and events. In contrast, the classical Hollywood musical has traditionally been associated with a kind of hyperreal escapism, 'the exaltation of the artifice' in the words of Thomas Elsaesser.[30] Because of its escapist aims, the musical is not predominantly concerned with realism and becomes the one genre that openly portrays performance, generally emphasising masquerade over characterisation in order to refer to traditions of live entertainment. Streep's performance in the film version of *Mamma Mia!* retains much of the original theatricality. For instance, in her performance of the song 'Mamma Mia' we watch as Streep pulls faces, runs her hands over her body in an exaggerated manner and wrings her hands, and her rendition of 'The Winner Takes It All' is noteworthy for her dramatic hand gestures and facial expressions evoking emotion *in extremis*. Streep's performance in both songs (and others throughout the film) becomes excessive, and excessiveness connotes a sense of freedom and liberation, a far cry from the idea of stiffness that has been so regularly associated with her throughout her career. It is this sense of freedom evoked in Streep's more recent performances that Molly Haskell offers as one of the reasons that mainstream audiences have finally warmed to her. In her article entitled 'Finding herself', Haskell writes that Streep's freedom from the 'need to prove herself or comply with the narrow romantic expectations of women that has been part of her make-up from the beginning' has meant that 'the audiences who have been lulled into a catatonia of admiration or vexation were forced to wake up and take notice of the dazzling dexterity and audacity of this woman'.[31]

The notion of performance is, of course, central to both the stage musical and the film narrative: after all, the story of *Mamma Mia!* centres on a woman who was once a stage performer herself, an occupation that relies heavily on the performer's ability to connect with an audience. In casting Donna as a one-time performer, *Mamma Mia!* could be read as a response to the many criticisms of Streep's supposed failure to reach her audience. The scene that appears to formally address this discourse is the performance of 'Super Trouper' at Sophie's bachelorette party by Donna, Tanya and Rosie, who make up the singing trio Donna and the Dynamos. In this scene the trio wear flamboyantly 1970s theatrical costumes (a clear reference to ABBA), and, despite their obvious initial nervousness, their performance is received with warmth and appreciation by the younger women attending the party. While this scene works to foreground the singing talents of Donna and the Dynamos and, by extension, the talents of Streep, Walters and Baranski, it also seems to serve as a request to the film's viewers to broaden their frame of reference for Streep's performances, just as Sophie has to broaden her frame of reference for her mother. Donna and the Dynamos perform together once again at the close of the film. This sequence is central to Streep's transgression and parody of her melodramatic persona as she and her co-stars perform *to* the camera in a first-person address, acknowledging the audience and the fact that they are performing onstage. This sequence is enacted extra-diegetically and directly addresses the cinema audience in a much more self-conscious fashion than even the diegetic musical numbers, particularly when Streep asks the cinema audience, 'Do you want another one?' Many of the musical numbers establish Donna/Streep as the centre of attention, the spectacle.

Of course, the focus on the body is a key element of the musical genre, which is designed to showcase the performer, the choreography and, indeed, the star. Contrary to Pauline Kael's belief that Streep relies on accents and is de-corporealised as a result, Streep foregrounds the physicality of her performance by dancing, a key strategy in making the body spectacle. Several long-shots portray her entire dancing and performing body. The most important scene in this regard is the performance of 'Dancing Queen', when Streep's character herself is actually addressed by the other characters as the 'dancing queen'. As Rosie and Tanya sing the lines 'you are the dancing queen' (and later when the large female cast perform the choreographed dance number on the pier) they point to Donna, who is constantly positioned in the centre of the dance troupe, and they sing the lines directly to her, formally addressing her performing body as spectacle. In addition, while Donna, Rosie and Tanya are making their way towards the pier, gathering women to dance with them, Donna remains the central focus so that the audience might contemplate and pay attention to her excessively performing, and highly active, body. Indeed, one of the most spectacular and memorable images of the entire film is Streep's performance of the splits mid-air while jumping on her bed, a moment made infamous because she was 58 at the time of filming. Not only was this move age-defying (see Claire Jenkins's chapter for further discussion of this), but it also provided a definitive contrast with Streep's static and stiff body in her earlier performances, indicating the spontaneity of an actress who was so often described as being the consummate actress, always prepared and always contained.[32] The upbeat tone of *Mamma Mia!* is in marked opposition to much of the rest of Streep's career. Contrary to the roles she is best known for, Streep plays a woman whose 'sunshine' demeanour is foregrounded throughout the exaggerated musical and bodily performances. This liberation from preconceptions about Streep grants her a playfulness that she had never had previously, as she explains: 'It was an opportunity to be, what's that line in Dancing Queen? To be 17 again, and be young and free. Everybody has that inside them.'[33] Thus, in *Mamma Mia!* Meryl Streep achieves exactly what Pauline Kael had previously said was absent from her performances, in that she is finally permitted to 'giggle more and suffer less'.[34]

Notes

1. Leibovitz, Annie, *At Work*, New York: Random House, 2008, pp. 58–61.

2. Anthony, Andrew, 'A super trouper for the silver screen', *Observer*, 29 June 2008, p. 41.
3. Kaplan, James, 'Nobody does it better', *Premiere*, November 2002. Available from *Simply Streep*. http://www.simplystreep.com/site/magazines/200211premiere/ (accessed 11 April 2011).
4. A term coined by Courtney Brannon Donoghue in her online article 'Rebooting Meryl Streep: from icon to boffo', *Celebrity Gossip, Academic Style*, 23 August 2009. http://www.annehelenpetersen.com/?p=352 (accessed 11 April 2011).
5. Dyer, Richard, *Stars*, London: BFI, 1986, p. 144
6. Ibid, p. 3.
7. Christiansen, Rupert, 'Meltdown', *Harpers and Queen*, July 1990. Available from *Simply Streep*. http://www.simplystreep.com/site/magazines/199007harpersandqueen (accessed 17 April 2011).
8. Papp quoted in Roll, Jack, 'A star born for the 80s', *Newsweek*, January 1980. Available from *Simply Streep*. http://www.simplystreep.com/site/magazines/198001newsweek (accessed 17 April 2011).
9. Haskell, Molly, 'Finding herself: the prime of Meryl Streep', *Film Comment*, May/June 2008. Available from *Simply Streep*. http://www.simplystreep.com/site/magazines/200805filmcomment (accessed 17 April 2011).
10. Vincentelli, Elizabeth, 'Meryl Streep: the great pretender', *Independent*, 8 May 2005. Available from *Simply Streep*. http://www.simplystreep.com/site/magazines/200505theindependent (accessed 17 April 2011).
11. Johnstone, Iain, *Streep: A Life in Film*, London: Psychology News, 2009, p. 6.
12. See Adnum, Mark, 'Meryl Streep: our lady of the accents', *Spiked*, 11 February 2009. http://www.spiked-online.com/index.php/site/article/6204 (accessed 13 April 2011).
13. Anthony, 'A super trouper for the silver screen', p. 41.
14. West, Kevin, 'Two queens', *W Magazine*, May 2006. http://www.wmagazine.com/celebrities/archive/lindsay_lohan_meryl_streep (accessed 16 April 2011)
15. Ibid.
16. Plaskin, Glenn, 'Meryl Streep's focus is work: private life is not for sale', *Seattle Times*, 21 September 1990. http://www.community.seattletimes.nwsource.com/archive/?date=19900921&slug=1094375 (accessed 17 April 2011).
17. Haskell, 'Finding herself: the prime of Meryl Streep'.
18. Maychick, Diana, *Meryl Streep: The Reluctant Superstar*, London: New English Library, 1984, p. 1.

19. Luzón-Aguado, Virginia, 'Star studies today: from the picture personality to the media celebrity', *BELLS: Film Studies Now*, Vol.13, 2008, p.12.
20. Ibid., p. 17.
21. Scott, A. O., 'That unmistakeable Streepness', *New York Times* (Arts), 18 February 2010, p. 1.
22. Anthony, 'A super trouper for the silver screen', p. 41.
23. Brown, Mick, 'Meryl Streep: mother superior', *Telegraph*, 4 December 2008. http://www.telegraph.co.uk/culture/film/3563965/Meryl-Streep-mother-superior.html (accessed 11 April 2011).
24. *Mamma Mia!* production notes, BFI Library.
25. Lane, Anthony, 'Euro visions: *Mamma Mia!* and *Journey to the Centre of the Earth*', *New Yorker*, 28 July 2008. http://www.newyorker.com/arts/critics/cinema/2008/07/28/080728crci_cinema_lane (accessed 18 April 2011).
26. La Sale, Mick, '*Mamma Mia!*, a musical vacation', *San Francisco Chronicle*, 18 July 2008. http://www.articles.sfgate.com/2008-07-18/entertainment/17172633_1_mamma-mia-phyllida-lloyd-amanda-seyfried (accessed 18 April 2011).
27. Ebert, Roger, '*Mamma Mia!*', *Chicago Sun Times*, 17 July 2008. http://rogerebert.suntimes.com (accessed 20 April 2011).
28. Hiscock, John, 'Meryl Streep, the singing and dancing queen', *Telegraph*, 4 July 2008. http://www.telegraph.co.uk/culture/film/3555667/Meryl-Streep-the-singing-and-dancing-queen.html (accessed 31 January 2011).
29. Ibid.
30. Elsaesser, Thomas, 'Vincente Minnelli', in Rick Altman (Ed.), *Genre: The Musical: A Reader*, London: Routledge, 1986, p.16.
31. Haskell, 'Finding herself: the prime of Meryl Streep'.
32. Jeffries, Stuart, 'A legend lightens up', *Guardian* (G2), 2 July 2008, p. 10. It is interesting to note that the image of Donna doing the splits in mid-air was regularly used in publicity material, a decision that has made this image a key one in consolidating Streep's transformation from serious actress to star.
33. Wloszczyna, Susan, 'Streep relishes *Mamma Mia!* role', *USA Today*, July 2008. http://www.airforcetimes.com/entertainment/movies/gns_streep_071508 (accessed 15 April 2011).
34. Horowitz, Jay, 'That madcap Meryl, really!', *New York Times*, 17 March 1991. http://www.nytimes.com/1991/03/17/movies/that-madcap-meryl-really.html (accessed 15 April 2011).

5

'Knowing Me, Knowing You': reading *Mamma Mia!* as feminine object

Caroline Bainbridge

As this collection of essays documents at various points, the success of *Mamma Mia!* in both its stage and cinematic forms has been phenomenal. Of particular note is the fact that, in the UK, the film rapidly became the fastest selling DVD of all time, an observation that has garnered extensive commentary in the national press. This is all the more remarkable given the generally derogatory critical appraisal of the film by reviewers. In the UK press, the narrative attracted far more brickbats than bouquets, and was described as 'naff', 'silly', 'cheeky', 'soulless', 'superficial' and 'at times, preposterously amateurish' with 'the atmosphere of a boisterous hen night'.[1] In this context, it is interesting to reflect on the fact that the *Mamma Mia!* phenomenon arose from a collaboration between three 40-something women. Significantly the film has evidently attracted a huge fan base[2] consisting, in the main, of women who seem to have enthusiastically taken this text to their hearts, using it as a means of finding joyful expression of their femininity and also as a means of forging and maintaining bonds of love and friendship with other women. There is widespread anecdotal and journalistic evidence to suggest that the film, in particular, with its slow-burning marketing strategy consisting of a protracted run supported by billboard and press-based advertising, culminating in the late release of the 'sing-along' screen version, has successfully tapped into a market that is generally described as 'niche': women with buying power.[3] This chapter sets out to explore the implications of these apparent contradictions between the critical perspectives on *Mamma Mia!* and its status as a feminine text at the levels of both production and consumption. It is, perhaps, no accident that the success of the phenomenon can be linked to a cultural context in which a particular moment of neoconservative post-feminism is in the ascendant. How might we grapple with the relationship between the popular appeal of the film to a broad base of women on the international scene, its origins in the collaborative working ethos of its female writer, female producer and female director and its deployment of a particularly feminine sensibility in terms of its representational themes and narrative focus?

As discussed by Williams elsewhere in this volume, one of the crucial elements underpinning the success of *Mamma Mia!* is its origin in the minds of women. The press has generally made a great deal of the relationship between Judy Craymer, Catherine Johnson and Phyllida Lloyd, tending to highlight their comparative inexperience at the point of *Mamma Mia!*'s inception. Significantly, press commentary frequently emphasises the effects of the large-scale success of the project for the financial well-being of each of these women, with an extraordinary amount of comment on how they had become 'stinking rich'[4] and with many witticisms about it being 'a rich gal's world' and 'winners taking it all'.[5] Throughout this press commentary, the women are frequently described as 'girls', despite being in their mid-40s with considerable amounts of professional experience, and discussion of their new-found wealth is often accompanied by extended commentary on the apparent luck of their timing with the creation of the show, their singleness and their 'savviness' and 'canniness' in looking after their own and deploying their 'affectionate, bantering friendship'.[6] It is worth noting here that Craymer, Johnson and Lloyd also opt into this discourse in the 'making of' documentary on the DVD, in which they liken themselves to the main characters in the narrative and comment on the ways in which they have become more 'high maintenance' since the success of their work and the financial reward it has entailed.

The discourses deployed here are familiar to us from the now widespread dominance in popular culture of the phenomenon of post-feminism, with its emphasis on the links between feminine subjectivity, conspicuous consumption, female friendship and an assumed aspiration to 'having it all' with regard to career success, (heterosexual) love relationships, babies and highly meaningful friendships. Many of these themes, of course, are echoed in the narrative concerns of Mamma Mia! itself. This raises a number of questions about the cultural and political significance of its success and its role in shaping what we might now understand as central concerns of contemporary women in their pursuit of opportunities for the expression of pleasure, subjectivity and identification with other women.

In an important intervention into the field of feminist media studies, Angela McRobbie has suggested that there is a significant absence of attention to the values of feminism as it was understood in previous years in the development of this post-feminist sensibility. McRobbie suggests that feminism has somehow been 'taken into account' in post-feminist discourse and she carefully shows how this 'permits an all the more thorough dismantling of feminist politics and the discrediting of the occasionally voiced need for its renewal'.[7] Similarly, Diane Negra and Yvonne Tasker have observed the ways in which the 'othering' of feminism entailed in the shift to a position of post-feminist dominance can be seen as an 'erasure of feminist politics from the popular'.[8] In other work, Negra has suggested that post-feminism is 'fundamentally uncomfortable with female adulthood ..., casting all women as girls to some extent'[9] and argues that 'a platitudinous post-feminist culture ... continually celebrates reductions and essentialisms as explanatory keys for women's psychological and social health'.[10] I have argued elsewhere that the unconscious losses sustained by women struggling against the kind of retrograde post-feminist climate described in the work of these theorists run deep and can be seen to underpin one notable trend in post-feminist discourse in which women enviously stage attacks on other women in order to preserve a fragile sense of self.[11] Negra suggests that this tendency demonstrates the extent to which post-feminism entails 'the aggressive (re)codification of female types' with a reversion to figures from previous eras such as bitches, gold-diggers, '"dumb blondes", spinsters, shrews and sluts' and that the deployment of such figures indicates the 'political and rhetorical "freedom"' of post-feminist women 'getting one over' on what she calls 'the imaginary feminist'.[12]

Whilst some of the press coverage of the success of the female trio who conceived of the *Mamma Mia!* phenomenon might call to mind the relevance of such work in examining the seemingly impossible task of gauging the success of the women behind the show and the film on its own terms within a post-feminist climate, there is more to the success of *Mamma Mia!* than its financial achievement and the consequent inscription of its creators as emblems/icons of post-feminism. As I have already suggested above, the extent of the appeal of *Mamma Mia!* for women across a range of national and generational demographics marks out an extraordinary desire on the part of women to find something to celebrate about femininity in a post-feminist climate. Generally there is little opportunity to forge spaces for such celebratory links between women outside the bounds of a predetermined terrain of conspicuous consumption. Nor is there much scope to do this in a way that creates a momentous feeling of shared experience, on which no pecuniary value can be placed. It strikes me that, despite its global visibility as a brand with selling power, the consumption of *Mamma Mia!* seems largely to have been determined on the basis of women's desire to share the experience of watching it with other women for the sake of the positive experience engendered by being in public spaces *en masse* and in witnessing their transformation because of the overwhelming presence of a feminine sensibility that has tended to characterise this experience.

Mamma Mia! perhaps inspires this at one level because of its narrative focus on relationships between women and between the mother and daughter in particular. There is a clear focus in *Mamma Mia!* on themes such as intergenerational relationships, the maternal bond, female friendship and, importantly, the kind of spaces of exchange that open up in woman-to-woman environments. At another level, the exploration of these themes in the context of the narrative of *Mamma Mia!* works partly because of the harnessing of the narrative to the array of highly popular and familiar songs by the pop group ABBA which work to create a backdrop of familiarity for viewers, enabling connections to be made with their own experiences of relationships, history, friendship and moments of celebration. It is arguably because of this intersection between fiction and a lived relation to popular culture that *Mamma Mia!* is able to transcend other exemplars of the post-feminist sensibility in a way that offers scope for new connections to be made between women in largely unanticipated ways, as I will go on to explore below.

There are echoes here of the writings of Luce Irigaray on the importance of shared objects of exchange and the creation of a mode of 'speaking (as) woman' (*parler femme*) that articulates aspects of feminine subjectivity that more usually go unspoken. Elaborated with reference to her discussion of female genealogy and the importance of charting the relationship between mothers and daughters, Irigaray's notion of *parler femme* attempts to signal the concomitant axis of relationships between women on the horizontal plane. In other words, the idea of 'speaking (as) woman' requires an intervention into the field of woman-to-woman relationships, relationships between female friends and other homosocial fields of relatedness. Margaret Whitford has suggested that, in creating her own work as an object to be exchanged between women, Irigaray attempts to show how women can invert their lived experience of a relation to culture and society that has tended to inscribe their role as commodities. Instead, in attempting to forge a model of *parler femme*, women are able to make use of objects they find amongst themselves so that they have a commodity of sorts to pass between each other, and this enables women to resist the kind of self-sacrifice that is usually required as the basis for social relations.[13]

Irigaray's notion of *parler femme* is closely related to notions of enunciation in cinema and questions of female subjectivity, and, elsewhere, I suggest that narrative elements of film such as scenes of magical realism and flashback sequences work to foreground themes and ideas that are central to any attempt to articulate the silences of feminine senses of self.[14] Irigaray has commented at length on the need for mothers and daughters to manipulate their histories, to reclaim stories of the origin of the feminine, highlighting the need for 'any individual, a woman or a man, [to] recreate his or her personal and collective history'.[15] In my own earlier work, I have set out to show how film can work as an example of *parler femme*, tapping as it does into the unconscious processes of fantasy and desire that underpin the spectatorial relationship, to the screen world, its characters and mechanisms. In most of the films where this can be seen to take place, there is a key narrative strand that centres on the mother–daughter relationship, and there is clear scope in which to apply such a model with regard to *Mamma Mia!* However, *Mamma Mia!* works simultaneously at another level, one that can be seen to fully articulate the psychological elements of the relation that Irigaray sketches out when she discusses the need of women to find meaningful, crafted objects for real and symbolic exchange between them in order to articulate the special terms of both their relationship and the feminine qualities of their senses of subjectivity.[16] There is a sense in this evocation of the feminine object that entails an understanding of how such an object not only would operate in terms of an actual object in the real world, exchanged as a means of symbolising the exchange being made, but would also play an important role in the mediation of psychological relationships between women.

This notion of the object is an important one in the broader psychoanalytic context of the development of the sense of self and a capacity to forge creative relationships with both other people and the world in general. In the work of the psychoanalyst Donald Woods Winnicott, this is expressed in terms of the notion of transitional or potential space (sometimes defined as an intermediary space). Such a notion is very helpful in understanding the importance of both our lived and our psychological relationship to real objects in external reality and their psychological equivalents, which furnish the fantasy spaces of our internal world, and this contributes to the shaping of our sense of subjectivity. For Winnicott, transitional objects, phenomena and space are fundamental to the subject's negotiation of individual identity and separation from the mother. The first transitional object is the m/other who acts as a facilitator for the child's emerging sense of creativity.[17] As the infant develops, these transitional qualities get projected onto a comforting material object such as a teddy bear or a blanket, and this object comes to serve as a point of psychological connection for the child, enabling her/him to hold together the experiences of both the inner and outer worlds. This enables the child, gradually, to bear the experiences of loss and separation anxiety and this contributes to the emerging sense of mastery over the world that comes for the child during this crucial stage of development.

These feelings of mastery are often bound up with the physical and sensory pleasures of the object, and the child takes comfort from this, cherishing the object and coming to associate its sensory pleasures with a broader capacity for feeling secure and happy. Critics drawing on the work of Winnicott to understand the ways in which we forge pleasurable connections with objects in later life have documented how such feelings and associations continue into adulthood.[18] Transitional objects also constitute the first experience of symbol-making and are therefore linked to our capacity for playfulness, thought and creativity, and, as adults, it is in the field of culture that we find ways of sustaining our capacity to find new transitional objects.[19]

Recently, the work of Winnicott has been taken up in the field of film studies, with the suggestion that it provides a particularly useful model for thinking anew about the relation of the cinematic spectator to the cinema screen and to the spaces of cinema as an institution.[20] The arguments here generally suggest that there is something about cinema that evokes our relationships with transitional objects and allows us to experience cinema as a transitional space that opens up possibilities for reworking ideas of the self, ideas of subjectivity and our relation to the emotional connections we have with the world around us. It is relatively straightforward, in this regard, to make links between the kind of object Irigaray has in mind when she sets out her ideal of women encountering objects for exchange between one another and the kind of object Winnicott has in mind.

Here, we might argue that *Mamma Mia!* comes to function as just such an object, enjoying a currency amongst women and serving to create spaces of feminine exchange and sociality in auditoria and beyond. This is, perhaps, particularly clear in the context of the staggering success of the film in terms of its DVD sales. As many sources have documented, the film became both the fastest and biggest selling DVD in the UK, selling more than 5 million copies, with estimated ownership in one in four UK homes.[21] This is highly interesting for a number of reasons. Firstly, it demonstrates the extent to which the success of *Mamma Mia!* is inscribed in its capacity to function as an object for its fans in both senses elaborated in the work of Irigaray and Winnicott. The desire for ownership of the DVD can be read in terms of a desire for women who appreciate the musical to be able to enjoy it on their own terms in their own domestic spaces and also to be able to recreate the experience of shared viewing experiences of the film by re-watching with friends and family. This can be interpreted as a means of seeking to hold onto the emotional qualities associated with the female sociality associated with the film (which has been well documented in press coverage of the *Mamma Mia!* phenomenon). Secondly, as I have suggested elsewhere, the DVD as a material object represents an interesting means of exploring cultural expressions of gendered identity.[22] In relation to masculinity, as Yates and I have argued, the DVD as a material object works to enable men to forge links between themselves as a means of sustaining spaces for pleasurable subjectivities in a culture in which hegemonic notions of masculinity are widely held to be 'in crisis'. The case of *Mamma Mia!* provides an interesting example of how women might also make use of media objects as a means of forging newly sustaining relationships in terms of female friendship and sociality and I wish to argue here that this can be read as a response to the strangulating effects of the losses of feminism and the neoconservative structures of post-feminism that have come to shape popular notions of femininity in recent years.

It is important to consider how *Mamma Mia!* might be seen to achieve this. As we have already seen, the narrative schema did not arouse what we might regard as critical acclaim, despite the extensive media coverage of the show in both its theatrical and cinematic formats. Unlike other examples that easily come to mind with regard to the fashioning of a woman-to-woman sociality, such as *Sex and the City* (HBO, 1998–2004),[23] *Mamma Mia!* did not emerge as an example of a 'water-cooler' televisual phenomenon with in-built extensive appeal. As a West End stage musical, its key selling point was its music, the songs made famous during the 1970s and 1980s by the Swedish pop group ABBA, and the narrative content of the show was largely absent from the marketing of the stage show and, subsequently, the film version of it. Instead, the emphasis was on the popularity of the musical content of the show, focusing on the ongoing appeal of ABBA as a group[24] whose music has enjoyed persistent popularity across the lifespan of a generation, and whose influence in the world of pop has been well documented.[25] In her work on gender and popular music, Norma Coates has suggested that popular music is generally understood as more 'artificial' than rock and is therefore commonly aligned with femininity.[26] This raises a number of interesting perspectives in terms of understanding how *Mamma Mia!* has come to take such a significant role as a feminine object, as I shall now suggest.

The meaning-laden quality of psychological objects explored in the work of Winnicott is further developed in the work of psychoanalyst Christopher Bollas, who suggests that we endow objects with our psychic states.[27] As a consequence, objects come to store aspects of 'self experience' in them that come to the fore when we witness them in new settings and encounter them as familiar and yet also as fresh.[28] Thus,

> the selection of objects is often a type of self utterance. This idiom of self expression is a potential means not only of representing unconscious phantasies but of conveying dense psychic textures that constitute a form of thinking by experiencing.[29]

Bollas goes further to discuss how we use objects in many different ways, according to the kind of stimulation required in any set of circumstances. For example, we may use objects sensationally or conceptually as well as symbolically. A key mode of object use for Bollas is the one that deploys the object 'mnemically', such that the object is understood to be endowed with prior self-experiences, signifying episodes in our past that are significant for the current use of the object. The suggestion here is that when we happen upon objects that are laden with such mnemic significance, they carry with them a sense of self-experience that may not have been anticipated in the fresh encounter with the cultural objects with which we interact. To clarify, in the case of *Mamma Mia!*, when we watch the stage show or the film, our relationship to the music can be understood as a mnemic one. Depending on one's generational experience and on the associations that one has to the songs of ABBA, there will be a renewed encounter with various self-experiences associated with previous (often emotional) engagements with the music as an object in its own right, and this is important in shaping the response that we have to its new context.[30]

The role of the musical object in the formation of the success of *Mamma Mia!* cannot be underestimated. As well as enabling women who watch the film to revisit aspects of self-experience related to their previous emotional encounters with the songs and their psychological associations with them, the music also allows a shared space of exchange to open up as women recognise the emotional experiences of other women as they consume the music together. The songs themselves, which deal with the stuff of relationships and emotion, come to stand in for the emotional and psychological dimensions of relatedness that is so central the formation of a sense of self, as object relations psychoanalysis makes clear. In encountering the songs anew in a fresh context of a stage or film musical, women are able to redeploy their relationships to them in ways that allow for a reconfiguration of the self and in ways that open up new opportunities for the recognition of shared experience amongst other women, who may or may not be known in advance. The use of music in the context of drama is a time-hallowed means of signalling emotional states of being and the experience of interiority, as much work on the significance of melodrama, especially in the context of cinema, makes clear.[31] In this way, music can be used as a means of women expressing the bonds between them.

In his work on fan cultures, Matt Hills has turned to an object relations psychoanalytic approach to ideas of fandom, suggesting that 'a fan culture is formed around any given text when this text has functioned as a primary transitional object in the biography of a number of individuals'.[32] This seems particularly pertinent when we consider the well-documented uses of the texts by fans of *Mamma Mia!* In the UK, the *Guardian* newspaper carried a column containing the opinions of a number of female public figures more usually associated with 'taste-driven' and/or 'feminist' artefacts of culture. The overwhelming character of the remarks made by these women was framed in terms of their joy at the experience of viewing *Mamma Mia!* repeatedly, whether alone or together with female relatives and friends. Author Jeanette Winterson remarked:

> It's the kind of film that you come out from feeling happy, and that's a rare experience. The politics are in there, but I'm not so interested in them: they're not the main focus. It's just a joyful, celebratory, happy experience. There are so many films where the women are sidelined and marginalised, just to turn that around is in itself a political act.[33]

In a similar vein, the feminist writer and activist Julie Bindel claimed that the film 'made [her] feel happy for the first time ever'.[34] The experience of watching *Mamma Mia!* often also entails descriptions of the desire to sing along with the songs and to dance with other members of the audience in the aisles. The sharedness of the experience of unbridled emotional joy and pleasure dominates in commentary around the pleasures of both the film and the stage show for their female spectators,[35] illustrating further the extent to which *Mamma Mia!* can be read as constituting a particularly feminine object for the women involved.

It is also worth noting that, for Luce Irigaray, the exchange of feminine objects between women is intended to transcend divisions between women, such as those experienced as a result of class, ethnicity or generational identification. Irigaray highlights the ways in which such objects often entail a focus on music or song, poetry, laughter or dancing and defines these moments of sensory pleasure in terms of the gestural codes of women's bodies being used in moments of song and dance that conjure up a sense of carefree whirling and turning. The sense here is that spaces are transformed into markedly feminine ones in such moments: 'in these places of women-among-themselves, something of speaking (as) a woman is heard'.[36] Irigaray's ideas here evoke very clearly the key elements of central sequences of *Mamma Mia!*, such as the 'Dancing Queen' one. This sequence highlights how music, dance and gender work together to produce laughter, merriment and joyous abandon that is infectious and irresistible for the film's entire array of female characters. The way in which feminine objects can work to unite women is forcefully represented here, although, of course, *Mamma Mia!* nevertheless privileges a vision of white, hegemonic, Anglo-European femininity that is overarchingly politically conservative.

In this way, then, the transitional or intermediary spaces opened up by the *Mamma Mia!* phenomenon can be read as producing innovative and creative containing structures for women who grapple with the contradictions of the contemporary post-feminist climate. In this chapter, I have sought to show how both the stage show and the film version have successfully provided opportunities for women to come together, in the formation of what we might describe, drawing on Irigaray's useful phrase, as a 'woman-to-woman sociality'. They do so by tapping into aspects of narrative form and textuality that are readily associated with femininity and emotionality: melodrama, images of female friendship, representations of the mother–daughter relationship, concerns about love relationships and the deployment of popular music to underscore each of these in more depth. In addition, in the modes of production, distribution, reception and consumption, there is also an overarching concern with the significance of woman-to-woman relationships in forging the original idea for the text as well as its ongoing success. The press coverage of themes related to femininity is indicative of the extent of their significance in this regard.

My suggestion, then, is that this film works symptomatically to express a desire amongst women to celebrate the specificity of their relationships to one another in a cultural climate in which feminism has fallen out of fashion. The spaces of resistance to the broad-based assumption that contemporary popular culture is always-already 'post-feminist' can thus be seen to be at play here. As we saw above, the advent of a dominant post-feminist sensibility has usually provided critics with an opportunity to lambast popular culture as unerringly laden with neoconservative values to the detriment of any desire for opportunities to speak a political position of resistance. However, psychoanalysis reminds us that the structures of subjectivity are always also inscribed in terms of resistance and, by using a psychoanalytic framework to illuminate the role of objects in enabling the quandaries of subjectivity to be reined in and redrawn according to a logic that may sometimes be directly unspeakable, I have attempted to show how spaces for resistance can frequently make themselves felt. With its clever deployment of emotion through song and music, *Mamma Mia!* offers a space for the articulation of the feminine on its own terms, and its use of popular songs with mnemic object qualities works to enhance the effectiveness of this by allowing the narrative to open up intermediary spaces between women that create opportunities for a shared experience of sociality to emerge.[37] In this way, women's engagement with *Mamma Mia!* creates a sense of 'Knowing Me, Knowing You' between the women who watch together, and the significance of this phrase resounds with the possibility of forging new friendships and new mutual modes of empathy and understanding.

In these terms, the success of *Mamma Mia!* can usefully be seen as opening up spaces in which women find a means of resisting the kind of hopelessness engendered in an age of postfeminism that has all too quickly moved beyond the objectives of feminism without due regard to the effect of this on women's senses of relatedness and subjectivity. In some ways, then, the *Mamma Mia!* phenomenon works to counter the tendency amongst women discussed earlier in this chapter to enter into patterns of mutual denigration as a means of surviving the losses implicit in the post-feminist turn. Instead, cultural objects such as *Mamma Mia!* offer women a chance to join together in a way characterised by gratitude rather than envy, emotional states of being that are seen as deeply interrelated by the psychoanalyst Melanie Klein.[38] Whereas envy is used to sanction destructive and denigratory behaviour and attitudes, gratitude is used to express appreciation for goodness and nourishment. In some ways, then, what the phenomenal success of *Mamma Mia!* demonstrates is the extent of good will between women, and the sense that post-feminism has not yet managed to eradicate the capacity for women to come together with creative and joyful intentions, despite the widespread assumption that feminism has had its day and survives as little more than a spectre from a bygone age. A feelgood moment indeed.

Notes

1. Both the stage show musical and the film were described in this way. See, for example, Anon., 'Review of reviews', *Guardian*, 14 July 2008, p. 29; Gardner, Lynn, 'Arts reviews, theatre: *Mamma Mia!*', *Guardian*, 8 April 1999, p. 11; Ide, Wendy, 'ABBA get drabber', *The Times*, 12 July 2008, p. 10; Tookey, Charles, 'So I say thank you for the musical!; now for the money! money! money!', *Daily Mail*, 11 July 2008, p. 54.
2. The Facebook fan page for the film had 790,168 friends as of 29 January 2011. http://www.facebook.com/#!/MammaMiaFilm?v=wall.
3. See, for example, http://www.peeledsnacks.com/blog/2008/12/mamma_mia_marketing_to_niches.html and http://www.prgossip.co.uk/tag/mamma-mia/ (accessed 19 December 2010).
4. Spencer, Charles, '*Mamma Mia!*', *Daily Telegraph*, 27 March 2004, p. 17.
5. Anon., 'It's a rich gal's world', *Mirror*, 9 July 2008, p. 23.

6. Ibid., and Spencer, 'Mamma Mia!'
7. McRobbie, Angela, 'Postfeminism and popular culture', *Feminist Media Studies*, Vol. 4, No. 3, 2004, p. 256.
8. Tasker, Yvonne and Negra, Diane (Eds), *Interrogating Postfeminism: Gender and the Politics of Popular Culture*, Durham, NC: Duke University Press, 2007, pp. 4–5.
9. Negra, Diane, *What a Girl Wants: Fantasizing the Reclamation of Self in Postfeminism*, London: Routledge, 2009, p. 14.
10. Ibid., p. 4.
11. Bainbridge, Caroline, 'They've taken her: psychoanalytical perspectives on mediating maternity, feeling and loss', *Studies in the Maternal*, Vol. 2, No. 1, 2009. http://www.mamsie.bbk.ac.uk.
12. Negra, *What a Girl Wants*, p. 10.
13. Whitford, Margaret, *Luce Irigaray: Philosophy in the Feminine*, London: Routledge, 1991, pp. 51–2.
14. Bainbridge, Caroline, 'Feminine enunciation in the cinema', *Paragraph: A Journal of Modern Critical Theory*, Vol. 25, No. 3, 2002, pp. 129–42; Bainbridge, Caroline, *A Feminine Cinematics: Luce Irigaray, Women and Film*, Basingstoke: Palgrave Macmillan, 2008, pp. 36–8.
15. Irigaray, Luce, *Je, Tu, Nous: Towards a Culture of Difference* (trans. Alison Martin), London: Routledge, 1993, p. 28.
16. Ibid., p. 48.
17. Bollas, Christopher, *Being a Character: Psychoanalysis and Self-expression*, London: Routledge, 1987.
18. Young, Robert M., 'Transitional phenomena: production and consumption', in B. Richards (Ed.), *Crises of the Self*, London: Free Association Books, 1989, pp. 57–72.
19. Winnicott, Donald W., 'Transitional objects and transitional phenomena: a study of the first not-me possession', *International Journal of Psychoanalysis*, Vol. 34, 1957, pp. 89–97.
20. See, for example, Kuhn, Annette, 'Screen and screen theorizing today', *Screen*, Vol. 50, No. 1, 2009, pp. 1–12; Lebeau, Vicki, 'The arts of looking: D. W. Winnicott and Michael Haneke', *Screen*, Vol. 50, No. 1, 2009, pp. 35–44. See also Bainbridge and Yates for a reading of how Winnicott enables us to develop new perspectives on the perceived 'crisis of masculinity' through the lens of film analysis and the cultural analysis of DVD consumption: 'Cinematic symptoms of masculinity in transition: memory, history and mythology in contemporary film', *Psychoanalysis, Culture and Society*, Vol. 10, No. 3, 2005, pp. 299–318; 'Everything to play for: masculinity, trauma and the pleasures of DVD technologies', in Caroline Bainbridge, Susannah Radstone, Michael Rustin and Candida Yates (Eds), *Culture and the Unconscious*,

Basingstoke: Palgrave Macmillan, 2007, pp. 107–22; 'On not being a fan: masculine identity, DVD culture and the accidental collector', *Wide Screen*, Vol. 2, No. 1, 2010. http://widescreenjournal.org/index.php/journal/article/view/39/48.
21. See, for example, coverage of the extent of DVD sales in Paphides, Pete and Foster, Patrick, 'The way old friends do?', *The Times*, 26 March 2009. http://entertainment.timesonline.co.uk/tol/arts_and_entertainment/music/article7076415.ece (accessed 11 April 2011).
22. Bainbridge and Yates, 'On not being a fan'.
23. Like *Mamma Mia!*, *Sex and the City: The Movie* (King, 1998) and *Sex and the City 2* (King, 2010) were both marketed to the 'women's niche audience' and succeeded in filling cinema auditoria with women who flocked to see these films in droves. In cities such as London, there were additional marketing ploys designed to heighten the 'experience' as one that women could share through their recognition of mnemic objects embedded in the original television series, such as Cosmopolitan cocktails and the idea that women should dress up in their most fashionable clothes in order to attend the screenings in a way that demonstrated an understanding of the TV show's chief themes and concerns. This created an atmosphere of carnival and celebration around the films as 'event movies' (see http://www.barbican.org.uk/film/event-detail.asp?ID=7543, accessed 17 May 2012), thereby heightening the gendered cultural significance of this phenomenon.
24. Marketing for *Mamma Mia!* describes the narrative as 'The smash hit musical based on the songs of ABBA', signalling in its marketing blurb that 'The story-telling magic of ABBA's timeless songs propels this enchanting tale of love, laughter and friendship, and every night everyone's having the time of their lives!' http://www.mamma-mia.com/ (accessed 17 May 2012).
25. For an exploration of ABBA's role in the globalisation of Swedish popular music, see Johannson, Ola, 'Beyond ABBA: the globalisation of Swedish popular music', *Focus on Geography*, Vol. 53, No. 4, 2010, pp. 134–41.
26. Coates, Norma, '(R)evolution now: rock and the political potential of gender', in Shelia Whitely (Ed.), *Sexing the Groove: Popular Music and Gender*, London: Routledge, 1997, p. 52.
27. Bollas, *Being a Character*, p. 13.
28. Ibid., p. 21.
29. Ibid., p. 30.
30. In this regard, it is worth noting that there is a significant tranche of women who have vociferously protested their dislike of *Mamma Mia!* For example, there are several pages on Facebook where the

emphasis is on the desire to express 'hatred' for the film in particular. Pages such as 'So how many Facebookers HATE *Mamma Mia* (the film)' (http://www.facebook.com/group.php?gid=61426156512#!/group.php?gid=61426156512&v=wall, accessed 17 May 2012), 'I hate *Mamma Mia* the movie! (But I still love ABBA)' (http://www.facebook.com/group.php?gid=43227565837#!/group.php?gid=43227565837&v=wall, accessed 17 May 2012), and 'I hate *Mamma Mia*' (http://www.facebook.com/group.php?gid=103459693029515#!/group.php?gid=103459693029515&v=wall, accessed 17 May 2012) have far fewer 'fans' than the *Mamma Mia!* Facebook fan page but nevertheless indicate the way in which the phenomenon has become emblematic of the post-feminist moment, creating something troubling and problematic for certain groups of women. Of particular interest here is the way in which women who profess their dislike of the film nevertheless wish to assert their appreciation of ABBA in particular. This suggests that the mnemic value of the songs for such groups of women might evoke self-experiences that are undermined by the film, thereby causing it to become a bad object and/or a source of projection of elements of the self that are intolerable.
31. Gledhill, Christine (Ed.), *Home Is Where the Heart Is: Studies in Melodrama and the Woman's Film*, London: BFI, 1987.
32. Hills, Matt, *Fan Cultures*, London: Routledge, 2002, p. 108.
33. Cochrane, Kira, 'The mother of all movies', *Guardian* (G2), 27 November 2008, p. 7.
34. Ibid.
35. For example, in the *Los Angeles Times*, Rachel Abramowitz observed, 'Every night, some 17,000 people watch Mamma Mia! somewhere in the world, joining the more than 30 million who have already seen it.' 'Mamma Mia! dances into theaters', *Los Angeles Times*, 16 July 2008. http://www.latimes.com/entertainment/la-et-brief16-2008-jul16,0,1488961.story (accessed 17 May 2012).
36. Irigaray, Luce, *This Sex Which Is Not One* (trans. Catherine Porter), Ithaca, NY: Columbia University Press, 1977, p. 135.
37. See Malcolm Womack's chapter in this collection.
38. Klein, Melanie, *Envy and Gratitude and Other Works 1946–63*, London: Hogarth Press, 1975.

6

The power of sisterhood: *Mamma Mia!* as female friendship film

Betty Kaklamanidou

According to Thomas Schatz, the first decade of the new millennium is the era of conglomerate Hollywood, which 'crystallized in the mid-1980s' and led to 'the formation of the so-called Big Six media conglomerates [Time Warner, Disney, News Corp, Sony, Viacom and GE, which own Warner Bros., Disney, Universal, 20th Century Fox, Columbia and Paramount] and their hegemony over the American film (and TV) industry'.[1] Schatz underlines that the millennial Hollywood strategy prioritises investments in 'a new breed of blockbuster-driven franchises specifically geared to the global, digital, conglomerate-controlled marketplace, which spawn billion-dollar film series installments while also serving the interests of the parent conglomerate's other media and entertainment divisions'.[2] Alongside these primarily male-centred blockbusters and film franchises – from the *Harry Potter* series to the *Pirates of the Caribbean* franchise – the female friendship film also grew beyond the mainly niche-targeted films of the 1980s and 1990s. *Charlie's Angels* (McG, 2000) and *Charlie's Angels: Full Throttle* (McG, 2003), *Sex and the City* (King, 2008), *Mamma Mia!* (Lloyd, 2008) and *Sex and the City 2* (King, 2010) generated impressive revenue (the films combined grossed more than $1.8 billion worldwide) and proved that female-centred stories are perhaps a new, untapped source in terms of big-budget films and corporate interest.³

Ashley Elaine York claims that two of the most financially viable female friendship films, *Mamma Mia!* and *Sex and the City*, changed 'the Hollywood moviemaking formula ... affecting the types of women's films that are produced in the future'.⁴ These 'women's blockbusters', to adopt York's definition, 'present a focused package of image, advertising, and text beyond the chick flick audience of 18–34-year-old heterosexual women'. *Mamma Mia* and *Sex and the City* were recognised for their appeal to a wider demographic 'that brought older and younger heterosexual women, lesbians and gays, heterosexual men, and transnational viewers together to transform what was once a small domestic following into a large, sutured, global audience'.⁵ As Guy Adams points out, this group of films and their common subject of female friendship 'has prompted talk among industry experts of the start of a new golden era for a genre known as the "girl-friend-flick" or GFF'.⁶ Adams' conclusions were based on the conviction that 'male teenagers still make up the biggest audience in US cinemas'.⁷ However, according to statistics drawn from the Motion Picture Association, of the 217 million moviegoers and total admissions sales of $1.4 billion in 2009, women made up 113 million of the filmgoers and bought 55 per cent of the tickets while men made up 104 million moviegoers and bought 45 per cent of the tickets. In other words, There were 9 million more women filmgoers than men.⁸ And it is these women who constituted the vast majority of the *Mamma Mia!* audience. Not caring about the unanimous unfavourable reviews, the mostly female viewers⁹ turned the film into the 5th highest grossing film of 2008 worldwide, as well as the 56th highest grossing film ever,¹⁰ surpassing such contemporaneous blockbusters as *Iron Man* (Favreau, 2008) and *I Am Legend* (Lawrence, 2007). Perhaps, as York suggests, for the first time in the history of the woman's film, 'women are able to enjoy the rewards of spectacular production in combination with millennial themes and narratives pitched from their own points of view'.[11] Although the smaller female-centred and/or female-produced films are, as York claims, still very important, the emergence of women's blockbusters makes these popular narratives sites of exploration of female issues such as friendship as well as global cultural products with an impact that should be explored.

The female friendship film

> It's all about the girls and their friendship. That is what matters after all in the end. (two Greek 60-something female spectators of *Mamma Mia!*, leaving the cinema)

Mamma Mia! was promoted as a musical romantic comedy that follows in the long tradition of one of the most classic Hollywood film genres. Its main tag lines confirm this generic category: 'Take a Trip down the Aisle You'll Never Forget', 'Everybody Is Coming to Sophie's Wedding', 'The Music. The Romance. The Movie'. Indeed, *Mamma Mia!* does include a love story; it has a wedding ceremony, albeit with a twist, and some of the most well-known songs in the history of pop music. However, more than 30 minutes of the total 108-minute duration of the film are devoted to scenes and/or sequences built around Donna (Meryl Streep) and her two girlfriends, Tanya (Christine Baranski) and Rosie (Julie Walters). If we juxtapose the three women's scenes with the seven minutes Donna's daughter, Sophie, shares with Lisa (Rachel McDowall) and Ali (Ashley Lilley), and the less than three minutes devoted exclusively to the three men, Harry (Colin Firth), Sam (Pierce Brosnan) and Bill (Stellan Skarsgård), it is clear that the narrative favours Donna and her two girlfriends. Of course, the existence of one or more sidekicks is almost mandatory in the grammar of the romantic film narrative – Jane's (Meryl Streep's) girlfriends in *It's Complicated* (Meyers, 2009), Sophie's (Drew

Barrymore's) supportive sister and confidante in *Music & Lyrics* (Lawrence, 2007) or Tripp's (Matthew McConaughey's) best friends in *Failure to Launch* (Dey, 2006) – but in *Mamma Mia!* Donna's girlfriends are not simply there to help her choose Mr Right or deliver witty one-liners to provide the comic relief such a generic narrative dictates, although they do fulfil that function too.

Tanya and Rosie's extended cinematic presence and their close interaction with Donna demonstrate that even though the film may tackle traditionally female subjects such as romance, motherhood, female autonomy, maturity and sexuality it also foregrounds female friendship as a central theme of the narrative. Indeed, it is Tanya and Rosie who are chosen by the film to provide support to Donna when she is dealing with her emotional chaos that ensues after Sophie's prospective fathers arrive on the island. Taking this narrative parameter into consideration, this chapter will suggest that *Mamma Mia!* is not 'just' a musical romantic comedy but can also be placed in the genre that Karen Hollinger calls 'the female friendship film'.[12] Drawing from Hollinger's work and other established genre theory, and using close textual analysis, I investigate how *Mamma Mia!* works to celebrate and consolidate the power of female friendship.

The generic category of women's film or women's cinema is not fixed; different meanings have been associated with the genre during the last decades, particularly with the emergence of feminist film theory in the 1970s. Molly Haskell viewed the 'woman's' film primarily with suspicion, since the term itself was 'used disparagingly to conjure up the image of the pinched-virgin or little-old-lady writer, spilling out her secret longing in wish fulfilment or glorious martyrdom, and transmitting these fantasies to the frustrated housewife'.[13] For Claire Johnston, women's cinema signified films made by women such as Dorothy Arzner and Ida Lupino,[14] while Annette Kuhn claims that women's genres included such diverse forms as 'television soap opera and film melodrama, popular narrative forms aimed at a female audience' regardless of the gender of their producers/filmmakers.[15] Similarly, Jeanine Basinger writes that the woman's film is very difficult to define, 'being something contradictory, elusive, hypocritical, and deceptive' and thus expanding to many different genres, such as the bio/pic, the melodrama, the western or the crime film.[16] It is interesting to note, however, that the parameter of female friendship as a significant narrative element or thematic axis of the woman's film was not a focal point of most of these writings. For instance, although Basinger's book on the woman's picture genre covers the years 1930–1960 and is divided into ten sections (among them fashion and glamour, men, marriage, motherhood and the woman in the man's world), there is little attention dedicated to female friendship; the word 'friendship' appears just seven times, only two of which refer to celluloid female friendships. Yvonne Tasker observes that 'the popular American cinema ... marginalised representations of female friendship' until the late 1980s, when films such as *Mystic Pizza* (Petrie, 1988) and *Steel Magnolias* (Ross, 1989) started to change the grammar and syntax of women's films – an argument that led Hollinger to focus exclusively on the female friendship film as a subgenre of the more generalised and inclusive woman's film.[17]

For the purposes of this chapter, I will begin by accepting that the woman's film is a separate genre – with all the questions and implications such a statement may rightly raise – which enjoys its special set of structural elements and conventions, like every other genre. According to Rick Altman the definition of a new genre or cycle can be determined through the identification of semantic elements such as 'shared plots, key scenes, character types, familiar objects or recognizable shots and sounds' and/or syntactic aspects such as 'plot structure, character relationships or image and sound montage'.[18] Hollinger uses only one semantic and one syntactic element, the female friends and their friendship(s), to define the female friendship film, which, as I previously note, she considered a 'subgenre of the woman's film'.[19] In this way, her corpus includes diverse films, such as the period drama *Julia* (Zinneman, 1977), the comedies *Nine to Five* (Higgins, 1980) and *Desperately Seeking Susan* (Seidelman, 1985), the ensemble drama *Steel Magnolias*, the action film *Thelma & Louise* (Scott, 1991) and the thriller *Single White Female* (Schroeder, 1992), among others, that Hollinger then proceeds to explore under six different headings.[20]

In the wider context of genre theory, Hollinger's corpus can be considered somewhat problematic, since a single syntactic element of the filmic plot is not enough to turn a bona fide comedy such as *Mad Money* (Khouri, 2008) and a conventionally structured action/adventure film such as *Charlie's Angels* into exclusively female friendship films. What Hollinger tries to do is to study the various representations of female autonomy and sisterhood in mainstream films through female friendships and to 'examine the complex and multidimensional nature' of their different filmic accounts.[21] The author's main concern is to approach the films in her corpus not as 'progressive challenges to the status quo' or 'as reactionary props of dominant patriarchal ideology, but rather as complex products of an intricate process of negotiation'.[22] Hollinger views the female friendship film as a system of multifaceted exchanges between the industry, the audience and the cinematic text. This follows the recent tendency in genre theory to claim that

> Genres do not consist only of films, they consist also, and equally, of specific systems of expectation and hypothesis which spectators bring with them to the cinema, and which interact with films themselves during the course of the viewing process.[23]

Indeed, the industry continues to produce female friendship films that the audience seems to 'demand', and the emergence of the new millennium women's blockbusters can easily attest to this symbiotic relationship.

Thank you for being a friend

Despite being marketed as a musical about romance, *Mamma Mia!*'s romance narrative is, as I suggested earlier, limited to a few brief scenes: Sophie and Sky's three-minute rendition of 'Lay All Your Love on Me', Donna's confession to Sam that 'The Winner Takes It All', his subsequent version of 'I Do, I Do, I Do, I Do, I Do' and their brief wedding that fades into the celebratory dinner, as well as Rosie's effort to seduce Bill whilst she sings 'Take a Chance on Me'. On the other hand, not only do the scenes and sequences that Donna shares with her girlfriends outnumber the aforementioned romantic sections but their longer duration creates a strong subtext that in the end surpasses the supposed centrality of the love story and ends up governing the narrative. According to Russian formalist Roman Jakobson, 'the dominant' is 'the focusing component of a work of art: it rules, determines, and transforms the remaining components' and 'guarantees the integrity of the structure'.[24] In *Mamma Mia!*, it is Donna, Tanya and Rosie who determine and dominate the film, transforming it from a romantic musical to a female friendship film.

The strong bond Donna has with Tanya and Rosie is shown not only through their many shared scenes but also through specific directorial choices. The women's first encounter takes place when Donna meets Tanya and Rosie at the island's smaller pier in the eleventh minute of the film, after the introduction of all the other characters. The reunion of the three women is staged as very special because the years that have intervened since they last met are dissolved by their immediate reference to their musical past, a past that bonds them and allows conventional etiquette to be abandoned. As soon as Donna, Tanya and Rosie see each other across the pier they start striking poses and shouting old mottos from their days performing as Donna and the Dynamos before they finally run and embrace. Behaving without inhibition and giggling like 15-year-olds – reminiscent of, or perhaps deliberately mirroring, the preceding meeting sequence of Sophie with Lisa and Ali – the three women head to Donna's island home. On the way to the house, their verbal exchange confirms their friendship bond. This four-minute sequence not only introduces Donna's two friends and consolidates our understanding of their close relationship; it also incorporates significant details pertaining to the importance of female friendship. It suggests that authentic friendship is a process that takes years to evolve, but, most importantly, does not necessarily depend on common class status, personality traits or beliefs. At first glance, the three women seem to have nothing in common: Donna is an independent single mother who settled on a Greek island, Rosie is single and a well-known cookery writer and Tanya is a divorcée in search of yet another husband. The narrative does not provide a detailed exposition of the background of their friendship but it nonetheless suggests a deep female bond through its emphasis on sparky interaction between the reunited friends.

Donna's business is in serious trouble and her pride does not allow her to accept the financial help Rosie and Tanya offer. However 'normal' Rosie and Tanya's reaction may be, money can become a thorny issue among friends that can lead to fights or break-ups. 'Money and friendship don't mix' is the initial firm response Charlotte (Kristin Davis) gives one of her best friends, Carrie (Sarah Jessica Parker), when the latter realises she will lose her apartment to her ex-boyfriend if she does not raise enough cash to buy it in the ultimate female friendship television series *Sex and the City* (HBO, 1998–2004).[25] But despite Rosie's and Tanya's offers of monetary assistance being rebuffed, this does not cause a schism between Donna and her friends, and the three of them share a few drinks and continue to catch up. The scene runs for a little over a minute and is divided entirely into eight medium three-shot shots, with the exception of a single and extremely brief medium shot of Tanya. The use of the three-shot is narratively significant; the three friends occupy the whole frame and become the centre of the diegesis at the same time. As such the three women become the centre of their own and the spectators' world. What makes this scene work so well is the actors' vast experience and their semi-improvisation. In the DVD commentary, director Phyllida Lloyd says that the scene begins with a 'genuine mistake' made by Christine Baranski that was instantly 'corrected' by both Streep and Walters in order to avoid another take. The actors' skills and their ability to physically and emotionally respond to each other's lines transforms the scene into a brilliant 'mimesis' of the power of female friendship. Indeed, the strength of their bond is highlighted in the presentation of female solidarity in the 'Chiquitita' scene that follows on from the women's light-hearted discussion of sex.

Their girl talk, interrupted by outbreaks of giggles and 'assisted' by alcohol, eventually touches upon the subject of sex. When Donna is asked whether she has been sexually active, she unconvincingly answers that she's glad that whole part of her life is over and that she doesn't miss it at all. However, she is soon reminded of 'what used to be' with the arrival of Sam, Bill and Harry. Terribly upset, she bursts into tears after their chance encounter and tries to hide from her friends. A closed door is of course not an obstacle for Tanya and Rosie, who start singing 'Chiquitita', a song whose title, which means 'little girl', further renders Donna as vulnerable and in need of support. Although often played for comedy, the women's rendition of the song makes it one of the more emotionally resonant songs within the film. Indeed, the fact that Tanya and Rosie sing in double harmony reinforces the idea of unity between these women.

The visual presentation of this scene also works to reinforce the three women's bond and demonstrates the unequivocal love they share. The 'Chiquitita' sequence is made up of 48 shots, the majority of which are medium three-shots that accentuate the characters' importance and encourages the spectator to invest emotionally in their relationship. Two-shots are also part of the sequence – Rosie buttoning Donna's overalls, Tanya offering her pills that Rosie takes instead in a humorous twist – but the frequency of the use of two-shots and their duration is significantly lower than that of the three-shots. In the DVD commentary, Lloyd underlines that this is the key scene 'where the relationship of these women really took off'. The director also reveals that although she had intended to do close-ups of the three women, she let her thespians improvise with props and the lyrics (the fourth line of the song is changed by Walters and Baranski). Impressed by the actors' skills in physical comedy and their ability to imbue a sense of comedy into what is ostensibly a more serious scene, Lloyd thought it would be best to convey their love for one another with the use of the three-shot. Although Donna seems to usually occupy the centre of the three-shot, the sequence includes several two-shots where either Tanya or Rosie dominates the frame. Back in Donna's room, Tanya and Rosie start singing 'Dancing Queen', and wearing the old Dynamo clothes Donna keeps stored, they try to instil positive thoughts into their frustrated friend, who finally comes to her senses and starts jumping up and down on her bed. As Donna does her famous splits in the air, time is seen to stand still and a few seconds of slow motion serve to suggest that this time-honoured friendship serves as Donna's liberating force.

The three friends' interaction and extended cinematic presence dominate the narrative even though it is Sophie's search for her father that drives the plot. Although a semiotic analysis of the plot would conclude that the major cardinal functions include the quest for a father, Sky and Sophie's decision to wait before they wed, and the final denouement in the form of Donna and Sam's subsequent nuptials, it is Donna's scenes with her girlfriends that imbue and determine the indexes; this is the film's atmosphere. It is important to note that even though the film begins and comes full circle with Sophie mailing the letters to her potential fathers and leaving the island with Sky by the close of the film, her on-screen time is limited compared with that of her mother and her friends. In addition, Sophie's scenes with Lisa and Ali usually accentuate her own importance and do not highlight their relationship. The 'Honey Honey' sequence, which is the only song in which the three younger women share extended screen time and sing together, ends with Sophie alone on the balcony. Other shots that include the three younger women tend to position Sophie as separate from her two friends, often employing close-ups that emphasise her distance from them. However, the narrative offers the supposition that the young women's relationship is, in fact, a mirror of the relationship of Donna, Tanya and Rosie. After the hen party that ends with Sophie collapsing on the dance floor, a 40-second parallel montage presents what Lloyd notes are intercutting shots of the 'two sets of friends', in two rooms. The fast pace of this scene reflects Donna's and Sophie's confusion and panic, and, uttering the same phrase – 'I have been tossing and turning all night' – adds to the comic effect. Nonetheless, this very brief juxtaposition of the young and older friends is not developed enough throughout the film to suggest that Sophie, Ali and Lisa's friendship will eventually progress to the bond shared between Donna, Tanya and Rosie.

Conclusion

The film's narratological and visual emphasis on the friendship between Donna, Tanya and Rosie complicates the generic categorisation of *Mamma Mia!* as a musical romantic comedy. The musical romantic comedy, by definition, follows the conventions of a love story, aided by comic situations as well as songs and dance. The Hollywood romantic comedy, one of the most durable film genres in the history of cinema, has survived through its ability to adapt to specific sociocultural circumstances. One of the most notable developments in the otherwise conventional narrative is the insertion of female friendships as significant narrative stratagems. Examining a number of romantic comedy paradigms from the 1990s, Celestino Deleyto observed that there is a 'broader tendency in romantic comedy to examine the importance of friendship in contemporary society and to explore the tensions that it creates in its rapport with heterosexual desire'.[26] Although the heterosexual union may more often seal the final sequence of these films, the incorporation and exploration of female friendships is continuing to preoccupy post-millennium romantic narratives. Films such as *The Sweetest Thing* (Kumble, 2002), *Sex and the City* and *Bride Wars* (Winick, 2009) are examples of recent films that appear to emphasise the importance and power of the female bond in preference to the romance narrative. *Mamma Mia!* is following suit, in line not only with these new millennium films but also with the female friendship films of the 1990s. Even though men may be the cause of problems to the women of these narratives, 'they are accorded little agency and very little screen time'.[27] Donna may end up marrying Sam and Rosie's serenade to Bill might eventually win him over, but their on-screen encounters are few, and, with the exception of 'The Winner Takes It All' sequence, they are not as powerful as the encounters between the women. Finally, one should not forget that whilst the film completes its narrative circle with Sophie and Sky leaving the island at night, the camera actually moves away from the boat and focuses on the moon's reflection on the sea, where the silhouettes of the Dynamos emerge to the first notes of 'Dancing Queen', followed by Donna, Tanya and Rosie on a stage performing the song in 1970s clothes. According to Bernard F. Dick, end credits of this kind do not contribute to the diegetic world; rather, they constitute a pleasant surprise.[28] In the case of *Mamma Mia!* not only do the lavish end credits try to recapture the feeling of the stage musical but, significantly, Donna, Tanya and Rosie are placed in the centre of the frame, together for the last time.

The incorporation of strong female friendships in many popular film narratives such as *Mamma Mia!* not only suggests genre evolution but might serve as a comment on societal concerns about the state of romantic relationships and female bonds. Varied family formulations such as 'smaller household sizes, the shift from extended families to nuclear families, the decrease in marriage and an increase in separation or divorce' and the 'appearance of new forms of unions such as unmarried cohabitation and living-apart-together and changing gender and intergenerational relations' may have resulted in people requiring and finding different emotional outlets other than the family.[29] Therefore, friendships seem to have become more important as the social space where an individual can experience the freedom of being herself/himself without the need to impress in order to secure a romantic partner. Taking into account Hollywood's capitalistic structure, Pam Cook observed that the return of the women's picture in the 1980s and 1990s was 'as much a recognition of the cultural power of feminism as ... an attempt to capitalize on and control it'.[30] Correspondingly, the rise of the women's blockbuster in the new millennium is also part of the patriarchal conglomerate plan to earn as much as possible from the large percentage of global female filmgoers. However, despite the financial reasons behind the resurgence of these films, their worldwide popularity is undoubtedly significant, as demonstrated by the way in which the female audience seemed to take *Mamma Mia!* to their hearts. Film narratives such as *Mamma Mia!* may not be explicitly subversive or propose solutions to the ongoing feminist debate about female subjectivity, but they do accentuate the relationship of the female protagonists to show there is much more to female fulfilment than just romantic love.

Notes

1. Schatz, Thomas, 'New Hollywood, new millennium', in Warren Buckland (Ed.), *Film Theory and Contemporary Hollywood Movies*, London: Routledge, 2009, p. 21.
2. Ibid, p. 20.
3. The box-office data are drawn from http://www.boxofficemojo.com (accessed 29 April 2011).

4. York, Ashley Elaine, 'From chick flicks to millennial blockbusters: spinning female-driven narratives into franchises,' *Journal of Popular Culture*, Vol. 43, No. 1, 2010, p. 4.
5. Ibid., p. 5.
6. Adams, Guy, 'There's a new genre in Tinseltown, and it's all about female friendship', *Independent*, 8 June 2008. http://www.independent.co.uk/arts-entertainment/films/news/theres-a-new-genre-in-tinseltown-and-its-all-about-female-friendship-842485.html (accessed 29 April 2011).
7. Ibid.
8. Silverstein, Melissa, 'Guess what? Women buy more movie tickets than men', *Women and Hollywood*, 11 March 2010. http://www.womenandhollywood.com (accessed 30 April 2011).
9. According to the UK Film Council, the 'overall UK cinema audience in 2009 was evenly split between male and female in contrast to the slightly female bias reported in 2008 due largely to the success of *Mamma Mia!* and *Sex and the City*'. http://www.sy10.ukfilmcouncil.ry.com/14.1.asp (accessed 30 April 2011).
10. http://www.boxofficemojo.com (accessed 20 April 2011).
11. York, 'From chick flicks to millennial blockbusters', p. 24.
12. Hollinger, Karen, *In the Company of Women: Contemporary Female Friendship Films*, Minneapolis: University of Minnesota Press, 1998, p. 2.
13. Haskell, Molly, *From Reverence to Rape: The Treatment of Women in the Movies*, Chicago, IL University of Chicago Press, 1973, p. 154.
14. Johnston, Claire, 'Women's cinema as counter-cinema', in E. Ann Kaplan (Ed.), *Feminism and Film*, Oxford: Oxford University Press, 2000, pp. 22–33.
15. Kuhn, Annette, 'Women's genres: melodrama, soap opera and theory', *Screen*, Vol. 25, No. 1, 1984, p. 18.
16. Basinger, Jeanine, *A Woman's View: How Hollywood Spoke to Women, 1930–1960*, New York: Knopf, 1993, pp. 15–17.
17. Tasker, Yvonne, *Working Girls: Gender and Sexuality in Popular Cinema*, London: Routledge, 1998, p. 139.
18. Altman, Rick, 'A semantic/syntactic/pragmatic approach', in Barry Keith Grant (Ed.), *Film Genre Reader*, 3rd edition, Austin: University of Texas Press, 2003, p. 31.
19. Hollinger, *In the Company of Women*, p. 2.
20. These are the Sentimental Female Friendship Film; the Female Friendship Film and Women's Development; the Political Female Friendship Film; the Erotic Female Friendship Film; the Female Friendship Film and Women of Color; and the Anti-Female Friendship Film.

21. Hollinger, *In the Company of Women*, p. 6.
22. Ibid.
23. Neale, Steve, *Genre and Hollywood*, London: Routledge, 1999, p. 147.
24. Jakobson, Roman, *Selected Writings III: Poetry of Grammar and Grammar of Poetry*, The Hague: Mouton, 1981, p. 751.
25. In episode 4:16 ('Ring a Ding Ding') of *Sex and the City* Carrie has only 30 days to find the money and despite offers from Miranda (Cynthia Nixon), Samantha (Kim Cattrall) and Mr Big (Chris Noth), and after a particularly painful rejection for a bank loan, she decides to confront Charlotte's unexpected reaction. Carrie believes that after everything she has been through with her friend, Charlotte can be certain she will pay her back. However, Charlotte initially defends her point of view and uses a story about how her father and a friend of his had fallen out after a similar situation. Although the episode ends with Charlotte finally realising her thoughtlessness and selling her expensive engagement ring to loan Carrie the money, the plot resonates with a widely disseminated social belief: friends and money are simply not a match made in heaven. Interestingly enough, if you Google Charlotte's phrase 'Money and friendship don't mix' you can choose among an impressive number of articles advising the reader in favour of this attitude.
26. Deleyto, Celestino, 'Between friends: love and friendship in contemporary romantic comedy', *Screen*, Vol. 44, No. 2, 2003, p. 171.
27. Tasker, *Working Girls*, p. 150.
28. Dick, Bernard F., *Anatomy of Film* (trans. Ioanna Davarinou), Athens: Patakis, 2005, p. 61.
29. Cliquet, Robert, 'Major trends affecting families in the new millennium: Western Europe and North America', in *Major Trends Affecting Families: A Background Document Prepared by the Programme on the Family*, New York: United Nations, 2003, p. 1.
30. Cook, Pam, 'Border crossings: women and film in context', in Pam Cook and Philip Dodd (Eds), *Women and Film: A Sight and Sound Reader*, Philadelphia, PA Temple University Press, 1993, pp. xii–xiii.

7

Embracing the embarrassment: *Mamma Mia!* and the pleasures of socially unrestrained performance

Ceri Hovland

Mamma Mia!, while a hugely popular film, was poorly received critically. This chapter examines this tension by focusing on the role of potential, or actual, embarrassment inherent in the viewing experience. On first seeing the film in the cinema, I was struck not only by the lively atmosphere, which ranged from clapping (now a common response to movies with a theatrical antecedent) to cheering, and even to singing along and/or dancing to certain musical numbers, but also by the thought that much in the film was slightly embarrassing.[1] Presenting her view that films tend to be either broadly melodramatic or comedic in form, Deborah Thomas argues,

> What's involved here is an extremely broad anticipation of the kinds of pleasure to be offered or withheld and the kinds of narrative world I'll be invited to inhabit ... on one hand, there are narrative worlds that feel repressive and full of danger and, on the other, those that feel more benevolent and safe. Settling down to watch a film is, crucially, a case of getting in the mood for the sort of film one is about to watch.[2]

Mamma Mia! has a benevolent film-world and, as a musical/romantic comedy, a viewer can expect song, dance, comedy and romance, or at least a focus on relationships. It also demands that the viewer get in an especially accepting mood. All fiction requires some suspension of disbelief, a willingness to accept artistic convention, sometimes at the expense of real-world conventions. Musicals are notoriously demanding in this respect, and particularly when numbers are not diegetically motivated: characters burst into song with little provocation; in song-mode they express emotion with unrealistic transparency and fluency; they can stand side by side without hearing each other sing; and finally the film-world may possess its own unnatural characteristics to make the transition into song seem less unnatural by comparison, such as brighter colours, stage-like features of setting, and performance styles that are more histrionic than verisimilar.[3]

Based on ABBA's oeuvre, a found score, *Mamma Mia!* has a particularly complex task integrating the songs into the narrative, as the lyrics do not always have an easy or obvious resonance with character situation. This makes it hard to create psychologically complex characters. So many characters, in narrative terms, are more typified than individualised, relying on performance and star persona to round them out. One effect is that both characters and performers are at greater risk of seeming embarrassing, or even, if you do not join in with the film's mood, grotesque. Pierce Brosnan, who played Sam, was singled out in reviews for his weak singing, and some critics were uncomfortable with the styling of the characters Donna (Meryl Streep), Rosie (Julie Walters) and Tanya (Christine Baranski).

This chapter critically reflects on *Mamma Mia!*, arguing that the characters are presented in such a way that they model liberation from various forms of social restriction. This is exhibited in the story and in the behaviour offered by the comic performances of Streep, Baranski, Walters and Brosnan. Moreover, the actors' (and characters') unrestrained and uninhibited presentation of both self and desire is a significant source of the pleasure that the text can provide in the viewing experience. Through comic and/or uninhibited performances by the actors, in the dual performance of character and song, the characters present newly found freedom through actions that defy not only restrictive and conservative social custom (sex outside marriage, gay love, sexual desire in older women) but also the possibility of social embarrassment (making a public fool of oneself). Through unrestrained and deliberately and unashamedly vulgar body movement, Streep, Walters and Baranski offer alternative ways of enacting femininity and desire. In a related but different way, Brosnan's uninhibited performance offers a model of release from social restraint. These performances encapsulate a key pleasure of *Mamma Mia!*: embracing the embarrassment.

Deborah Thomas has examined her embarrassment at the maids' behaviour in *La Cérémonie* (Chabrol, 1995) as they rifle through their employers' possessions prior to a killing spree.[4] She found that the characters' flouting of social convention made her so anxious she was forced to switch off the film. While Thomas's embarrassment came in conjunction with an uncomfortable viewing experience, and a less benevolent world, we can draw on her discussion of embarrassment to examine what the characters and actors *do* in *Mamma Mia!* that makes the viewing experience potentially both embarrassing and freeing.[5] Thomas suggests that embarrassment is

> an emotional reaction to the transgression of social conventions … experienced in two ways. First, it can flood over us when *our* transgressions make *us* the centre of unwelcome attention (or … where we are self-conscious … finding ourselves at the centre of attention … it can make us anxious that we will not be able to carry off our expected social role … so the imagined prospect of transgression may be embarrassing as well as its actuality). Second, it can be felt when we are forced to witness the transgressions or social gaffes of others, or, once again, anticipate the prospect of their

> occurring before our eyes. ... Thus ... embarrassment is the result of our position as witnesses, and therefore well suited to the experience of watching films.[6]

Several points from Thomas's argument are relevant to *Mamma Mia!*: that embarrassment is an effect of social transgression; that we can become embarrassed not only as a result of our own behaviour but also as a witness to others' behaviour; and finally that sometimes even the possibility of a transgression is sufficient to create embarrassment or anxiety.

Mamma Mia! provides rich ground for potential and actual embarrassment. Through its 'remarriage' structure it focuses on overcoming past social transgressions so that relationships can be created or renewed.[7] Illegitimate Sophie (Amanda Seyfried) searches for the father she has never known, and that search culminates at her weekend of wedding festivities, as she prepares to marry Sky (Dominic Cooper). Her invitations to three possible fathers, Sam, Harry (Colin Firth) and Bill (Stellan Skarsgård), bring her mother, Donna's, sexual past (and sexual 'shame') back into the limelight, as even Donna is unsure which of these men fathered her daughter. As the wedding festivities unfold, in an eternal 'Green World' of a Greek Island, the fantasy of a free and permissive society is born, as the characters overcome past fears of being socially ostracised, and relationships are mooted between all sexes, ages and degrees of marital status.[8] As a musical/romantic comedy, the fantastic and fantasised world of the film has licence to explore less conservative and hegemonic romantic unions than marriage between white, heterosexual couples.[9] Through its dual focus on the romantic (and sexual) happiness of mother and daughter, the film explicitly addresses female sexuality, particularly in older women, and its relationship with marriage. However, while Sophie feels free to choose not to marry by the end of the film, Donna, and her rediscovered sexual appetite, are safely contained within marriage. The genre and narrative format demand this particular kind of narrative closure, and finishing with a wedding is traditional as a way of celebrating the role of couples within society.[10] The genre impacts what the film can do with the characters and their relationships, in an inherently conservative manner. The interpretation of the characters and narrative, on the other hand, particularly as offered through performance, represents gender and social interaction with a degree of liberalism. This can particularly be seen in the depiction of the older generation of women.

At first, Donna is ashamed of having had three sexual partners in quick succession in her youth, and of her subsequent single motherhood. She now sees her behaviour as transgressing certain social mores and conventions, referring to herself as a 'stupid, little slut'. Rosie and Tanya laugh this off, but Donna has punished herself for her youthful sexuality; it is strongly implied that she has not had another sexual partner since. She verbally defends her celibacy, saying she is 'fine' how she is and glad 'that part of her life' is over. Her abstinence is also declared by her costume, rolled-up dungarees (with their lesbian connotations), as though she is refusing a sexist feminisation of herself, and a tool-belt with a phallic electric drill that she rears up on occasion, as though she has no need of any other phallus, and which also acts as metaphorical protection, as a chastity belt might. However, the reappearance of her former lovers places Donna in a situation in which she has to negotiate embarrassment about her youthful behaviour, and the possibility that it might make her a negative focus of attention. It is through negotiating and eventually discounting this potential embarrassment that Donna is able to renew her relationship with Sam and with herself as a sexually active woman. For Sophie's wedding, she dons a patterned blue dress and red scarf as the reappearance of several old flames reignites her sexuality and, in the film's terms, femininity. While this attitude towards gender and sexuality is constructed in a binary way through costume, Streep's physicalisation of the role complicates these oppositions, as her tomboyish embodiment of Donna infuses her decision to reincorporate romance back into her life with a physical freedom.

There are moments in which Streep as Donna offers liberated depictions of gender and sexuality: the playful greeting as Donna, Rosie and Tanya reunite on the pier, and Donna 'writhing' on the roof during the number 'Mamma Mia'. The reunion involves a re-enactment of the introduction they performed as the pop group Donna and the Dynamos.[11] They take up poses while Donna is still a considerable distance away, making their reunion public and presentational. Streep stands so that her dungaree-clad body creates a curvaceous shape; she leans into one hip, crooking the other leg slightly in front, and holds one shaped arm aloft above her head. Baranksi and Walters, at the opposite end of the pier and with their backs to each other, offer themselves as bookends, turned to the side with one leg bent in front, and the shaped arm similarly held aloft. All three mimic holding a microphone up to their mouth, their raised heads evocative of confidence and pride. Their pose creates overtly womanly silhouettes, designed to be seen as much as enacted.[12] Once the woman have finished reminiscing through posing, they run towards each other squealing, Tanya and Rosie flapping slightly and kicking up their legs (girlishly by Baranski, and like a child trying to win a race from Walters), while Donna runs in a zigzag fashion. Streep holds her feet far apart to do so, and her run involves an out-step-cross movement that expresses an exuberant energy but also freedom and pleasure in the movement, disregarding how it may appear to others watching.[13] As they meet, Streep takes up a stance with legs still wide apart, hands in pocket, so that Donna swaggers and bounces like an enthusiastic ranch hand in her straw cowboy hat. This oscillation between movement and posing, demonstrating a physical freedom and more overt sexuality in turn, becomes a significant motif throughout the film. While Donna seems physically free in many ways, she has also been repressing herself sexually, with the posing a remnant of long-lost behaviour. On the pier, the more overtly feminised and sexualised movement is playfully reenacted, but it is not undertaken with meaning until 'Mamma Mia'.

Entering her goat house, Donna discovers that her three ex-lovers are there. Their presence prompts confusion, curiosity, panic and sexual reawakening in Donna, and her conflicted emotional response triggers the musical number, sung as she processes her feelings and seeks to satisfy her curiosity while remaining out of sight. Through the lyrics she voices her regret at losing her lover, her disbelief that she has managed to do without him and her anxiety over whether she will be able to resist him now.

It is unclear which man, if any, she misses the most, and so the generalised lyrics, combined with choreographic decisions, instead suggest that Donna is remembering her sexual desire, and, as she recognises what she has lost, it is transformed into an insatiable curiosity. Over the course of the song, this leads her to climb onto the roof, until at the climax of the song, curiosity overcoming her desire to hide, she slips and falls through a trapdoor onto a waiting mattress below, where she lies dishevelled, legs wide open. Donna's position possesses the potential for social embarrassment: how can she explain falling in on them without admitting to spying? Furthermore, her physical attitude is accidentally sexually provocative, with dishevelled clothes, and in the company of three men, with whom personal history makes her feel awkward. Donna's response, however, brushes off the embarrassment as she responds with unashamed laughter.

During the song, she begins to negotiate her conflicted feelings about her reawakening sexuality. On the roof, before she falls (from grace?), she sings lying down next to the trapdoor, and, in her delivery of the choreography and the lyrics, Streep articulates the dichotomy, set up in her earlier movement, between physical freedom and posing as the presentation of female sexuality.

Lying down, limbs spread out like a starfish, she sings the song's lyrics about suddenly losing control and having a 'fire within my soul'. As she sings she moves between positions in which her legs are open and in which her legs are closed. Her position as she lies there initially mimics the more sexualised posing of her Dynamos days; her left arm crooks over her head, and her left leg crooks over right, while her right arm folds down over her body as through to protect her modesty. With her flowing blond, wavy hair fanned out behind her head, she is reminiscent of a Venus or Aphrodite figure, a goddess of love, familiar from Renaissance paintings.[14] In this position she moves her head from side to side, as she despairs that she won't 'ever learn', until this fleeting negativity is channelled into the loss of 'control', demonstrated physically but also meant figuratively. Streep's body pulses upwards from the chest into a sitting-up position, legs hip-width apart and hands clenched, which while a sexualised movement in one respect, as though the needs of her body are overtaking those of her mind, is also emotional, as though led from the heart. This movement and tension then continues to flood out, as Streep, singing, 'There's a fire within my soul', flexes her arms and legs in and out so that her arms stretch upwards, as though reaching for something she needs, and the movement in her limbs causes her body to shift and move at the ribs and hips. The large scale, multiple directions and abandon of these movements register physical freedom and sensuous enjoyment of the body, and in a much more sexualised format than Streep's earlier 'asexual' movements. By the word 'soul' Streep has come to rest back in a 'Venus' pose, legs crooked one over the other, but this time with both hands resting across her lower body, and during her movements, the camera has swivelled on its axis, as though mimicking the sensory flooding of sexual arousal. Streep also deepens her voice to put a slight, smiling growl into the lyrics as Donna takes ownership and pleasure in her own desire. However, Streep performs the choreography so that it is not titillating; the only person Donna is seducing is herself. Her uncertainty still manifests itself as she reaches towards the trapdoor as though the object she wants (the men below) might burn her. Having acknowledged her desire, Donna can seek a way of being both sexually aware and physically free.

While Streep's Donna negotiates the peril of *character* embarrassment, the other performances under consideration here present a greater likelihood of creating *witness* embarrassment in a viewer through character behaviour and/or actor performance. Baranski's Tanya is, from first appearance, presented as a sexually voracious woman with several failed marriages.[15] She is a foil to Donna's self-enforced celibacy, with Rosie, the hermit who has never married, representing the other end of the spectrum. Tanya represents active sexuality in older women; however, in the form offered by the narrative, this is no simple thing. She is slender, toned and attractive, but there are references throughout to the cost of remaining so unnaturally well preserved through expensive clothes, face creams and cosmetic surgery. 'Does Your Mother Know' presents her as an attractive older woman gaining the attention of younger men, but also colours her as a 'cougar', a sexually predatory older woman who targets younger men. Her mooted coupling with Pepper (Philip Michael) represents an interracial union, a progressive representation in another way (although the 'young, black stud' is a cliché not always shown with representational sensitivity). However, the flirtation does not develop, suggesting that a full sexual coupling between them might perhaps be viewed as less acceptable. Baranski's number received mixed reviews: Hugo Rifkind refers to it as 'rather gruesome',[16] while for Robey, it is 'the hands-down highlight. It is a bit strange that Benny and Björn's rockin' ode to cradle-snatching ... should have had me wanting to neck ouzo and join the party, but there you go.'[17] Baranski has had some training in song and dance (although less than Streep and Seyfried, who both had operatic training), and her singing and dancing is accomplished, the product of three months' training and rehearsal, within the camp style demanded by this film. Owen Gleiberman actually writes, 'It's tempting to say that *Mamma Mia!* has the worst choreography of any big-screen musical in history.'[18] However, choreographer Anthony Van Laast emphasises the difficulty of designing dance and movement so that it appears spontaneous and improvised. In this way, the eccentricity of the choreography negates stereotypes and models a way of dancing unhampered by a public setting.

Moments in the routine enhance the glamorous image presented by Tanya, for example when she sashays away at the end, cocktail in hand, her movement mimicked by the younger women, or, alternatively, as she is held aloft by young male dancers as she reclines in mid-air. In contrast, some of the choreography is more playful in relation to gender roles and sexual activity. Tanya is firmly in control, forestalling Pepper's lustful crush. As he climbs aboard her pedalo, her energy levels swiftly change from an elegant recline, arms resting behind her head bathing-beauty style, into forceful pedalling, rapidly steering the pedalo inland. As she starts to sing, she enunciates the lyrics (particularly the 't' sound) sharply to bring out a challenging edge to her words, 'You're so hot, teasing me', and marches across the sand, arms and hips swinging, to tip Pepper onto the floor as she whips her towel out from underneath him. At the bar, they briefly dance together in-hold, performing a few rock 'n' roll-style steps that they both try to lead, contrary to the dance convention that men lead, until a push from Tanya sends Pepper flying off the deck. She then teases him even more when she crouches in front of him at crotch height. The camera's refused gaze, as it remains firmly on Michael's face not on Baranski's action, and Michael's performance, as he gasps with an expression of pleasurable alarm while Baranski's painted talons snake up his torso, suggest fellatio, until it is swiftly revealed she has actually been swaddling the fluffy, white towel into a makeshift nappy.

While Pepper is briefly aghast and embarrassed, the number does not dwell on Tanya's control over Pepper and does not seek to continually mock and embarrass the character. Instead, the whole number becomes increasingly wild and free-spirited as all those present on the beach join in (arms and legs flung wide in side steps) and Baranski's choreography escalates into increased silliness. Some moments remain sexually aware, for example as she manually thrusts her breasts upwards or performs some crotch-clutching moves Michael Jackson style. There is also a memorable moment as one male dancer manically and unashamedly thrusts his pelvis back and forth, head held back ecstatically with his arms flung wide. In contrast, Baranski's small solo routine, while presenting Tanya as the centre of attention, does not overemphasise either her powerful presence or her sensuality. Instead, she is proficient but also goofy, with a nodding, bobbing head, funky chicken style, and actual use of legs and arms akimbo as she flaps them around. The routine is evocative of aerobic-style dance crazes like 'Saturday Night' or 'Macarena', with their rhythmic movement alternating between different poses. However, it is more complex through its speed and the multistage movement of each limb, and lacks the hip rolls and hand placements that draw attention to the female form in these routines.

While Baranski's performance treads a fine line between silliness and sexiness, and handles ageing female sexuality in a broadly progressive manner, Walters' performance of Rosie, particularly during the character's pursuit of Bill in 'Take a Chance on Me', is, in its depiction of an older woman pursuing a reluctant man, evocative of sexually voracious women and reluctant men familiar from *Carry on ...* films or seaside postcard humour. Enjoyment of the number is perhaps predicated on whether one views this as sexist or as humorous self-deprecation by women in which the mockery relates quite directly to a negotiation of the ageing process. Like many of the performances, it divides critics; for Rifkind, 'Walters cackles away like the old pro she is' (a description with unfortunate connotations of prostitution);[19], while for Robey, '*Mamma Mia!* degenerate[s] into the best available version of itself – a so-bad-it's-good, never-mind-the-singing campathon, with Julie Walters … in … a "Take a Chance on Me" solo that would clear the average bingo hall.'[20] On the other hand, the 'average' appearance of Walters' physique, particularly as presented via the styling of Rosie through costume and make-up (which makes the slim Walters appear slightly overweight), is a portrayal of a more ordinary woman who possesses a sexual appetite than those offered by Streep's professionalism or Baranski's lithe athleticism. Their skill at singing and dancing creates clearer distinctions between the proficiency of the actor and the behaviour of the character, conveying deliberateness less obviously present in Walters' performance, and almost absent from Brosnan's performance. In this way, the questions of how seriously we take the number and whether it has managed to stay on the right side of grotesque become increasingly pertinent.

'Take a Chance on Me' is one of ABBA's campest songs, and Walters commences Rosie's pursuit of Bill with an actual nudge and a wink as she initially sings under her breath, as though she doesn't want to publicly proposition Bill in case it causes embarrassment. However, this reticence is short-lived, as Rosie loudly proclaims 'speech', before singing and dancing along the tabletop with pelvic thrusts and manually heaving her breasts forward. This is followed by choreography consisting of hip rolls with one hand spanned across the top of her head, like a bizarre misinterpretation of vogue-ing à la Madonna. As the song continues, movement and choreography also literalise lyrics that were written to be metaphoricaly, for example hanging from a rooftop while singing that she 'can't let go'. The number's rapid progression from a privately negotiated flirtation to a public demonstration of both desire for a man and the intention to act upon it fervently denies that Rosie feels any embarrassment. In this respect, is it possible that any embarrassment felt by viewers is witness embarrassment, implying that the text is not presenting women in a socially acceptable manner? Does it transgress social convention because the behaviour is too loud and brash (thus going against old-fashioned dictums regarding women's behaviour) or because the humorous presentation of older women's sexuality represents it negatively? The alternative is to accept Walters' devil-may-care performance, with its disregard for decorum and public outspokenness, as offering a kind of authenticity or sincerity. Feelings or intentions usually disguised by appearance or good manners are, instead, available for all to see.

The public declaration of love is a common trope of romantic comedies. 'Take a Chance on Me', in this respect, is adjunct to *Mamma Mia!*'s wedding section as Sam proposes to Donna in 'I Do, I Do, I Do, I Do, I Do'.[21] A public location has increased resonance when the opposition to the relationship is social. Bill and Rosie's relationship hesitates due to Bill's uncertainty and Rosie's fleeting concern over whether an older woman (or any woman?) should publically pursue her desire. In contrast, Sam and Donna's relationship faltered for social reasons, as they were involved with other partners and feared reprisal. Through a public declaration, they affirm that outside forces will no longer interfere with their relationship. The public location, however, increases the likelihood that by speaking out they will appear foolish, either through having misjudged their partner's feelings or simply through making a spectacle of themselves in public. This trope, a willingness to be a fool to demonstrate your love, is also important in romantic comedies.[22] As Donna and Sam marry, the potential embarrassment is minimised, despite the need to deliver both proposal and answer in song. However, earlier moments in the film offer greater potential for embarrassment as feelings are revealed through song in 'SOS' and 'The Winner Takes It All'. These numbers spring from the need to express character emotions that are too raw and pressing to be delivered in any manner other than song. Richard Dyer refers to this convention of musicals as an increased transparency and intensity offered via the musicalisation of romance, feelings and relationships. Entertainment has the capacity 'to present either complex or unpleasant feelings ... in a way that makes them seem uncomplicated, direct and vivid, not "qualified" or "ambiguous" as day-to-day life makes them.'[23]

In 'The Winner Takes It All', Streep's skilled musical performance and the character's confidence negate much of the potential for embarrassment. It is, therefore, Brosnan's valiant effort in 'SOS' that offers the potential for awkwardness and indeed embarrassment on both the character's and actor's behalf. Reviews were scathing: comments on Brosnan's performance include that it was, 'a crime against popular music';[24] that he 'cannot sing at all';[25] that his 'stab at SOS is the sound of a man gargling TCP';[26] and on his casting, 'I don't know who ... thought Pierce Brosnan should sing in it. How on earth could it not be shit?'[27] However, despite Brosnan's shortcomings as a musical performer, the producers persisted with his casting; he offered something in addition, his persona. As an actor who has played James Bond, Brosnan's persona carries with it a hyped masculinity; Bond is charming but restrained and lethal. In contrast, Sam has to declare himself and express his feelings without restraint. The theme of 'SOS' is literally a request for rescue, a dropping of barriers and pretence in order to get to the metaphorical heart of the matter. While much of the song, with the play on 'Darling, can't you hear me', is conducted as though Donna and Sam cannot hear each other, in the opening section Sam sings directly to Donna.[28] She is trying to avoid a serious conversation, while he wants to discuss the past and the possibility that Sophie might be his daughter. The characters' engagement in the conversation is subject to widely varying tones. Brosnan's Sam is serious, while Streep offers Donna's denial via continued sexual parody as she accidentally rears up her phallic drill, saying, 'Here's the thing' while trying to block conversation. Even so, Sam continues to try to reach out to Donna. In a rather excruciating and punishing close-up, Brosnan starts to sing the opening lines about reaching out to Donna even though she has shut him out. Brosnan does sing in tune; however, as one review points out, 'you can really hear him trying'.[29] Rifkind is commenting upon Brosnan's performance rather than upon Sam's progression into MERM (Musically Enhanced Reality Mode).[30] Even so, Brosnan's strain colours the characterisation. The emotion and the risk to the character come across forcefully: he could easily be rejected and look a fool. It is more poignant because Brosnan cannot sing well; if you *can* sing, serenading your partner may make you look good, but when you cannot it is easier to create an embarrassing spectacle of yourself. The other benefit from Brosnan's limited skills, however, like Walters' ordinariness, is the hope that he offers to the majority who are not talented. It is easier to ignore the potential embarrassment of singing along to ABBA badly when you are in such good company. In this respect, it is possible, as Glieberman suggests, to be 'charmed' by this rather inept performance.[31]

The varying degrees of skill possessed by the performers, the styling of the choreography and the character situation combine to create many occasions on which either the character or the actor ends up in situations that are embarrassing or offer the potential for embarrassment. As viewers we can also be subject to witness embarrassment on their behalf for these potential or perceived transgressions. However, the manner in which *Mamma Mia!* negotiates these positions and the viewing experience it promotes presents the potential for both character and viewer to throw off the embarrassment and embrace alternative ways of behaving.

Notes

1. I would like to thank the Sewing Circle, my family and other friends for their thoughts on the film, particularly Stephanie Hovland, Lucy Fife Donaldson and Simone Knox.
2. Thomas, Deborah, *Beyond Genre: Melodrama, Comedy and Romance in Hollywood Films*, Moffat, Scotland: Cameron and Hollis, 2000, p. 9.

3. See Altman, Rick, *The American Film Musical*, Bloomington: Indiana University Press, 1987, and Knapp, Raymond, *The American Film Musical and the Performance of Personal Identity*, Princeton, NJ: Princeton University Press, 2006, for accounts of the conventions of Hollywood musicals. Dyer, Richard, *Only Entertainment*, London: Routledge, 1987, Chapter 3, 'Entertainment and Utopia', and Mueller, John, 'Fred Astaire and the integrated musical', *Cinema Journal*, Vol. 24, No.1, 1984, pp. 28–40, directly address the integration of number and narrative.
4. Thomas, Deborah, '"Knowing one's place": frame-breaking, embarrassment and irony in *La Cérémonie* (Claude Chabrol, 1995)', in John Gibbs and Douglas Pye (Eds), *Style and Meaning: Studies in the Detailed Analysis of Film*, Manchester: Manchester University Press, 2005.
5. Thomas is indebted to sociologist Erving Goffman's works, *The Presentation of Self in Everyday Life*, London: Penguin, 1959, and *Frame Analysis: An Essay on the Organisation of Experience*, Cambridge, MA: Harvard University Press, 1974. Goffman examined both the structure of social encounters and spectatorship as a form of social encounter; see, for example, Chapter 6, 'The Arts of Impression Management (*The Presentation of Self in Everyday Life*) and Chapters 10, 'Breaking Frame', Chapter 11, 'The Manufacture of Negative Experience' and Chapter 12, 'The Vulnerabilities of Experience' (*Frame Analysis*) for discussions of potential or actual embarrassment.
6. Thomas, 'Knowing one's place', p. 170.
7. Cavell, Stanley, *Pursuits of Happiness: Hollywood Comedy of Re-Marriage*, Cambridge, MA: Harvard University Press, 1981, refers to some Hollywood romantic comedies as belonging to the 'genre of re-marriage'. Cavell suggests that these films model relationships that are renewed as a result of shared pasts and mutual re-education.
8. Frye, Northrop, *Anatomy of Criticism: Four Essays*, London: Penguin, 1990. Frye coined the term 'The Green World' to refer to the alternate spaces visited by characters in pursuit of romantic resolutions (Shakespeare's plays are prime examples). The Green World is outside normal social realms and thus can allow leeway from ordinary social custom. This is a frequent trope of romantic comedy, and a well-established critical theme in analyses of Hollywood romantic comedy; see, for example, Cavell, *Pursuits of Happiness*, and Glitre, Katrina, *Hollywood Romantic Comedy: States of the Union, 1934–1965*, Manchester: Manchester University Press, 2006.
9. Frye points out that the 'romance' structure is based on wish fulfilment, and Dyer discusses the fantasy element of musicals and entertainment, suggesting that a central thrust of them is imaging Utopias (*Only Entertainment*, p. 20).

10. Frye, *Anatomy of Criticism*, pp. 43 and 163.
11. Earlier Sophie and friends greet each other in a similar way, so the routines are designed to show intergenerational bonds; however, Donna and friends' reunion is much more public and presentational than Sophie and friends' insular and private routine.
12. I would like to thank Melanie Williams and Louise FitzGerald for pointing out the similarity between the Donna and the Dynamos pose and that of the women in *Charlie's Angels*. An intertextual reading further highlights the strength and independence of Donna, Tanya and Rosie, as well as the sexualisation and potential objectification embodied in the transformation of the female form into spectacle.
13. At this point, the only potential witnesses, other than Rosie and Tanya, are Greeks. It is possible, therefore, to relate Streep's disregard for how others perceive her to the film's depiction of Greek people and culture. As discussed earlier, the island is constructed as a fantasy space, and in this respect the liberated environment perhaps fosters an increased physical freedom. This is also the place that Donna retreated to after she was disowned by her mother for being pregnant and unwed and is therefore a safe haven for her and a kind of extension of her private, home environment. On the other hand, it is also possible to view the depiction of the island as infantilising Greek culture, as Donna feels no need to regard how the Greeks perceive her, suggesting that their opinion has less value than that of Americans or English people.
14. See *Venus of Urbino* (Titian, 1538), *The Birth of Venus* (Botticelli, 1486), *Sleeping Venus* (Giorgione, 1510). Also note the hotel is positioned over Aphrodite's spring, which bursts through the courtyard at the end.
15. I wonder whether the peek at the 'baby' on the ferry, which turns out to be a large, dead fish, is, whether intentionally or not, an ironic comment about ageing female sexuality. The fish is an alarming object through its unexpectedness, and its gaping, circular mouth with sharp, pointy teeth proffers loose comparison with the vagina dentata.
16. Rifkind, Hugo, '*Mamma Mia! The Musical*: first review', *The Times*, 1 July 2008. http://entertainment.timesonline.co.uk/tol/arts_and_entertainment/film/article4245117.ece (accessed 6 January 2011).
17. Robey, Tim, 'Film reviews: *Mamma Mia!* and more', *Telegraph*, 11 July 2008. http://www.telegraph.co.uk/culture/film/filmreviews/3556138/Film-reviews-Mamma-Mia-and-more.html (accessed 6 January 2011).
18. Glieberman, Owen, '*Mamma Mia!*', *Entertainment Weekly*, 19 July 2008. http://edition.cnn.com/2008/SHOWBIZ/Movies/07/18/ew.review.mammamia/index.html (accessed 8 January 2011).
19. Rifkind, '*Mamma Mia!*'

20. Robey, 'Film reviews'.
21. A wedding is also the 'real-world' version of a public demonstration of love and commitment. Among other things, a marriage is a social and legal contract between two people undertaken partly as a demonstration to the social community of conformity to the rules of that society.
22. As discussed in Glitre, *Hollywood Romantic Comedy*.
23. Dyer, *Only Entertainment*, p. 25.
24. Landesman, Cosmo, '*Mamma Mia!*', *Sunday Times*, 13 July 2008. http://www.entertainment.timesonline.co.uk (accessed 9 January 2011).
25. Rifkind, '*Mamma Mia!*'
26. Robey, 'Film reviews'.
27. Bradshaw, Peter, '*Mamma Mia!*', *Guardian*, 10 July 2008. http://www.guardian.co.uk/culture/2008/jul/10/film.reviews (accessed 6 January 2011).
28. Much of the number, like the rest of the film, is performed in a 'camp' style. As they sing the chorus, for example, they are separated by a wall that suggests they cannot hear each other and which is reminiscent of ABBA-esque side-by-side staging and use of profiles, as used in Lasse Hallström's original videos for the group.
29. Rifkind, '*Mamma Mia!*'
30. See Knapp, *The American Film Musical and the Performance of Personal Identity* for discussion of MERM.
31. Glieberman, '*Mamma Mia!*'

8

The same old song? Exploring conceptions of the 'feelgood' film in the talk of *Mamma Mia!*'s older viewers

Kate Egan and Kerstin Leder Mackley

Labelled as a 'communal extravaganza'[1] and 'the first Saga karaoke musical',[2] *Mamma Mia!* has enjoyed phenomenal box-office success of the seemingly unlikely, though clearly carefully designed, kind.[3] For Ashley Elaine York, the film is a key example of what she describes as the 'millennial women's blockbuster', a new form of 'chick flick' that has moved beyond the original target audience of 18- to 34-year-old women by appealing more widely to younger and older viewers.[4] At the same time, the opportunities *Mamma Mia!* has offered for repeat viewing and some highly vocal and visible audience participation are akin to practices associated with cult classics like *The Rocky Horror Picture Show* (Sharman, 1975) and, more recently, the *Sing-a-Long-a Sound of Music* screenings.[5]

The audience research presented in this chapter is informed by such debates and developed out of an interest in *Mamma Mia!*'s cultural status; its appeal as a repeatable and pleasurable film experience potentially problematised academic conceptions of cult as chiefly non-mainstream and male-oriented.[6] However, what emerged in the very early stages of our research, and continued throughout, was the overwhelming sense that a taken-for-granted element, the film's 'feelgood factor' (a term repeatedly employed in newspaper reviews and marketing materials), had come to play an organising role in people's enjoyment of *Mamma Mia!* Specifically, it seemed to unlock a whole range of meanings and pleasures for members of the very audience group that had been held responsible for some of the film's success, the not-so-regular cinemagoers aged 40 and above.[7] Consequently, this chapter addresses the pleasures and enjoyment of *Mamma Mia!* as evidenced in the responses of 12 repeat viewers (three male, nine female, aged 47 to 81), with specific focus on the meanings and significances behind the use of the ostensibly unambiguous term 'feelgood' as a descriptor for the *Mamma Mia!* film experience.

Our research employed two main methods: multi-method questionnaires, followed by semi-structured interviews. Initially, recruitment centred on a screening at the Aberystwyth Arts Centre cinema, a popular *Mamma Mia!* screening venue, in late August 2010. The post-screening questionnaire was designed to identify repeat viewers, assess kinds and levels of enjoyment of the film and elicit information about people's engagements with the formal aspects of *Mamma Mia!* as well as the potential importance of viewing context (including possible differences between watching the film on DVD and in the cinema). Questions were also anchored around the issue of the kind of film *Mamma Mia!* was for these audiences, and how industry and more vernacular categorisations of the film (e.g. blockbuster, chick flick, cult, feelgood, romcom, etc.) might relate to viewers' general enjoyment of the film. We received 29 questionnaire responses from a mixed audience – young families, students, middle-aged women and men – with eight participants providing their contact details for follow-up interviews. Strategic sampling led to the recruitment of six *Mamma Mia!* viewers from a village in South Wales, five of whom had enjoyed a screening of the film at a resident's hen night in the village hall. General snowballing resulted in 16 further contacts across England and Wales, providing us with a total of 51 questionnaire responses.

The scope of this chapter allows for a detailed discussion neither of the Aberystwyth screening nor of the overall questionnaire responses. Instead, we focus on the materials gathered during the project's follow-up interview stage. As indicated above, questionnaire responses pointed towards *Mamma Mia!*'s status as a 'feelgood' film for older people who had seen the film repeatedly (i.e. at least twice). Twelve of these participants had indicated their willingness to be interviewed. They were Cath (47), Pete (52), Steph (60) and Janet (64) from Aberystwyth; Alice (59), Amy (69), Jean (71) and David (81) from the village in South Wales; and Jane (58), Ken (59), Helen (62) and Marilyn (66) from London, Swansea and the Isle of Wight.[8] Although our socio-demographic information about interviewees is limited, we consider all interviewees to be broadly middle class and, in most cases, educated to degree level. Respondents had seen the film between two (Alice) and six (Ken) times. Except for Jane and Ken, all participants had seen it at least once at the cinema. Ten interviews were conducted in person (partly in pairs, in the case of Alice/Amy, Jean/David and Jane/Ken), while Helen and Marilyn were interviewed over the telephone. All interviews were audio-recorded and transcribed.

While the film was often discussed in interviews as a 'woman's film' (and, to a lesser extent, a 'chick flick'), 'feelgood' was these respondents' first choice in describing *Mamma Mia!* as a kind of film. Moreover, participants who raised its possible 'woman's film' status often added that, in their experience, it could also be enjoyed by men (in fact, for one of the married couples we interviewed, it was almost the only film that managed to bridge their otherwise divergent film tastes). As a result of participants' emphasis on 'feelgood', and due to the scope of this chapter, issues of gender play only a minor role in the context of this study.

We also cannot do full justice to the complexities of individual interviews here. Instead focus will lie on overall patterns across responses (e.g. repetitions, key concepts, distinctions, discrepancies, modalities of talk), while bearing in mind that the scope of our research does not allow for any representative claims or demographic distributions.[9] While we paid attention to participants' discursive strategies (in relation to wider socio-cultural processes and 'public' discourses), we also took their reflections seriously as representations of their cognitive, emotional and embodied sense-making.[10]

In film studies, 'feelgood' has been discussed by Charles Burnetts in terms of the way in which it works as a mode associated with the sentimental, life-affirming endings of Steven Spielberg's films.[11] Its meanings for audiences who choose to make sense of a film experience as 'feelgood' have, however, not been sufficiently explored. Within the context of respondents' talk, there was a sense that 'feelgood', though at times difficult to define, functioned to place and make sense of *Mamma Mia!* in relation to other films and film-going experiences, and that this worked in a number of ways (associated, for instance, with issues of affect, realism and notions of the 'fun' and the 'serious'). In the spirit of conciseness, this chapter identifies and explores four main ways in which the terms 'feelgood' and, by extension, 'fun' were mobilised in participants' talk.

'Feelgood' in relation to personal, cultural and musical familiarity

Our respondents, some of whom considered themselves to be long-term ABBA likers, felt that the use of ABBA's music was key to the appeal and success of *Mamma Mia!* They were aware that the film had special significance for people in their age group, and this related to the ability of ABBA's music to 'bring back memories' of, and 'take [them] back' to, their youth and things they did when they were young (e.g. Marilyn, Steph, Alice, Helen). In some ways, this specific appeal connects with David Shumway's and Estella Tincknell's arguments about the 'rock 'n' roll soundtrack' or 'compilation score' film. For them, the use of pop or rock music's 'back catalogue' serves as a 'vehicle for nostalgia', with films ranging from *American Graffiti* (Lucas, 1973) to *Pulp Fiction* (Tarantino, 1994) using songs whose style conjures up ideas of, or a longing for, a past cultural era.[12] For Shumway (drawing on Fredric Jameson), this strategic appeal can be termed 'commodified nostalgia', in that these songs are seen to evoke a broad, widely disseminated sense of a decade or era rather than conjure up memories linked to an audience member's life history. As Shumway argues,

> if hearing a song on the radio invites us to remember our own past, movies use the same technique to evoke the fiction of a common past. Popular music works because it was and is widely shared, but not necessarily because the audience literally remember the songs.[13]

However, the ideas of youth that the music conjured up for our respondents were very much related to the intrinsic tie between ABBA, their songs and what Annette Kuhn would term 'repetitive' or 'habitual' memories from respondents' youthful past.[14] In some cases, the film's music was seen to bring back memories of ABBA themselves (particularly their appearance on the Eurovision Song Contest, or 'when ABBA were up on the stage', to use Marilyn's words). Yet, most often, it was seen to take respondents back to a period in their own life history, in that the 'period when ABBA were famous' was also 'their youth' and 'their era' (Steph, Helen and Cath). In particular, the songs reminded Cath, Helen, Jane and Steph of events in their lives (relationships, having young children, disco dancing, things they did after college) that occurred when ABBA were topping the pop charts. Even respondents who did not self-identify as long-term ABBA likers noted that the songs were 'in the background' (Jean) when they were younger. Indeed respondents linked the film's special appeal for their age group precisely to having grown up with these songs, with their immediate familiarity functioning as a source of pleasure (Janet) and enjoyment (Cath) when watching *Mamma Mia!* Liking the songs and familiarity with the songs thus served, for these respondents, as the 'immediate cue' or 'point of entry' (Amy and Alice) into the film and this, more than anything else, made it a film that was naturally and inevitably enjoyed.

In *Watching Dallas*, Ien Ang draws on Pierre Bourdieu's conception of 'popular pleasure', arguing that 'what matters is the possibility of identifying oneself with it [the object of pleasure] in some way or other, to integrate it into daily life'.[15] For Ang, 'popular pleasure' is therefore 'first and foremost a pleasure of recognition'.[16] Interestingly, a number of our respondents noted that the film's focus on characters who are forced to think about their past had encouraged them to reflect nostalgically on the freedom associated with life before parenthood, involving discussions of 'spontaneous carefree days before mortgages and children' (Cath) and 'looking back over ... relationships you've had' (Steph). However, the use of ABBA's music in *Mamma Mia!* seemed to function for our respondents less as an elicitor of longing for a past era and more in the terms described by Ang. The film 'pulls you in' because ABBA, their songs and their lyrics are known and recognisable. These respondents *do* literally remember these songs, rather than nostalgia being evoked through a style of popular song that is a vague marker of a past era. And this 'pleasure of familiarity' (as Janet terms it) is inextricably entwined with 'habitual', everyday memories from each respondent's youth to which the ABBA music served as sonic background.

Importantly, respondents noted that there was something specific about the ABBA songs that aided this process – that they are catchy or, in Janet's words, have a 'tendency to get on your brain'. For these respondents, ABBA songs are songs 'you remember straightaway even if you haven't heard them for years' (Helen); they are songs one can easily sing along to. It was the songs' specific characteristics, then, which seemed to make the pull back to respondents' youth quick, straightforward and easy. Moreover, respondents' relationship with the ABBA music informed the sense that *Mamma Mia!* was a particularly unique experience, shedding light on the appeal of *Mamma Mia!* as a film that hovers between popular music soundtrack film, classical Hollywood musical and an ABBA-specific 'jukebox musical'.[17] 'Feelgood', in this sense, encapsulated the range of ways in which the film was seen to pleasurably and instantly speak to respondents through the vehicle of the ABBA music: taking them back, pulling them in, conjuring up ABBA-inflected memories from their past and connecting with them through catchy, culturally and personally familiar songs. Indeed, as will become evident, ABBA's music was almost inseparable from the wider *Mamma Mia!* film experience, and continued to resurface in participants' 'feelgood' talk.

'Feelgood' in relation to affective and embodied response

Watching *Mamma Mia!* was seen as a hugely positive experience for our participants because of the 'happy' state that they were left in as the film finished (Jean). They felt they had been 'lifted' by the film (David), that it had made them smile and 'feel positive about life' (Steph) as well as just 'physically happy' (Jane). Both Jane and Helen associated this with the fact that the end of the film features the actors singing ABBA songs over the credits. Marilyn also noted that the actors in the film all seemed to be enjoying themselves, and this seemed to feed into the film's ability to be contagiously joyful and happy.

Of course, this aspect of the 'feelgood' experience could be seen to relate to the oft-acknowledged appeal of musicals as films whose 'musical performances' are associated with 'a joyous and responsive attitude to life' and a 'live and immediate performance of feeling'.[18] It also accords, to a certain extent, with Linda Williams' conception of 'body genres', in that 'the success of these genres is often measured by the degree to which the audience sensation mimics what is seen on the screen'.[19] Indeed, associating a film with the term 'feelgood' can be seen, on one level and as with the term 'horror', as a labelling of a film in relation to the kind of bodily sensation it evokes. Certainly, the affective responses described above could be termed emotional or sensational mimicry, in that the 'affective states' of the characters/actors were mimicked or, in Carl Plantinga's terms, 'caught' by our respondents during their viewings of the film.[20] However, this seems to have worked in a more multifaceted way than Williams' notion of 'mimicry' suggests, and to have related to a range of textual and extra-textual factors associated with the film and its screening contexts.

Firstly, for our respondents, ABBA's songs had always been supremely effective at being affective. Repeated words used to describe ABBA's music (and its beat, rhythms and melodies) were 'vibrant', 'bouncy', 'powerful', 'dynamic', 'fun', 'energetic', 'upbeat' and 'happy', and these were seen to cause (in the film and, previously, when they had listened to the songs outside of the film) the following affective or embodied states: being uplifted or 'lifting you up and out', releasing endorphins and making you want to get up and dance (Alice, David, Jane, Cath). Consequently, the ABBA songs were seen as key to the film's ability to literally make you feel-good. If, in Leslie M. Meier's words, 'popular music's ability to rouse a physical and emotional response' is 'much of its appeal',[21] then, for our respondents, ABBA are the exemplar of this and the perfect source material for a musical's 'live and immediate performance of feeling'.[22]

Secondly, the emotionally contagious nature of *Mamma Mia!* was also attributed, for cinema screening attendees, to the emotions or affective states of their fellow audience members, with participants commenting on the pleasures of attending and responding to other viewers' enjoyment of the film (e.g.

contagious laughter, singing and dancing). Indeed, Helen, Amy, Alice, David and Jean all responded in kind, by getting up and joining in, and this was seen to mark the film, and the experience of watching it in the cinema, as distinctive and special.

Thirdly, Marilyn and Jean noted that watching the actors sing and dance in the film made them feel that they wanted to be (or could imagine being) in the film dancing with the actors. While watching the film, Marilyn had realised that she 'was moving, tapping [her] feet', while Jane, in a related vein, had felt 'like skipping and carrying on' with the dancing and singing once the film had ended. This kind of embodied response to the film could be considered to be a combination of sonic and 'kinesthetic engagement'.[23] In her work on audience responses to the BBC television series *Strictly Come Dancing*, Karen Wood argues that her participants experience 'kinesthetic contagion' in that they 'passionately describe' (as many of our respondents did) 'the feeling of joyful pleasure in uplifting ... movement'.[24] For Wood, 'wanting to join in and feeling involved with the dance are key indicators of kinesthetic engagement', leading to viewers feeling 'active or energised' and having a 'desire to move'.[25] In the case of our respondents, the contagious happiness of the film's characters and (in some cases) fellow audience members, the intrinsic bodily affect of the ABBA songs themselves and the kinesthetic engagement elicited by the film's combination of music and movement thus allowed, to borrow Wood's expression, for 'a multiplicity of converging senses' while the film was viewed.[26]

While, as noted earlier, such appeals have long been attributed to film musicals, *Mamma Mia!*'s potential to elicit such a range of affective and embodied responses meant that discussions of affect in the interviews were more consistently linked with the category of 'feelgood'. Consequently, while, for Steph, *Mamma Mia!* has 'got a touch of musical because of the singing and dancing', it is more accurately classified, for her, as a 'positive sing-along make you feel happy and good about life type of film' or, for Pete, as a 'happy family sort of enjoy it film'. This illustrates that these respondents are more inclined to categorise the film in relation to its affective nature than in relation to more established genre categories. Indeed, for Janet and David, *Mamma Mia!* could be most closely aligned with the category of 'feelgood' because, for them, the film was obviously designed, by its makers, to be a 'feelgood' film 'from its inception', and this seems to connect with Marilyn's comment that the actors all seemed to be enjoying performing in the film. In other words, the film's makers and stars were seen to be working in the mode of 'feelgood', and our respondents were conscious of this – an idea that will be returned to later in the chapter.

'Feelgood' as a (functional) viewing choice

Throughout the interviews, *Mamma Mia!* was loosely classified (using terms like 'type of film' or 'kind of thing') as a film that performed a key function. A repeated remark across the interviews was that 'if you're feeling light-hearted' (Alice) or if you're feeling down and need cheering up, this film could be pulled out and watched and would make you 'feel good about [yourself]' (Steph). In addition to being able to listen to the songs again, this was a key reason given for why the film would continue to be re-watched on DVD in the future. Indeed, for Cath and Marilyn, a pleasurable aspect of the film is that their 'feelgood' response to it is predictable: 'each time, you know what's going to happen and how you're going to feel' (Cath).

In addition to chiming (to an extent) with functionalist approaches to the study of media/audience relations, this perspective on the film could be seen to support the kind of popular and academic arguments that Charles Burnetts and R. L. Rutsky and Justin Wyatt note have long been made about films associated with 'fun', sentiment or entertainment.[27] For them, these kinds of film, in political terms, are often construed as instruments of mass manipulation, inviting escapism and artificially heightening people's morale, rather than dealing with real-world issues or problems. One counter to this kind of interpretation is that *Mamma Mia!* was discussed by respondents as somewhat extraordinary, not only because of the ABBA music but also because it stood out in relation to these participants' usual viewing habits and tastes. Pete, Janet and Amy noted that they generally like 'serious' films, ranging from *Raise the Red Lantern* (Yimou, 1991) to *Schindler's List* (Spielberg, 1993), while Steph generally enjoys thrillers, and Ken is predominantly a viewer of westerns and war films. A number of other respondents noted that they enjoy a range of films for different reasons because films can come 'at different levels' (Alice) or reach you in 'different ways' (Jane). Consequently, when asked whether *Mamma Mia!* was one of their favourite films, many respondents noted that it was their favourite within 'its line' or in a 'light-hearted way', whereas other favourite films would be valued for different reasons. It is possible to read these qualifications as discursive markers of taste, as justifications for enjoying what others might consider less adequate entertainment. Participants' talk certainly displayed awareness of possible objections to the film, and of being judged as part of its audience. Alice noted that 'young men with an image to protect' may not enjoy (or admit to enjoying) a film like *Mamma Mia!*, which hints towards a gendered reading but also towards the film's invitation to 'let go'. Furthermore, the film's value as a guaranteed 'feelgood' experience did not preclude respondents from being critical of aspects of the film, such as implausible aspects of its plot. Indeed, the film's story, overall, was seen as an 'absolute scream' or 'cheesy', because of these plot implausibilities (Amy and Helen) or because the three prospective father characters in the film were seen to be thinly characterised (Cath and Janet).

However, when considering the film's function as 'feelgood', respondents tended to discuss the film (positively) in terms of the lack of demands it made on them. Unlike 'serious' films that 'get your mind working' or 'go to a deeper place inside' or 'require thought and concentration' (Jane, Alice, Amy), you 'don't have to think' about *Mamma Mia!* afterwards: it's 'undemanding', 'pleasant', 'uncomplicated' or 'like reading a good book and it's finished and you've enjoyed it' (Janet, Alice, Pete, Helen). For Janet, if you 'go on thinking' about a film afterwards, then it does not work as a 'feelgood' film, because 'feelgood' is 'instant ... like chocolate biscuits or something' (a comment that seems to connect with respondents' discussions of the familiarity and catchiness, as well as the oft-discussed, non-political, fun-focused nature of ABBA's music).[28] Discussing alternative ways in which the pleasures of 'fun' films can be understood, Rutsky and Wyatt argue that 'fun' films can be seen to offer 'an autonomous space that resists, and in fact levels, the presumed superiority of seriousness'.[29] In its 'instant' ability to make you feel good, and in terms of the lack of demands it places on the viewer, *Mamma Mia!* can therefore be seen to give respondents an 'autonomous space' to enjoy and gain pleasure from a film that, despite the criticisms they and others have made of it, is a conscious respite from the 'serious' films that they also value and gain other kinds of pleasure from.[30]

'Feelgood' as an idealistic mode or sensibility

The most prevalent way in which *Mamma Mia!* was distinguished from other musicals was related to what some participants saw as the film's consistent focus on happiness at the expense of any 'underlying seriousness' (Amy). Drawing on such examples as *Carousel* (King, 1956) and *The Sound of Music* (Wise, 1965), Janet, Amy, Pete and Jane noted that musicals are 'sometimes serious' and 'don't always have happy endings' and that, in the case of *The Sound of Music*, one would not 'necessarily come out smiling' but perhaps be 'spiritually uplifted' by a storyline focused around good overcoming evil. For these respondents, *Mamma Mia!* was therefore distinctive because of the absence of evil, villainy, crisis and tragedy from the film's narrative and story world, which was considered a positive, or at least unusual, attribute of the film. *Mamma Mia!* is seen to leave no 'loose ends' as 'everyone ended up with somebody' (Jane); there are 'no real serious ... tragedies like you get in some of the other films today' (David); and although other films may have a happy ending, 'usually they'll have some crisis in the middle' (Pete). This might again suggest that the film is being valued because of its 'escapism' (a term used less frequently by respondents than we expected). However, Alice, in particular, sees this absence of villainy and crisis as 'refreshing' because it allows the film 'just for once' to be 'peopled by characters' who are 'like the people in [her] life'. For her, *Mamma Mia!* is distinctive because it is not about 'good and evil' but just about a lot of people who 'care about each other' and who are 'trying their best to get on with life and maybe not doing it quite right'. In this sense, *Mamma Mia!*'s characters bring the film closer to her real-life experiences, partly because they are, for her, imperfect and normal rather than heroic or villainous.

For David, Alice and Cath, this absence of antagonistic forces from *Mamma Mia!*'s narrative is seen, then, as a distinctive factor in the film's categorisation as 'feelgood'. This suggests that 'feelgood' works as a kind of 'modality' for these respondents, which relates to the film's focus on happiness and problematises the film's straightforward categorisation into more established, or widely used, genre categories. Indeed, it is notable that, when respondents were asked to give examples of other films that they would place with *Mamma Mia!* in the 'feelgood' category, they either struggled to give examples (with Steph noting that she 'can't really think of any other film that's quite the same') or gave a wide range of eclectic film examples that cross traditional genre categories, including Disney films, *Four Weddings and a Funeral* (Newell, 1994), *The Full Monty* (Cattaneo, 1997),

Slumdog Millionaire (Boyle, 2008) and even, in Ken's case, *The Outlaw Josey Wales* (Eastwood, 1976).

Indeed, *Mamma Mia!*'s status as a film that sits precariously on the edge of the conventional musical genre was also related to the perceived playfulness and imperfection of some of the singing and dancing in the film. For Helen, the fact that the film's cast weren't professional singers or dancers made them 'unlikely' choices for a musical. Discussions of the imperfections in Pierce Brosnan's vocal performance were particularly interesting in that they seemed to connect with Alice's conception of *Mamma Mia!* as a film full of imperfect (and therefore ordinary and not heroic) characters. While Ken and Jane acknowledged the criticism that Brosnan had received for his weak singing abilities, they (along with Marilyn and Pete) noted that this made the film 'more real' and less 'contrived'. For these viewers, Brosnan's imperfect singing 'made him more of a real person than this sort of superhero', illustrating that 'you can't have great perfection in life' and that 'life's not perfect' (Jane and Marilyn). As a result, for Pete, Brosnan's as well as Colin Firth's and Stellan Skarsgård's apparent inability to sing made their characters seem like 'ordinary guys', rendering *Mamma Mia!* 'a kind of film about ordinary people'.

This focus on the (vocal) performances of the stars in the film therefore relates to a tension in the respondents' talk between seeing the film as 'fun' and 'real'. While imperfect star performances made the characters seem more 'ordinary', they also informed respondents' appreciation of *Mamma Mia!* as a film that is 'fun' and does not take itself (and its narrative and characters) too seriously. In the same stretch of talk where Jane discussed the realness of Brosnan's imperfect voice, she also noted that this aspect of the film 'was fun'. Furthermore, both Pete and Janet felt that the decision to cast actors who could not sing illustrated that the film was not 'bothered about going for any kind of realism' and that it was fundamentally 'humorous'. This complicated, and quite contradictory, assessment of the imperfections in actors' performances therefore seems to slide between seeing the actors in the film as characters and as stars, with imperfections seeming to suggest an 'ordinariness' that can be contrasted with the perfect, polished performances associated with traditional musicals. Furthermore, these imperfections seemed to remind respondents that the film's story was not to be taken seriously and (as noted earlier) was all about the actors having fun. In this sense, the film's effectiveness as entertainment was related to Brosnan and company's willingness to have a go at the singing (and the kind of dancing that, to Helen, was 'pretty hectic for actors of their age') and succeeding in entertaining them. This factor, then, seemed to further extend and enhance the film's life-affirming qualities and the sense that (in terms of the story world and the star performances) the film was operating in the mode of 'feelgood' – a mode that, for the respondents, associates notions of imperfection with fun, ordinariness and a lack of seriousness.

Conclusion

For our respondents, a range of factors informed *Mamma Mia!*'s status as a film that could be most readily associated with the loose, but 'useful' (in Janet's terms), category of 'feelgood'. This category seemed to encapsulate the film's appeal as a culturally and personally relevant, affective, deliberately non-serious and refreshingly tragedy-free experience that distinguished it from many of their other filmic encounters. In terms of the range of ways in which the film was seen to speak to our respondents, 'feelgood' could be seen to function as what Matt Hills (quoting Thomas Austin) would call a '"privatised" or "personal" quasi-genre label' with particular uses and meanings for these respondents that related to 'their own established social interests and cultural identities'.[31] Indeed, the term 'feelgood' functioned in respondents' talk rather like the way in which Hills has conceptualised the term 'cult'. It seemed to hover 'below genre' (as a personalised film category) while also, at points, taking 'on the qualities of a meta- or supra-genre' or modality 'via its ability to transgress, transcend, and articulate other genres' (most prominently in relation to the respondents' conceptions of the musical).[32] For these respondents, 'feelgood' constitutes a way of approaching films like *Mamma Mia!* It clearly draws on the term's wider public circulation but also has a specific use and value for them: working to encapsulate the film's pleasures in relation to its specific appeals and characteristics and in the context of their life histories, cultural tastes and film-watching habits.

Acknowledgements

We are indebted to all participants for their contributions to this project. In addition, we would like to thank everyone who assisted during the recruitment process and through conversations about all things *Mamma Mia!* Special thanks go to Emma Pett and Gareth Bailey for their support.

Notes

1. Feltz, Vanessa, 'Give us girls the feelgood films we want', *Express*, 20 January 2009, p. 11.
2. Hunter, Allan, 'So thank you for the music', *Express*, 11 July 2008, p. 48, with 'Saga' alluding to the well-known corporation that aims its products and services exclusively at the over-50s.
3. For a discussion of *Mamma Mia!*'s audience targeting, see Gant, Charles, 'ABBA hit top note', *Sight and Sound*, September 2008, p. 9, and Akers, Anne, '*Mamma Mia!* An analysis of the UK's most popular film of all time', University of York MA dissertation, 2009. http://www.stripeyanne.org/MammaMiaDissertation.pdf (accessed 17 May 2012).
4. York, Ashley Elaine, 'From chick flicks to millennial blockbusters: spinning female-driven narratives into franchises', *Journal of Popular Culture*, Vol. 43, No. 1, 2010, p. 4.

5. See Conrich, Ian, 'Musical performance and the cult film experience', in Ian Conrich and Estella Tincknell (Eds), *Film's Musical Moments*, Edinburgh: Edinburgh University Press, 2006, pp. 115–31, and Mathijs, Ernest and Mendik, Xavier, 'Editorial introduction: what is cult film?', in Ernest Mathijs and Xavier Mendik (Eds), *The Cult Film Reader*, Maidenhead, UK: Open University Press, 2008, pp. 1–12.
6. Hollows, Joanne, 'The masculinity of cult', in Mark Jancovich, Antonio Reboll Lazaro, Julian Stringer and Andy Willis (Eds), *Defining Cult Movies: The Cultural Politics of Oppositional Taste*, Manchester: Manchester University Press, 2003, pp. 35–53.
7. Gant, 'ABBA hits top note'.
8. Names have been anonymised.
9. Barker, Martin, and Brooks, Kate, *Knowing Audiences: Judge Dredd, Its Friends, Fans and Foes*, Luton, UK: Luton University Press, 1998.
10. Leder, Kerstin, 'Audiences talking "fear": a qualitative investigation', Aberystwyth University doctoral thesis, 2009. http://cadair.aber.ac.uk/dspace/handle/2160/2738 (accessed 18 May 2012).
11. Burnetts, Charles, 'Steven Spielberg's "feelgood" endings and sentimentality', *New Review of Film and Television Studies*, Vol. 7, No. 1, 2009, pp. 79–92.
12. Tincknell, Estella, 'The soundtrack movie, nostalgia and consumption', in Ian Conrich and Estella Tincknella (Eds), *Film's Musical Moments*, Edinburgh: Edinburgh University Press, 2006, pp. 133–4.
13. Shumway, David, 'Rock 'n' roll sound tracks and the production of nostalgia', *Cinema Journal*, Vol. 38, No. 2, 1999, p. 40.
14. Kuhn, Annette, *An Everyday Magic: Cinema and Cultural Memory*, London: I.B.Tauris, 2002, p. 10.
15 Ang, Ien, *Watching Dallas: Soap Opera and the Melodramatic Imagination*, London: Methuen, 1985, p. 20.
16. Ibid.
17. Gant, 'ABBA hits top note'.
18. Feuer, Jane, 'The self-reflective musical and the myth of entertainment', in Steven Cohan (Ed.), *Hollywood Musicals: The Film Reader*, London: Routledge, 2002, p. 32; Tincknell, 'The soundtrack movie', p. 134.
19. Williams, Linda, 'Film bodies: gender, genre, and excess', *Film Quarterly*, Vol. 44, No. 4, 1991, p. 4.
20. Plantinga, Carl, 'The scene of empathy and the human face on film', in Carl Plantinga and Greg M. Smith (Eds), *Passionate Views: Film, Cognition and Emotion*, Baltimore, MD: Johns Hopkins University Press, 1999, p. 243.
21. Meier, Leslie M., 'In excess? Body genres, "bad" music, and the judgment of audiences', *Journal of Popular Music Studies*, Vol. 20, No. 3, 2008, p. 248.

22. Feuer, 'The self-reflexive musical', p. 32.
23. Wood, Karen, 'An investigation into audiences' televisual experience of *Strictly Come Dancing*', *Participations*, Vol. 7, No. 2, 2010, pp. 262–91.
24. Ibid., p. 278.
25. Ibid., pp. 280 and 285.
26. Ibid., p. 284.
27. Cf. McQuail, Denis, 'With the benefits of hindsight: reflections on the uses and gratifications paradigm', in Roger Dickinson, Ramaswami Harindranath and Olga Linne (Eds), *Approaches to Audiences*, London: Arnold, 1998, pp. 151–65.
28. For instance, see Broman, Per F., '"When all is said and done": Swedish ABBA reception during the 1970s and the ideology of pop', *Journal of Popular Music Studies*, Vol. 17, No. 1, 2005, pp. 45–66.
29. Rutsky, R. L. and Wyatt, Justin, 'Serious pleasures: cinematic pleasure and the notion of fun', *Cinema Journal*, Vol. 30, No. 1, 1990, p. 16.
30. We should note that, for some participants, *Mamma Mia!* also gave rise to intense emotion, contemplation and even tears, especially regarding the main characters' mother/daughter relationship. However, the film's ability to deal with 'every human emotion' (Jean) in a fleeting, non-tragic manner clearly added to the 'feelgood' factor.
31. Hills, Matt, 'The question of genre in cult film and fandom: between contract and discourse', in James Donald and Michael Renov (Eds), *The Sage Handbook of Film Studies*, London: Sage, 2007, p. 439.
32. Ibid., p. 443.

9

My, my, how did I resist you?

I. Q. Hunter

I've said it before and I'll say it again, 'No more fucking ABBA.'
Bernadette (Terence Stamp) in
The Adventures of Priscilla, Queen of the Desert
(Elliott, 1994)

That is a film that if Winona Ryder, Zooey Deschanel and Liv Tyler came round my house together and said 'we will make mad passionate love to you forever but only if you watch Mamma Mia with us first' I would have to seriously think about whether it was worth it.
Comment on a Facebook thread about *Mamma Mia!*

'Beyond awfulness'

Ten minutes into *Mamma Mia!* and I have shrunk back into the sofa, rigid with disbelief at the highest-grossing British film of all time. I had shunned it in the cinema, fearing for my self-respect as a cinephile and perhaps also for my masculinity. Rumour hinted at women-only screenings with sing-alongs and impromptu dancing, a prospect as forbidding to me as Shelob's lair. Curiosity and professional duty finally compelled purchase of the DVD, so here I was, with my equally bemused first wife, struggling to grasp the appeal of a slackly plotted, indifferently lensed pantomime of out-of-tune cover versions; a British film starring Americans, set in Greece, with songs by Swedes and a title in Italian; a film more gruelling than torture porn and so stupid it drooled.[1] Ninety long, draining minutes of forced jollity and torch-song abuse later, we agreed: an unpleasantly alienating experience, baffling and never to be repeated. When Anthony Lane of *The New Yorker* described his agonised recoil from the film, which he half-watched 'staring down at my clenched fists and curled toes in a calvary of embarrassment', I could sympathise and feel his pain.[2]

That was in 2009. I did not commit to becoming an 'anti-fan', Jonathan Gray's handy term for one whose emotional investment in hating a film defines his self-image, but I wasn't slow to revile *Mamma Mia!* given the chance and a captive audience.[3] Not until one of the editors of this book conscripted me to justify my hatred in print did I start to reflect on *why* the film had so repulsed me. Bluff called, I admit that it was gut prejudice rather than any kind of considered aesthetic response. After all, it is no surprise that I hated the film. A middle-aged straight white man, a middle-class *soi disant* cinephile and academic, doesn't fit the target demographic of a camp musical romcom embraced by 'older women' and young girls. While I am now, alas!, too old to pass convincingly as a 'fan-boy', my film choices are the expected cult movies and 'male classics' of a cineaste of a certain age, from *A Clockwork Orange* (Kubrick, 1971) to *Fight Club* (Fincher, 1999). My natural 'habitus' of 'postmodern irony' – 'the last refuge of middle-class white male intellectuals' – is much the same as described over a decade ago in my widely reviled encomium to Paul Verhoeven's camp-fest *Showgirls* (1997).[4] So from the opening soul-curdling sabotage of 'Honey Honey' (a song I *like*) to Meryl Streep's final threatening squawk of 'Do you want another one?', *Mamma Mia!* was destined to elicit a fight-or-flight response. Irrational aversion – a bodily rather than intellectual reaction – stiffened the sinews of aesthetic disapproval. I hated *Mamma Mia!* as completely and unhestitatingly as I had hated *Jerry Maguire* (Crowe, 1996) and *Bridget Jones's Diary* (Maguire, 2001), which made me retch and gibber like Alex DeLarge during the Ludovico Treatment.

My, my, how did I resist you?

Lane and many other critics (and I) were clearly not alone. In reply to a Facebook post, a half-hearted attempt at crowdsourcing opinions about *Mamma Mia!*, a (male) friend commented: 'Crap, the worst thing ever to be put onto film or on to the stage. It is truly, truly awful. Beyond awfulness in fact, sitting through it was probably the worst experience of my life so far.' This chapter is an attempt to explain why the film affected me (and him, and quite a few of my other Facebook friends) as it did. It is a story with an unexpected twist.

'A little bit sick in my mouth'

By any reasonable standards *Mamma Mia!* is a second-rate movie. *Variety* pounced on its technical faults ('poor dubbing', 'tech work often feels more rushed than mastered') and 'over-polished glitzy texture'.[5] Other critics denigrated the miscasting, incompetent singing (especially hapless Pierce Brosnan's) and the clumsy blocking and over-cutting of the musical numbers. A smell of amateurism about the whole enterprise evokes karaoke, holiday videos and bawling into a hairbrush in front of the mirror. The plotting is loose to the point of capricious misdirection: we never find out who the father is; the marriage at the end is not the one the story arc requires; and the outing of Colin Firth's character as gay, presumably a nod to ABBA's gay fan base, is so offhand that it foxed the *Guardian*'s reviewer.[6]

This is all evidence of poor and inexperienced film-making, but hardly enough to justify abhorrence and disgust. Why then did I hate the film beyond all reason? I confess that it is disconcertedly hard to explain, but I can hazard a list:

- Glutinous sentimentality about cartoonish characters I couldn't care less about.
- The seemingly random insertion of ABBA songs into an already illogical set-up, heedless of their narrative or emotional relevance.

- The shabby betrayal of great pop music.
- An unearned and contemptuous air of celebrity self-satisfaction. The cast is evidently enjoying itself more than any sane audience is likely to. This might just be the dark pulsating heart of my hatred: resentment at rich people lazily flaunting their inferior musical skills and expecting fame alone to secure our simpering indulgence. I hate *Strictly Come Dancing*, too.
- Julie Walters. She irritates me.

But is this enough? Jason Mittell, explaining why he dislikes *Mad Men* (AMC, 2007–), cites his inability to 'reconcile the show's critical representations of idealised advertising-constructed visions of American culture with the show's seemingly authentic (and simultaneously idealised) glossy presentation of 1960s New York'.[7] But my hatred of *Mamma Mia!* was not politically inspired. I can certainly imagine taking offence at the wafer-thin characterisations, gender stereotypes and insultingly clichéd depiction of Greece as a timeless sunny backlot, but, aside from envious distaste for capering celebs, I thought the film no more ideologically repellent than the run of contemporary movies. Something else was going on.

For its haters *Mamma Mia!* belongs to a kind of 'body genre' – in Linda Williams's sense of the term – of unwatchable films.[8] Critical detachment is short-circuited by inexplicable physical distress – notably embarrassment, anger, repulsion, disgust. As a (female) Facebook friend commented on the 'Horrible, embarrassing and cringeworthy' experience of *Mamma Mia!*, 'Brosnan made me a little bit sick in my mouth when he started singing on that boat.' The film is an experience of the *abject*, so that as yet another nauseated Facebook commentator said: 'The very thought of it makes me want to vomit.'[9] Mittell writes, 'In the end, watching *Mad Men* leaves me feeling unclean and unpleasant, having spent time in an unenjoyable place with people I don't care about, and coming out smelling of stale cigarettes.'[10] The world of *Mad Men* is 'not a place of comfort'. That is how I felt about *Mamma Mia!*, though I remain shamefully ineffective at rationalising why. I did not want to be there, frozen to a sofa, sharing my life with these ridiculous shouty people indiscriminately strangulating ABBA songs in their shinily unreal tourist hell.

'My mum absolutely loves it though'

Mamma Mia! is sloppy hackwork rather than a 'badfilm' as cultists put it. It is not *Plan Nine from Outer Space* (Wood, 1959) or *The Room* (Wiseau, 2003), which deliver the pleasurable shocks of bad taste and subversive style. I don't sense in those who enjoy *Mamma Mia!* an ironic pleasure in its failings, which seem a product of willed mediocrity, almost a principled lack of interest in achieving slickness and diegetic consistency. To judge from comments on IMDb, aesthetic considerations, for those who like the film, are subordinated to cheerful acceptance of its untidiness and boisterous indifference to good taste. Critical faculties are suspended in favour of being harmlessly entertained. At any rate audiences proved more forgiving than the critics. While rottentomatoes.com lists the film with a 53 per cent critical approval rating (29 per cent from 'top critics'), its audience rating is 76 per cent.[11]

This is where things get tricky, for explicating a personal if widely shared dislike segues rapidly into vulgar generalities. Bluntly, most fans of *Mamma Mia!* seem to be women – especially 'the much neglected female audience who ... are "north-of-middle-age"'.[12] (This audience seems to be a fragment of a larger audience, which boosted the takings of *The King's Speech* (Hooper, 2010), of people who rarely go the cinema at all and are similar to what Barker and Brooks call 'film refusers'[13].) My dislike of the film may have little to do with the fact it is clichéd, badly put together and as sickly sweet as Babycham.

It might have something to do with masculinity. If I didn't 'get' the film, well, maybe as a bloke I simply wasn't supposed to. Or perhaps there was a more basic and discreditable repulsion – a male dismissal of something made for and by women and loved by teenage girls, their mothers and grandmothers. In the reception of *Mamma Mia!*, comments about the actors and the audience suggest something similar. One commentator on rottentomatoes twittered, 'anyone with a slight bit of manliness would run',[14] while a short-lived Facebook group, Men United Against Mamma Mia (MUAMM), declared, 'This group of men cringes at the very thought of being subjected to a film that stands against all things manly.'[15] My instinctive loathing therefore smacked of knee-jerk sexism and ageism, an offhand refusal not only of misconceived chick flicks but of women's taste itself. Was I both victim and unthinking conduit of preconceptions about the triviality of female pleasures?

Cultural critics have long argued that women's tastes are associated with low, easy pleasures, mindless conformism and the detachment of brain from aesthetic judgement.[16] Soap operas, four-handkerchief weepies, *Hello!* magazine, *Fifty Shades of Grey*, Mills & Boon, the *Twilight* films, heritage stuff, the poisonously reviewed *Sex and the City 2* (King, 2010) and *Eat Pray Love* (Murphy, 2010) – the cultural world of women, or rather the cultural texts served up to women, rank low in aesthetic estimation; at best they are 'guilty pleasures'. Highbrow critics accuse women's films and TV of damaging vulnerable female audiences by reinforcing their belief in romance as a solution to deeper social problems, weakening their critical defences with the acid of sentiment and slushy emotion. Bubbly tosh like *27 Dresses* (Fletcher, 2008) locks women into a femininity defined by romance, dippy introversion and the bogus empowerment of shopping, and the happy ending of marriage rather than self-fulfilment.

All this doubtless informs disdain for *Mamma Mia!*, a disdain also perhaps for its core audiences. But explaining a taste choice can seem like airily explaining it away. Some men like *Mamma Mia!* with heroic cross-gender solidarity, and many women I know dislike it, not least because they resent the assumption this type of film is intended for them. One female Facebook friend commented:

> I think the film is terrible. It has an amateur feel about it that makes it feel like a school play. The performances are poor and the protagonists come across as more caricatures than characters. ... My mum absolutely loves it though.

She is a film academic, however, which may 'inoculate' her against feminine populism. Yet even I can see that the film's candy-floss pleasures might be re-described as 'positive' for many women, not only the life-affirming on-screen energy of its lip-synched divas, but the rousing off-screen saga of triumphant, woman-led progress from underdog musical to world-conquering phenomenon. As in Richard Dyer's description of the utopian world of the musical, the film showcases strong, confident, sexually assertive women and brings together all the elements of a female-centric 'utopian sensibility'.[17] There are positive spins, too, on baby boomers' sexuality, as in other recent romcoms such as *Something's Gotta Give* (Meyers, 2003) and *It's Complicated* (Meyers, 2009). And opportunities abound to revel in the mature beauty of Colin Firth and Pierce Brosnan. Even bad films can be upliftingly progressive for their committed fans. As Barbara Klinger says:

> Repeated experiences with the same film can operate normatively, continually reaffirming appropriate gender identities, for example. By the same token, favorite texts can continue to inspire feelings of liberation in women looking for strong role models (even in what appears to be a compromised genre such as the chick flick).[18]

The film's heart (unlike its cameras) might be in the right place.

If simple masculinity was insufficient to explain my excessive hatred of *Mamma Mia!*, had it something to do with my being a film cultist, the type of cinephile explored in my article on *Showgirls*? In rejecting *Mamma Mia!* was I also rejecting what might be called 'the wrong kind' of cult film? This too, however, brings us inexorably back to questions of gender.

'A Marmite cult?'

Given its enthusiastic reception by certain audiences, could *Mamma Mia!* be described as a cult film? Before dismissing this out of hand, consider that it has all the makings of a bona fide cult. There are the sing-alongs and other activities of enthusiastic repeat viewers; the screenings are occasions for collective ritual performances; the film's success came out of nowhere critical disapproval. *Mamma Mia!* despite shares textual characteristics with other cult films, which have what Umberto Eco describes as a 'glorious ricketiness'.[19] It is playfully intertextual, with knowing nods to Bond (Bond sings! Badly!) and Firth's soggy-shirted turn in *Pride and Prejudice* (1995), and Streep and Skarsgård's trashing of their high-minded star personae. It is also, like many cult films, a shambolically hybrid text (a musical, albeit without much musicality) and has no truck with verisimilitude. The use of songs by ABBA, a group poised between ironic camp and mainstream affection, is in itself culty. Using songs as a ready-made soundtrack to life, regardless of their strict relevance, blurs the distinction between life and film and, assuming shared knowledge of ABBA as a lingua franca, binds the audience into a celebration of archetypal female experience. From summoning memories of old boyfriends to sanctifying the ties between mother and daughter (the 'Slipping through My Fingers' sequence, of which Björn Ulvaeus said, 'It's a very powerful emotion, for all parents. I've seen that in the audience at performances ... over the years, people getting very emotional about that particular song'[20]), the songs are instruments of nostalgic recall. (Anecdotally I am told that mothers take pleasure in watching the film with their daughters, sharing ABBA's songs in earnest of intergenerational solidarity.) This is a film, too, about release (for the audience, but also for a cast letting its collective hair down) and carefree self-acceptance in supportive company – a *holiday* ('a virtual holiday', as Colin Firth put it[21]) from taste and seriousness, rather like a hen party or boozy wedding reception. Is that so different from J. P. Telotte's description of cult: 'In essence, therefore, every cult constitutes a community, a group that "worships" similarly and regularly, and finds a strength in that shared experience'?[22]

Yet it is counterintuitive for good reasons to describe *Mamma Mia!* as a cult film, even as what one Facebook friend called 'Marmite Mia' – 'a Marmite cult' because 'people seem to love it or detest it'. There is a general assumption that the cult audience will relish the film for reasons different from the intended or original audience. *Mamma Mia!* can be compared with a definitive cult 'midnight movie', *The Rocky Horror Picture Show* (Sharman, 1975), but both its popular success and its audience profile are problematic. There has been some debate about whether mainstream and blockbuster films can be labelled cult. Danny Peary excluded from his canon-building *Cult Movies* films, such as *Gone with the Wind* (Fleming, 1939) and *Star Wars* (Lucas, 1977), that had numerous fans but no cultists: 'The word cult', he insisted, 'implies a minority.'[23] And while Matt Hills has argued for *Star Wars* and *The Lord of the Rings* trilogy (Jackson, 2001–2003) as cult films, cult does tend to imply a cinema of marginality and subversion – films about shit-eating transvestites and eyeball-popping zombies rather than all-singing-and-dancing romcoms.[24] If *Mamma Mia!* were appropriated by a subcultural audience different from its intended one, as *The Sound of Music* (Wise, 1965) or *Showgirls* have been by gay audiences, then its cult status, and that of the audience participation events, would be more secure. *Mamma Mia!* is, from this point of view, not only not-cult but precisely the kind of mainstream pap that cult tastes define themselves against. Cinephile cultists (like me) have a sworn duty to reject happy-clappy stuff like *Mamma Mia!*, even if it means being snotty killjoys and party poopers and upsetting our mums. We pride ourselves and acquire subcultural capital by what Greg Taylor called our 'oppositional discernment'.[25]

Building on the idea that female tastes tend to be looked down on, Jacinda Read and Joanne Hollows argue that the idea of cult itself is gender-specific, not so much a subversion of mainstream taste as an intensification of its masculinist ideology.[26] According to Hollows, 'mainstream cinema is imagined as feminized mass culture and cult as a heroic and masculinized subculture'.[27] That is why chick flicks like *Dirty Dancing* (Ardolino, 1987) – '*Star Wars* for girls' – and *Titanic* (Cameron, 1997) are not seen as cult films. Moreover, these films have tended to be rapturously consumed in the domestic sphere, on TV or video, where, as Barbara Klinger has shown, repeat home viewing may turn films into personal cult movies within specifically gendered traditions of sleepovers, girls' nights in and so on:

> In the case of chick flicks, their frequent rewatching by groups of friends as a form of female bonding enhances the status they have as bildungsromans or coming-of-age stories that model female subjectivity and desire as inextricably bound up with romance-and-rescue scenarios.[28]

But this is rarely considered an experience of cult viewing. In truth, a girl watching *Dirty Dancing* on DVD for the twentieth time is probably more characteristic of cult practice nowadays than the remnants of midnight movie culture. Cult viewing has become much more about private viewing and personalised cults than about collective public displays of fandom. Even so, cult is still conventionally defined as incompatible with women's films and what Hollows calls 'the passive, distracted and complicit female viewer ... against which cult fans define themselves'.[29] The result is an 'Othering' of the mainstream and women's culture – at best an ironic appropriation of it (as with Douglas Sirk's movies). What made *Mamma Mia!* stand out is that it seemed a return, like the sing-along screenings of *The Sound of Music*, to a classic midnight movie tradition of cult appreciation (or, for resistant cultists, a vanilla parody of it).

Even if *Mamma Mia!* does not fit the standard definition of a cult film, it certainly shares with cult films a thematic interest in bonding, on and off screen, and in alternative and extended families. Cult films are often about male bonding linked to structures of nostalgia. They are curiously utopian in depicting free love and unlikely pairings – as in *Harold and Maude* (Ashby, 1972), *Pink Flamingos* (Waters, 1972) (even if its model alternative family is based on Charles Manson's) and *The Rocky Horror Picture Show*. Cult films are male guides to slacker outsiderdom and the negotiation of otherness through Zen resistance or psychosis (*Fight Club*), *Taxi Driver* (Scorsese, 1976)). Cultists find comfort in the films' exploration of homosocial male units (*The Big Lebowski* (Coen, 1999), *Withnail and I* (Robinson, 1986), *Repo Man* (Cox, 1985), *The Thing* (Carpenter, 1982)), indulgence of antisocial individualism (*A Clockwork Orange* (Kubrick, 1971), *If...* (Anderson, 1968)) and yearning for lost or impossible masculinities (Bogart, Carter in *Get Carter* (Hodges, 1971)) and obsolete male codes through which a kind of cool difference can be achieved (*Blade Runner* (Scott, 1982)). Like a cinephile Huck Finn, the cultist lights out for a territory without women where he can bind nostalgically with other exiles from the commercial mainstream.

Mirroring this, *Mamma Mia!* also focuses on female bonding in an atmosphere of utopian escapism, a world where, as Dyer said of the musical generally, 'song and dance "are in the air", built into the peasant/black culture and blood', and not without a tone of 'nostalgia or primitivism' (the Greek locals, whose island is colonised by foreigners, are kept in the background as an undifferentiated chorus).[30] The Golden Ages alluded to in *Mamma Mia!*, however, are multiple and layered, ranging from bucolic visions of ancient Greece and memories of package tours and *Shirley Valentine* (Gilbert, 1989) to the permissive 1960s and 1970s (the 1960s are a significant object of cult nostalgia). True, the dates do not work (if Streep's daughter was conceived in the Summers either of Love or Platform Shoes she'd be into or nearing her forties), but the point is to evoke for the audience pastness, embarrassing youth, nostalgia for freedom and a time before conspicuous ageing and to promote an upbeat vision of 'middle youth'. (Though, one friend confided, the movie got her down because her life was conspicuously absent of sunshine and Colin Firth.) It evokes, too, memories of the stage show and crucially, with repeat viewing, nostalgia for the experience of seeing the film itself (the DVD acknowledges this with a 'sing-along' option that enables domestic reproduction of the 'live' event). It is this that links it with cult films: *Mamma Mia!* – an anti-cult cult film – becomes an occasion for audience-generated pleasure rather than an object of pleasure in itself.

'There, I feel better now'

And then, of course, I saw *Mamma Mia!* again. An entirely unscientific focus group of a couple of girlfriends, their daughters and I put the DVD on one Friday night in early 2011, and after a few glasses of wine the inevitable happened. I sang, I danced, I fell over. I felt the beat of the tambourine and we chased the shadows away. The bad singing didn't matter because I couldn't hear it; I was too busy singing even more badly myself. Before I knew it the film was over and I had had *fun*.[31]

In fact, everything I disliked about the film turned out to be *a good reason to like it* – from the bad singing (which seemed a mark of transparency and honesty), to the meticulously reproduced clichés, to the unrelieved girliness (my spellchecker suggests *grisliness*), make-believe and wish-fulfilment. Its failings, technical and otherwise, lend it a certain gauche homemade charm, a defiantly British rebuff of Hollywood gloss, while the sense that the cast is off-duty suggests a kind of let's-do-the-show-right-here spontaneity.

It turned out that never having seen it 'live' I had *not seen the film at all*, just as someone who has only seen *2001: A Space Odyssey* (Kubrick, 1968) on video or a video nasty on shiny Blu-ray rather than as a fuzzy fourth-generation copy has not really experienced them either. As another, male Facebook friend commented:

> OK, I'm going to come clean: I greatly enjoyed the film when I saw it with a warm, unpretentious audience at the multiplex. I liked the cheerful am-dram quality and the attemps [sic] to give narrative sense to nonsensical lyrics. I liked the music, because I like ABBA. There, I feel better now.

Mamma Mia!'s full enjoyment seems to require a public collectivity of unembarrassed response, for which re-viewing the film on DVD is at best an experience of nostalgic recall. Seeing the film again had offered a glimpse, a simulacrum of liveness, and that was enough. When I first saw *Mamma Mia!* I was not dressed up and diggin' it in the aisles with friends on my umpteenth cinema visit, or gaily having the time of my life at some sing-along event. There was no possibility of getting caught up in a spontaneous emotional moment, as, when watching *The Full Monty* (Cattaneo, 1997) for the first time in a packed provincial cinema, I felt the audience connect with the film, a collective welling up of recognition and delight repeatedly capped by shared laughter. It wasn't until I saw the film in the right company, as an interloper at a girl's night in, that I comprehended its powers of liberating release. I was seduced and my inner camp self burst free from its crabbed middle-class male film snob Englishness. 'In the end,' as Brosnan said, 'I surrendered to the whole experience, and had a great time doing it.'[32] It reminded me of that scene, the archetypal moment of cult experience, memorialised in *Fame* (Parker, 1980), when an uptight girl, losing her *Rocky Horror* virginity at a midnight screening, suddenly finds herself excitedly doing the Time Warp on stage in front of the whole congregation and is never the same again. *Mamma Mia!* had become a different kind of 'body genre' experience. David Church notes that 'the spectacle of body genre manipulates the viewer into involuntarily imitating the pain, fear, or pleasure of the onscreen female body', so perhaps in learning to enjoy *Mamma Mia!* I had been interpellated, thanks to alcohol, by female pleasure.[33] God knows what I'd be like at a full-blown sing-along. As a cinephile and supposed scholar of cult film I should have known all this. Watching films is not just about having appropriate foreknowledge, learned skills of comprehension and sufficient cultural capital to make smart comments about it afterwards, but about being emotionally attuned, physically aligned and ready to lose oneself in an experience only partly confined to what is happening on screen.

What in the end have I learned? That bad films can be fun, especially when one is in love, mildly intoxicated and surrounded by friends, was hardly a revelation. Without the imperishable ABBA songs to draw me in, *Mamma Mia!* would still have been an ordeal. But it impressed on me that responses to films (all films, not cult ones or ones seen though a haze of alcohol consumption) are situational: not just emotional investment in a film but understanding its structure of feeling depends on seeing it under the right conditions and recollecting it in apt ways. What struck me, when I sobered up and reconsidered my dislike of this awful film, was how little aesthetics and narrative coherence mattered to my experience of it. In a sense the film didn't matter all that much; context was everything. I certainly don't know whether that later viewing of *Mamma Mia!* was a 'cult' experience, since, though it propelled me out of my usual comfort zone of cinephile irony, cheerful enthusiasm was how most audiences seemed to respond to the film. Cultists like me tend to resist the emotional as well taste choices of ordinary 'mass' audiences; that is one aspect of what Hollows and Read might consider a laddish disavowal of the mainstream and its monstrously feminine pleasures. Equally, I am unwilling to write off my initial repulsion from the film as wrong or 'inauthentic'; I did feel it, intimately, and cannot discount it as 'merely' symptomatic of some toxic combination of ageist misogyny and cinephile snootiness.

What I am left with is this. Emotional and *physical* rather than cognitive engagement was crucial, and *caring* about the film experience, whether that meant hating it or throwing myself bodily into its pleasures, drew me far more deeply into the whole *Mamma Mia!* 'thing' than either textual analysis or diagnosing the aesthetic errors of those I had initially, and thoughtlessly, dismissed as 'hysterical' cine-illiterate fans.[34] I learned that sometimes I have to have a little faith in ordinary people, stop being a cultist and start believing that, as Muriel says in *Muriel's Wedding* (Hogan, 1994), 'my life is as good as an ABBA song. It's as good as "Dancing Queen".'

Acknowledgements

Thanks to Elaine, Sam, Georgia and Alice, who educated me in the pleasures of *Mamma Mia!* while never bothering to argue that it was a 'good' film, and to Andy, Andrea, Laura, Vincent, Kate, Jim, Kathy, Jamie and James and my other Facebook friends, who provided not only highly quotable comments but invaluable evidence of the passions aroused by even the most apparently inoffensive romcom.

Notes

1. *Sex and the City 2* attracted several comparisons with torture porn. See Leupp, Thomas, 'This is the new torture porn'. http://www.hollywood.com/review/Sex_and_the_City_2/6875329 (accessed 15 March 2011).
2. Lane, Anthony, 'Euro visions', *New Yorker*, 28 July 2008. http://www.newyorker.com/arts/critics/.../2008/.../28/080728crci_cinema_lane (accessed 15 March 2011).
3. Gray, Jonathan, 'New audiences, new textualities: anti-fans and non-fans,' *International Journal of Cultural Studies*, Vol. 6, No.1, 2003, pp. 64–81. Hating a film passionately is as rare and definitive of identity as loving one as a fan or cultist, but more common is not caring about or engaging with a film and then forgetting about it afterwards. There seems to be little research on the intriguing topic of indifferent, bored or disengaged audiences.
4. The offending article, to which this essay is a kind of sequel, is Hunter, I. Q., 'Beaver Las Vegas! A fan-boy's defence of *Showgirls*', in Xavier Mendik and Graeme Harper (Eds), *Unruly Pleasures: The Cult Film and Its Critics*, Guildford: FAB Press, 2000, pp. 187–201.
5. Mintzer, Jordan, '*Mamma Mia!*', *Variety*, 14 July 2008, p. 36.
6. Bradshaw, Peter, '*Mamma Mia!*', *Guardian*, 10 July 2008. http://www.guardian.co.uk/culture/2008/jul/10/film.reviews (accessed 15 March 2011).
7. Mittell, Jason, 'Smoke gets in my eyes: on disliking *Mad Men*', *Just TV*, 29 July 2010. http://justtv.wordpress.com/2010/07/29/on-disliking-mad-men/ (accessed 15 March 2011).
8. Williams, Linda, 'Film bodies: gender, genre and excess', *Film Quarterly*, Vol. 44, No. 4, 1991, pp. 2–13.
9. The link between the unwatchable and the abject was suggested to me by Tim O'Sullivan's paper 'Intensity, taste and other judgements: unwatchable television', Screen Studies Conference, Glasgow University, 3–5 July 1998. I have found relatively little work on films as objects of disgust (unless they are deliberately revolting ones like *Pink Flamingos*), but see Plantinga Carl, 'Disgusted at the movies', *Film Studies*, No. 8, 2006, pp. 81–92. David Church has suggested that cult viewing practices are themselves masochistic: 'Wilfully and (un)pleasurably submitting oneself to the often transgressive content of cult films is a profoundly masochistic act.' This implies that a cultist might return repeatedly, like a dog to vomit, to films he hates precisely in order to experience variations on the 'visceral affects' he relishes in cult favourites like *Pink Flamingos*. Anti-fans stake their identities on it. Interestingly, the cultist's masochistic

exposure to cinematic displeasure may function to test and reassert his masculinity: 'Consumption of cult films may outwardly appear as masculine territory, but the actual viewing experience is predicated on a(n) (un)pleasurable feminization that is only defenced against when the house lights come up again and gendered power relations resume in everyday life.' Enjoying *Mamma Mia!* threatens the masculinity of an anti-fan, but the painful ritual of watching it paradoxically involves experiencing masochistic feminisation. Church David, 'Notes toward a masochizing of cult cinema: the painful pleasures of the cult film fan', *Offscreen*, Vol. 11, No. 4, 2007. http://www.offscreen.com/index.php/pages/essays/masochizing_of_cult_cinema (accessed 15 March 2011).
10. Mittell, 'Smoke gets in my eyes'.
11. http://www/rottentomatoes.com/m/mamma_mia (accessed 15 March 2011).
12. Cochrane, Kira, 'The mother of all musicals', *Guardian*, 27 November 2009, pp. 7–8.
13. Barker, Martin and Brooks, Kate, *Knowing Audiences: Judge Dredd, Its Friends, Fans and Foes*, Luton, UK: University of Luton Press, 1998, pp. 232–7.
14. http://www.rottentomatoes.com/m/mamma_mia. Comment by Maxamillion, 5 December 2010 (accessed 15 March 2011).
15. http://www.facebook.com/group.php?gid=18361249763 (accessed 15 March 2011).
16. A point made with some over-statement by the cultural critic Bidisha in the wake of the critical mauling of *Sex and the City 2*. See Bidisha, 'Why the *Sex and the City 2* reviews were misogynistic', *Guardian* (G2), 4 June 2010, p. 18.
17. Dyer, Richard, *Only Entertainment*, 2nd edition, London: Routledge, 2002, pp. 30–1.
18. Klinger, Barbara, *Beyond the Mutliplex: Cinema, Technologies, and the Home*, Berkeley: University of California Press, 2006, p. 188.
19. Eco, Umberto, '*Casablanca*: cult movies and intertextual collage', in *Faith in Fakes: Essays* (trans. William Weaver), London: Secker & Warburg, 1987, p. 198.
20. Andersson, Benny, Ulvaeus, Björn and Craymer, Judy, *Mamma Mia! How Can I Resist You? The Inside Story of Mamma Mia! and the Songs of ABBA*, London: Phoenix Illustrated, 2008, p. 112.
21. Cochrane, 'The mother of all movies'.
22. Telotte, J. P., 'Beyond all reason: the nature of cult', in J. P. Telotte (Ed.), *The Cult Film Experience: Beyond All Reason*, Austin: University of Texas Press, 1991, p. 13.
23. Peary, Danny, *Cult Movies: A Hundred Ways to Find the Reel Thing*, London: Vermilion, 1982, p. xiii.

24. Hills, Matt, 'Realising the cult blockbuster: *The Lord of the Rings* fandom and *residual/emergent cult* status in "the mainstream"', in Ernest Mathijs (Ed.), *The Lord of the Rings: Popular Culture in Global Context*, London: Wallflower Press, 2006, pp. 160–71; Hills, Matt, '*Star Wars* in fandom, film theory and the museum: the cultural status of the cult blockbuster', in Julian Stringer (Ed.), *Movie Blockbusters*, London: Routledge, 2003, pp. 178–89.
25. Taylor Greg, 'Pure *quidditas* or geek chic? Cultism as discernment', in Jeffrey Sconce (Ed.), *Sleaze Artists: Cinema at the Margins of Taste, Style and Politics*, Durham, NC: Duke University Press, 2007, p. 260.
26. Hollows, Joanne, 'The masculinity of cult' (pp. 35–53) and Read, Jacinda, 'The cult of masculinity: from fan-boys to academic bad-boys' (pp. 54–70), in Mark Jancovich, Antonio Lazaro Reboll, Julian Stringer and Andy Willis (Eds), *Defining Cult Movies: The Cultural Politics of Oppositional Taste*, Manchester: Manchester University Press, 2003.
27. Hollows, 'The masculinity of cult', p. 37.
28. Klinger, *Beyond the Multiplex*, pp. 172–3.
29. Hollows, 'The masculinity of cult', p. 43.
30. Dyer, *Only Entertainment*, pp. 30–1.
31. Having written this chapter, I discovered that another film cultist, the journalist and critic Mark Kermode, had a similar epiphany watching this 'knee-tremblingly terrible' film, as I did not, in a cinema: 'Even as every critical faculty I possessed told me to run screaming from the theatre right now, I felt my heart swelling, my eyes welling up, my pulse starting to jump, and my general aura going all pink and cuddly.' See Kermode Mark, *It's Only a Movie: Reel Life Adventures of a Film Obsessive*, London: Random House, 2010, pp. 116–21.
32. Anderson Ulvaeus and Craumer, *Mamma Mia! How Can I Resist You?*, p. 249.
33. Church, 'Notes toward a masochizing of cult cinema'.
34. I pursue this theme in Hunter, I. Q., 'From adaptation to cinephilia: an intertextual odyssey', in Thomas Van Parys and, I. Q. Hunter (Eds), *Science Fiction across Media: Adaptation/Novelisation*, London: Glyphi, 2012.

10

Not too old for sex? *Mamma Mia!* and the 'older bird' chick flick

Claire Jenkins

The on-screen representation of older women has become a frequently discussed issue within recent British and American popular culture. For example, the decision by the BBC's *Strictly Come Dancing* to replace the 66-year-old judge Arlene Phillips with the much younger Alesha Dixon in 2009 raised questions about the visibility of older women on the screen, particularly after 'thousands of viewers complained to the broadcaster about perceived ageism'.[1] In 2011, the BBC came in for criticism again when it was successfully sued for age discrimination by former *Countryfile* presenter Miriam O'Reilly after the show terminated the contracts of all of their female presenters over 40, despite retaining older male presenters.[2] In Hollywood, actresses ranging from Scarlett Johansson to Meryl Streep have publicly lambasted the film industry for its persistent marginalisation of older women.[3] Meanwhile, British actresses such as Juliet Stevenson and Dame Helen Mirren have also voiced their concerns about ageism towards women within the British film and television industries.[4] Whilst the popular press has tended to side with these women in their protests against marginalisation, in certain forms the older woman still remains highly problematic and at times near-horrific. When news emerged in 2010 that the 60-something grandmother of *The X-Factor* contestant Katie Waissel was working as a prostitute, the attitude of the press was markedly critical and derisive, demonstrating some of the tensions implicit in the cultural presentation of overtly sexualised older women.[5]

Some academic work in media studies has also focused on images of and narratives about older women. For example, Sadie Wearing's analysis of the ageing woman within a post-feminist, youth-oriented cultural landscape introduced the notion of the 'girl-ing' of the older woman through transformative rejuvenation narratives.[6] Film scholar Imelda Whelehan's exploration of representations of older women within British cinema notes the political potential of these depictions of the ageing female body, suggesting that films such as *Calendar Girls* (Cole, 2003) and *The Mother* (Michell, 2003) work to 'destabilise deeply held preconceptions about the social place and function of the ageing woman'.[7] In her analysis of Michell's film, Whelehan demonstrates the ways in which the older woman is offered a position usually reserved for her younger counterpart in a narrative about sex and fulfilment. Although sexual reawakening is a key theme in the film, Whelehan argues that the film is as much about the mother finding her 'self' and becoming visible after her husband's death as it is about older female sexuality.[8] Margaret Tally's discussion of older women's sexual reawakenings in Hollywood's 'older bird' chick flicks (a term coined by the *Guardian* columnist Cherry Potter in her article about Hollywood's recent foregrounding of middle-aged women[9]) explores the ambiguities and tensions at play in representations of older women's sexual expression in films such as *Something's Gotta Give* (Meyers, 2003), *The Banger Sisters* (Dolman, 2002) and *Freaky Friday* (Waters, 2003).[10] This interest in older women, particularly sexually active older women, is coupled with a renewed screen presence in an increasing number of films from both sides of the Atlantic, encompassing the examples referenced in Whelehan's and Tally's work as well as films such as *Because I Said So* (Lehmann, 2007) and *Under the Tuscan Sun* (Wells, 2003).

Although the middle-aged female lead is not necessarily a new phenomenon, there has undoubtedly been a shift in the kind of narratives in which she is placed that contrasts with how women of similar ages were featured in classical Hollywood cinema. Whelehan discusses this, with reference to Bette Davis's performances in *All About Eve* (Mankiewicz, 1950) and *Whatever Happened to Baby Jane* (Aldrich, 1962) and Gloria Swanson's role in *Sunset Boulevard* (Wilder, 1950), in film narratives that quite self-consciously drew attention to the ageism of the silver screen. As Whelehan explains, commentators and actors have long noted the paucity of roles for older women, who have inevitably been positioned in the cinematic margins as 'mother, grandmother, domestic servant, spinster [or] infirm person' once they reached a certain age.[11] This is not to say that more recent configurations of older women on screen have necessarily represented an exponential leap beyond negative stereotyping; Jane Fonda's and Meryl Streep's titular roles as monster and devil respectively in *Monster-in-Law* (Luketic, 2005) and *The Devil Wears Prada* (Frankel, 2006) are both reminiscent of the traditional rendering of the older woman as monstrous, demonstrated in earlier films such as *The Nanny* (Holt, 1965), in which Bette Davis plays the terrifying older female authority figure.

However, this chapter seeks to explore the trend of casting the middle-aged woman as a romantic heroine exemplified by *Mamma Mia!* and its repositioning of Meryl Streep from *The Devil Wears Prada*'s boss-from-hell into a warm, funny and maternal figure. Although the initial romantic storyline of the film is driven by the impending wedding between Sophie and Sky, Donna's romantic entanglements soon usurp those of her daughter and it is ultimately her romantic union with Sam with which the film ends. Whilst *Mamma Mia!* is undoubtedly the most successful 'older bird' chick flick to date, and in many ways fits the template of this new cycle of film-making, I want to suggest that in some respects it is also atypical of this group of films, especially in the way that it deals with sexuality and the question of sexual awakening.

How old?! Female ageing and film

Imelda Whelehan notes that 'ageing is too often associated with diminishing of powers, or loss of maternal resources, friends and health' and that femininity is overwhelmingly defined in line with biological 'stages of menarche, pregnancy, motherhood and menopause' and socially constructed rituals such as marriage.[12] Given the emphasis on sexual attractiveness and fecundity as key markers of female identity and female value, ageing thus becomes specifically problematic for post-menopausal women. That is not to say ageing men do not also suffer from the waning of their virility and attractiveness, and while older men may be often depicted as wise they can also be feminised.[13] Ageing women and men inevitably stand in contrast to the ideals of their sex. That said, there is still not the same level of scorn reserved for older men as there is for older women, with no male equivalent for the notion of the 'hag' aimed at ageing women.

Although far from unproblematic in their representation of ageing, 'older bird' chick flicks have made some attempts to counteract the lack of roles for mature women by allowing them to take on more diverse and 'sexy' roles than they may have done previously, suggesting that women of a certain age no longer have to opt out of relationships. Also, the notion of the 'older' woman is becoming ever more fluid, as there are an increasing number of actresses in their 40s taking on the role of the 'single girl'. Films such as *Sex and the City: The Movie* (King, 2008), *The Proposal* (Fletcher, 2009) and *The Switch* (Gordon and Speck, 2010) have actresses in their 40s taking on romantic leads and embodying the ingénue identity usually associated with youth. Placing 'older' women in this role allows greater diversity in women's roles but also recalls Wearing's thesis about the 'girl-ing' of more mature women, wherein she argued that this process has the potential to subvert age, making the older female figure simultaneously more acceptable but also problematic. This paradox is evident, argues Wearing, in the film *Something's Gotta Give*, where Harry (Jack Nicholson) tells Erica (Diane Keaton) that she is 'the funniest girl [he] had ever had sex with'. Wearing suggests this dialogue, played for comedy, represents the anxieties about the girl-ing of older women and asks whether we are laughing at the incongruity of his description of Erica as a 'girl' or whether the scene is indicative of the growing preoccupation of post-feminist culture that only foregrounds the older woman as a desirable character if she invokes youth. Wearing raises important questions here about the subversive potential of girl-ing but she also notes that the girl-ing of the older woman can reinforce clearly defined demarcations of age. For example, when Carrie in *Sex and the City* finds herself getting married in her 40s it is celebrated by the film even as it is treated as near unique for a woman her age to be a first-time bride. In fact, when she is asked to appear in an issue of *Vogue* focusing on weddings for all ages of women, Carrie is the only example of a 40-year-old bride the editors can find; indeed, 40 is announced as the last appropriate age to get married, with the magazine feature ending on images of Carrie as the 'blushing bride', perhaps depicting her extended 'girlish-ness' into her 40s as a kind of spectacle.

Golden girls or dancing queens? *Mamma Mia!*'s older women

The representation of older women in *Mamma Mia!* is a complex one; whilst the film itself, and its commercial success, celebrates the middle-aged woman, there is, at times, a more ambiguous approach to age. Within the world of the film, ageing is referred to (Sophie's comments about her mother's youth being 'the olden days', slighting remarks about Tanya looking ancient), but actual age is almost never explicitly articulated. The exception is the age of Sophie, who, the film informs us, is 20 years old. The articulation of Sophie's age allows us to assume that Donna is aged somewhere between 40 and 45, a fact that is reinforced in Donna's recollections about her mother banishing her from the family home when she was pregnant with Sophie. But Donna's age is never specified, and when coupled with the fact that she is played by an actress around 15 years senior to Donna's presumed age, this creates further complications around the film's representation of the older woman.

Although age is not specifically articulated, it is conveyed in more general ways, such as costuming. Kathleen Woodward suggests that youthful dress can be a masquerade used to disguise the ageing body, through a denial of or an attempt to erase age.[14] But this potential masquerade is continually scrutinised and policed for 'age appropriateness', with a saying such as 'mutton dressed as lamb' functioning as a commonly recognised derogatory phrase used against older women who dress in clothes seen as more fitting for someone younger in an attempt to disguise the ageing process. In *Mamma Mia!*, Donna's costuming suggests a youthful masquerade of a different kind. In the first act of the film, Donna is clad in a white blouse worn underneath dungarees, with plimsolls on her feet, and her hair left to hang loose. Her body then is presented as youthful to such an extent that she is dressed like a child; her outfit infantilises her body and sanctions her girly behaviour.

Female childlike behaviour permeates the early part of the film, not least in the words and the performance of the 'Dancing Queen' musical sequence, where Donna's 'girlish-ness' is expressed most clearly with the help of her friendship with Rosie and Tanya. The musical number begins as Donna is curled in a foetal position hiding her face amongst the covers in a pose more reminiscent of an embarrassed or upset child. The lyrics encourage Donna to be childlike, to be young, and sweet and seventeen. That Tanya and Rosie 'dress up' in clothes taken from a large wooden chest in Donna's room reinforces the argument here about how the scene works in highlighting the youthfulness of its older female protagonists. Furthermore, the youthfulness of Streep's body and agility became a feature of interest for many who found it difficult to reconcile Streep's gymnastics on screen with her physical age. In an interview with Stuart Jeffries, Streep explains, 'I keep getting asked about the scene with the splits. They ask, was there a body double? ... Yeah, right! Or was it CGI? Of course! They grafted my face on to Olga Korbut's body.' Jeffries' response: 'She's joking ... Olga Korbut was an adorable, Olympic gold-winning Soviet gymnast of the early 1970s, who will always be remembered in her teenage state; Meryl Streep is an actor who turned 59 barely a week ago.'[15] In the same article, Jeffries also refers to Streep, Walters and Baranski as a 'kind of Golden Girl Trio',[16] referring to the popular 1985–95 American sitcom following the antics of four house-sharing retired women, and implicitly suggesting a reading of the women in Mamma Mia! as similarly elderly.

The 'Super Trouper' scene also sees Donna and the Dynamos return to their youthful glory. The women appear on stage in their seventies-inspired Lycra catsuits, worn in their youth when performing in their own band (of course, they also pay homage to ABBA). Similar costuming is used in the finale performances of 'Dancing Queen' and 'Waterloo' that close the film. Once again, the childish act of 'dressing up' is employed here, perhaps as a denial of age but more significantly as an evocation of youthful abandonment and endorsement of the sentiments of the 'Super Trouper' lyrics about 'smiling, having fun'. The catsuits, whilst figure hugging, display little in the way of female flesh, but despite their relative inoffensiveness, the Sunday Times journalist Cosmo Landesman still felt compelled to comment that 'the spectacle of these middle-aged women, in ABBA-esque costumes, giggling and indulging in girlie antics as they murder Dancing Queen, is grotesque'.[17] Landesman claims his comments are not ageist, yet he makes a clear suggestion that the (mis)representation of older women as 'girls' is as grotesque as their flouncy Lycra costumes. The older female body, even when barely on display, becomes a site for criticism, often tinged with barely concealed disgust. Acting inappropriately for one's age is also the focus of Chris Tookey's *Daily Mail* review of *Mamma Mia!*, which begins, 'The film is as naff as a Club 18–30 holiday, embarrassingly enacted by people 36–60.'[18] Here, 'ageing' is categorised as beginning as early as 36, more often designated as late youth or early middle age, suggesting something of the fluidity and unpredictability with which 'age' or 'being older' is demarcated.

Although Donna is initially coded as behaving in a childish manner, she does undergo a transformation through the course of the film. In fact, in the latter part of the film, where the narrative emphasis shifts towards her daughter's wedding, Donna is dressed in a mid-calf-length flowing dress and wears a red pashmina (the fashion remedy for older women to cover their wobbly arms), pointing towards her maturing femininity, soon to be sealed by her reacceptance of partnership with Sam. The film's costuming choices for Donna signify her journey from youthfulness to mature femininity, which is rewarded with her romantic reunion, but Donna is not the only model of ageing femininity in the film. Whilst not so feminine or girly in her clothing, Rosie's attire through the film echoes Donna's transformation from girlish to suitably mature. She initially wears a T-shirt featuring The Bangles, the iconic all-female pop group from the 1980s. That Rosie is still wearing this T-shirt codes her as a woman who refuses to move on from that period or, more precisely, as a woman who refuses to 'grow up'. However, by the close of the film, during the wedding sequence, she dons a pale trouser suit that would not be out of place in a grandmother's occasion-wear wardrobe. Tanya's clothing is less conservative than that of her fellow Dynamos. Nonetheless, she still shows relatively little flesh and remains covered up by a sarong when in swimwear. Although figure-hugging dresses point towards Tanya's more sexual demeanour, there is nothing vulgar about the way in which she dresses. That said, Tanya's body becomes the site for discourses of age avoidance to be explored, particularly in terms of her artificially rejuvenated body. Tanya's concern to look youthful, demonstrated by her reference to plastic surgery and use of expensive face creams, fits in with wider anxieties about the older female body highlighted earlier. Indeed, that Tanya's face cream might be, as Rosie jokily suggests, made from extract of donkey's testicle positions her as a figure for derision and disgust. Tanya's age, or denial of ageing, regularly becomes the object of ridicule by Donna and Rosie and is treated comedically by the film, from the character's first appearance accompanied by Rosie's announcement 'S'cuse me, I have a senior citizen coming through … my mother needs a perch.' Such ridicule within the film reinforces Jane Arthurs' argument that female transgression of appropriate bodily behaviour invokes either comedy or horror,[19] further cemented by Hugo Rifkind's review labelling Tanya's performance of 'Does Your Mother Know' as 'gruesome'.[20]

Much too old for sex: revising 'older bird' chick flicks

Margaret Tally's discussion of the 'older bird' chick flick notes that this cycle of films explores the mother's sexual reawakening, a subject matter neglected in customary narratives of older women, which usually contain them within a family framework. In *Something's Gotta Give*, a near obsession with age and age differences provides the thematic core of the film which uses pairings of old and young suitors. Through the initial coupling of Harry, a 63-year-old man who only dates women under the age of 30, and Marin (Amanda Peet), the 20-something daughter of Erica, the film draws attention to the 'trend' of older men dating younger women. The burgeoning relationship between Erica and the much younger doctor, Julian (Keanu Reeves), serves as a counterpoint to Marin and Harry's relationship. By employing two cross-generational relationships as its central focus the film raises issues about age and sexuality and codes the ageing female protagonist as sexually attractive and sexually active. This is repeated in a later film by the same writer-director, Nancy Meyers, *It's Complicated* (2009). Jake (Alec Baldwin) and Jane (Meryl Streep) are a divorced couple in their late middle age. Jake is remarried to a much younger woman, but, after attending their son's graduation, Jane and Jake rekindle their relationship. Meyers continues to subvert expectations about relationships between older men and younger women by reversing the stereotype of the infertile older woman during a wonderfully poignant moment in a fertility clinic waiting room where the camera pans across the faces of numerous couples, all made up of middle-aged men accompanying their youthful and fecund wives. Despite their flirtation with a more challenging tone about age-appropriate romance, these two 'older bird' chick flicks eventually re-situate the older woman in a more traditional role by reuniting her with a former lover or spouse who is of similar age.

Both *It's Complicated* and *Something's Gotta Give* foreground the successful, independent, divorced older woman as their central protagonist but also suggest that these characters are frustrated and in need of the intervention of a romantic heterosexual relationship to provide fulfilment. *Mamma Mia!* fits into the generic parameters of the 'older bird' chick flick in this sense by promising the single, work-focused woman metamorphosis through romance and/or sex. In many ways, it follows a similar narrative pattern to *Something's Gotta Give* and *It's Complicated* (and shares a star with the latter): Donna is an older woman, a mother and an independent businesswoman who rekindles her past relationship with Sam, her first 'true' love. But whereas films about older women's relationships are often about their sexual awakening or reawakening, *Mamma Mia!* partially subverts or sidesteps the idea of sex as being of central importance. Tanya mocks and rejects the possibility of a relationship with a much younger man in 'Does Your Mother Know', the film codes the burgeoning relationship between Rosie and Bill as both comedic and slightly pitiful during 'Take a Chance on Me', and Donna's colourful sexual life is all safely located in the past. Sam raises the issue of sex when he sings the lyrics about being 'not too old for sex' during 'When All Is Said and Done' after the wedding ceremony, a move that neatly reinforces the idea of sex within the confines of marriage. *Mamma Mia!* does make it clear that Donna has had a sexual past, but for the most part, the film's references to sexual desire remain within the realms of comedy or fantasy. In fact, the presentation of Donna and Sam's reunion is a chaste one, and in marrying her first and only true love, the romantic resolution for Donna is an idealised one, with marriage rapidly proceeding after little more than a quick kiss between the couple. The first real moment of overt sexual expression between the two of them occurs when Donna rips Sam's shirt off during the eruption of Aphrodite's spring, which is also located post-wedding, and therefore within conjugal boundaries.

Interestingly, *Mamma Mia!* shares its narrative traits and ideological schema with single-parent romantic comedies such as *Sleepless in Seattle* (Ephron, 1993) or *One Fine Day* (Hoffman, 1996), where the relationship is never coded as sexual but rather works to provide a sense of security by reinforcing traditional family values through the recuperation of the single parent back into a nuclear family. Likewise, *Mamma Mia!* sees Donna's romantic relationship positively linked to her daughter's coming of age and the recuperation of the family. The strong link between the mother's romantic life and the daughter's life choices evident in *Mamma Mia!* is echoed in other 'older bird' chick flicks, like *Something's Gotta Give*, where the mother's sexual reawakening is intrinsically linked to the daughter's improved prospects for personal fulfilment or romance. As such, the conclusion of *Mamma Mia!* is in keeping with the restorative conventions of single-parent romantic comedies.

That said, the romantic reawakening of a middle-aged female lead in *Mamma Mia!* clearly suggests parallels with the 'older bird' chick flick. Akin to this cycle of films, *Mamma Mia!* also offers something different from the romcom mainstream in terms of its approach to the older woman. Furthermore, its generic status as a musical provides another dimension. The alleged weariness of 'middle age' can be cast off by the upbeat and energetic numbers, and, for the duration of the film, audiences can vicariously participate in this ageless Utopia that throws off conventions and expectations of age. Thus *Mamma Mia!* encourages its audience to regress (to 'grow down a little', as Tanya instructs Donna) and embrace a carefree youthfulness, even if only fleetingly.

Notes

1. Khan, Urmee, 'BBC promises more older women on television', *Telegraph*, 19 September 2009. http://www.telegraph.co.uk/finance/newsbysector/mediatechnologyandtelecoms/media/6206321/BBC-promises-ore-older-women-on-television.html (accessed 20 March 2011).
2. See Singh, Anita, 'Older women axed from *Countryfile* in new BBC ageism row', *Telegraph*, 9 December 2008. http://www.telegraph.co.uk/news/celebritynews/3690708/Older-women-axed-from-countryfile-in-new-BBC-ageism-row.html. See also Plunkett, John, '*Countryfile*'s Miriam O'Reilly wins BBC ageism claim', *Guardian*, 1 January 2011. http://www.guardian.co.uk/media/2011/jan/11/country-file-miriam-oreilly-tribunal.html (both accessed 20 March 2011).
3. Minaya, Marcell, 'Actresses fight against ageism in entertainment industry', *Digital Spy*, 30 May 2010. http://www.digitalspy.co.uk/movies/news/a222599/actresses-fight-ageism-in-entertainment.html; Singh, Anita, 'Scarlett Johansson: "Women actresses are victims of Hollywood ageism"', *The Telegraph*, 12 August 2010. http://www.telegraph.co.uk/news/celebritynews/2547469/Scarlett-Johansson-Women-actresses-are-victims-of-Hollywood-ageism.html (both accessed 20 January 2011).
4. Nikkah, Roya, 'Leading actresses hit out at discrimination in entertainment industry', *Telegraph*, 3 May 2010. http://www.

telegraph.co.uk/culture/culturenews/7782247/Leading-actresses-hit-out-at-discrimination-in-entertainment-industry.html (accessed 9 April 2011).
5. Littlejohn, Georgina, 'Car crash Katie Waissel in shock after discovering her favourite grandmother is £250-an-hour prostitute', *Mail Online*, 22 November 2010. http://www.dailymail.co.uk/tvshowbiz/article-1331750/Katie-Waisells-grandmother-Shelia-Vogel-prostitute-X-Factor-stars-shock.html (accessed 20 January 2011).
6. Wearing, Sadie, 'Subjects of rejuvenation: ageing in a postfeminist culture', in Diane Negra and Yvonne Tasker (Eds), *Interrogating Postfeminism: Gender and the Politics of Popular Culture*, Durham, NC: Duke University Press, 2007, p. 277.
7. Whelehan, Imelda, 'Not to be looked at: older women in recent British cinema', in Melanie Bell and Melanie Williams (Eds), *British Women's Cinema*, London: Routledge, 2010, p. 172.
8. Ibid, p. 180.
9. Potter, Cherry, 'Sex and the older woman', *Guardian*, 23 February 2004. http://www.guardian.co.uk/world/2004/feb/23/gender.film.html (accessed 20 March 2011).
10. Tally, Margaret, 'Something's gotta give: Hollywood, female sexuality and the "older bird" chick flick', in Susan Ferris and Mallory Young (Eds), *Chick Flicks: Contemporary Women at the Movies*, London: Routledge, 2008.
11. Whelehan, 'Not to be looked at', p. 170.
12. Ibid.
13. See Peter Lehman on the example of Stumpy in Howard Hawks' *Rio Bravo* (1959), whose 'age has eroded his masculinity. In many ways, he fulfils the traditionally feminine function within the group; he cleans, cooks and keeps house.' Lehman, *Running Scared: Masculinity and the Representation of the Male Body*, Philadelphia, PA: Temple University Press, 1993, p.63.
14. Woodward, Kathleen, *Aging and Its Discontents: Freud and Other Fictions*, Bloomington: Indiana University Press, 1991, p .148.
15 Jeffries, Stuart, 'A legend lightens up', *Guardian* (G2), 2 July 2008, p. 10.
16. Ibid.
17. Landesman, Cosmo, '*Mamma Mia!* – The Sunday Times review', *Sunday Times*, 13 July 2008. http://entertainment.timesonline.co.uk/tol/arts_and_entertainment/film/film_reviews/article4304527.ece (accessed 18 March 2011).
18. Tookey, Chris, 'Mamma Mia: thank you for the musical! Now for the Money! Money! Money!', *Mail Online*, 10 July 2008. http://www.

dailymail.co.uk/tvshowbiz/reviews/article-1034188/Mamma-Mia-Thank-musical-Now-Money-Money.html (accessed 13 March 2011).
19. Arthurs, Jane, 'Revolting women: the body in comic performance', in Jane Arthurs and Jean Grimshaw (Eds), *Women's Bodies: Discipline and Transgression*, London: Cassell, 1999.
20. Rifkind, Hugo, '*Mamma Mia! The Musical*: first review', *The Times*, 1 July 2008. http://www.timesonline.co.uk/tol/arts_and_entertainment/film/article4245117.ece (accessed 30 April 2011).

11

Dancing queens indeed: when gay subtext is gayer than gay text

Georges-Claude Guilbert

Autobiographical snippets count among the regular features of cultural studies/gender studies books and articles; this is to be expected, for in such disciplines one always acknowledges that one is speaking from somewhere. In December 1976, I was a 17-year-old illegal immigrant in London. Those were the heroic pre-EU days, when custom officials would search me the minute I tried to cross a border. Officially I could not even enter discotheques at my young age, but I actually worked at a straight Kensington nightclub from Tuesday to Sunday, without the least semblance of a legal existence, let alone a work permit. On Mondays I was off, and what did I do but go clubbing, of course – a busman's holiday if ever there was one. My Monday haunt was BANG, a weekly gay nightclub at the London Astoria, 157 Charing Cross Road. That venue opened as a cinema in 1927 and hesitated in the 1970s as to its status (theatre? cinema? discotheque?).

A small gang of us always dressed up for the occasion: pink work overalls complete with plastic hammers and screwdrivers in the workman's pockets, numerous earrings and sequined jelly shoes. The night was wild and we indulged in all sorts of excesses. Our favourite moment was when they played a 'video' of ABBA's 'Dancing Queen' on a huge screen above the dance floor (a technological feat in those pre-MTV days). 'Dancing Queen' had been released in Sweden and the UK in August 1976, and in the US in November 1976. Hysterically joyful, we yelled with Agnetha and Frida, camping around for every penny's worth, thoroughly identifying with the heroine of the song, getting in the swing. The only adjustment we had to operate was to replace 'Friday' with 'Monday'.

I was indeed a queen looking for a king. That song could function for heterosexuals, but on Mondays that was not the point: what else could it depict but a promiscuous gay young man ('queen') out in search for anonymous sex ('anybody') with a hunk ('king') and a great time on the dance floor. I was also a drug user, like everybody else, and when ABBA sang 'the music's high', I thought of another kind of high, just like the Christine Baranski character, Tanya, in *Mamma Mia!*, who mimes joint-smoking (with a tampon) as she sings that line. And, as it happens, when I did 'get the chance', I *was* 'the dancing queen' (of BANG), I was 'young and sweet, only seventeen', and I was 'having the time of [my] life', totally in sync with the song's lyrics about teasing and then leaving men burning.

The words 'you can jive', beyond the obvious historical references to specific dances, could also refer for anyone versed in slang to the way young things like myself could talk nonsense, chat away or kid around without worrying about consequences, or indeed could cajole older patrons of the venue and mislead gentlemen into agreeing to various arrangements – in other words, find jive sugar daddies, 'Diggin' the dancing queen' being the relevant pun, though as far as most of them were concerned, you 'leave 'em burning and then you're gone'. Some people I knew, with a taste for S&M games, could take the line 'Getting in the swing' more seriously than others, of course, but they did not frequent the same venues: theirs were smellier and darker. As for 'watch[ing] that scene', this is precisely what we were doing, taking 'scene' in the sense of gay scene as well as fancying ourselves on a stage playing scenes, theatrical little things that we were.[1]

The year 1976 was also when I discovered feminism, mixing with Roman girls who had got into so much trouble with the Italian police that they had been compelled to flee to London. That song could obviously, and can to this day, be interpreted in a feminist way: a sort of proto-'Girls Just Wanna Have Fun'. The personal is political. Here's a 17-year-old girl who wants to be in control of her own private life. No one has the right to legislate upon her body, she can have fun dancing to her heart's content, and she can have sex with any boy she wants – a new one every night, no strings attached. She can even be a mere cocktease (excuse my Swedish) if it strikes her fancy. She's in charge. This is admirably illustrated by the comic feminist *mise-en-scène* of the song in the movie *Mamma Mia!* Was there ever a more empowering song? All the women who follow Donna down to the little Greek port, kicking away the symbols of their work (ironing board, vacuum cleaner, plates of food, ladders, aprons, wooden spoons, laundry, bundles of firewood) communicate an extraordinary sense of joy to the viewers, and even though you cannot help supposing that they will go back to their usual condition once the number is over, it works admirably. Donna (Meryl Streep), Rosie (Julie Walters) and Tanya (Christine Baranski), AKA Donna and the Dynamos, are feminist role models; they are, in their own words, 'the world's first girl power band', as if they had somehow anticipated the likes of Madonna and Lady Gaga, back in the 1970s.

It is all the more efficient as it follows an amusing dialogue between the three girlfriends about Donna's unease at the ambiguous male parentage of her daughter:

> Donna: And I have brought this all on myself because I was a stupid, reckless little slut!

> Tanya: Whoa! Don't you sound like your mother?
> Donna: I do not!
> Tanya and Rosie: Yes, you so do!
> Donna: Oh, my God, I do not.
> Rosie: Yes you do, it's Catholic guilt. You've been living like a nun.
> Tanya: Yeah, whatever happened to our Donna? Life and soul of the party, el rock chick supremo?
> Rosie: Yeah, come on.
> Donna: *I* grew up.
> Tanya: Well, then, grow back down again.
> Tanya and Rosie: Screw them if they can't take a joke.

Like Madonna's in the 1980s and 1990s, the girls' pop here is enrolled in the service of women's liberation, as opposed to Catholic oppression and repression. Gays also know a thing or two about that. Donna supposes that her daughter is a little more given to old-fashioned morals than she is, which is true to a certain extent, but Sophie will later say, 'I don't care if you slept with hundreds of men, you're my mom and I love you.' Donna specifies (mostly for the priest's benefit) that she didn't sleep with *hundreds* of men, but she does grab her crotch when she sings 'there's a fire within my soul'.

In December 2001 Londoner friends of mine took me out dancing. The place was called G-A-Y, one night a week. For some unfathomable reason I did not recognise the venue until actually inside, when (and I swear this is true) I heard the first notes of 'Dancing Queen' and suddenly found myself on the dance floor, under a video screen showing ABBA. Finally I understood perfectly what every sci-fi time traveller feels (and I have read all their adventures), as I was transported in a nanosecond to a whole quarter of a century before. What was happening? Was the entrance to the club a gateway back to the past? Was I experiencing an extraordinarily delayed acid kickback? The effect – one of the eeriest in my existence – lasted but a minute. I hugged myself. I was inside the London Astoria. The night was not called BANG; it was called G-A-Y, but it was *exactly* the same. Twenty-five years and 25 kilograms later I was dancing to the same video on the same dance floor, except this time I was sober – and if I hadn't been, I would have rapidly sobered up at the sight of half a dozen very decorative 17-year-old dancing queens who made me feel irrevocably bloated and decrepit. I rejoiced immensely, however, as I perceived their own joy: they loved the song (as) much as I had in 1976, with perhaps the added fun of temporally and aesthetically distanced PoMo appreciation. Kitsch ruled, and ABBA could be proud; their song defied time.

I hear the London Astoria was demolished in 2009 and it saddens me a great deal. I won't be rolling my wheelchair to 'Dancing Queen' there in 2026. But the song lives on. One of the reasons for this longevity has to do with the craftsmanship of the inspired authors of 'Dancing Queen', obviously. Much in the way of the Beatles before them or Michael Jackson after them, Benny and Björn had an admirable flair for pop, but I believe another reason is those lyrics and what I am tempted to see as their intrinsic gayness. This, thankfully, has crossed over into *Mamma Mia!* the stage musical, which premiered at the Prince Edward Theatre on Old Compton Street (hailed by production designer Mark Thompson as 'great. ... It's in the heart of Gayworld'[2]), and now into the movie. The two Australian movies *Muriel's Wedding* (Hogan, 1994) and *The Adventures of Priscilla, Queen of the Desert* (Elliott, 1994) had paved the way. Steeped in ABBA's music, those movies redefined 'feelgood', and the latter redefined camp in a quintessentially Australian way. It is absolutely no coincidence that ABBA remain so huge in Oz.

Camp is the key word to describe *Mamma Mia!*, but not in the debased sense it has unfortunately acquired in the US in recent decades – not in the reductive sense of so-bad-it's-good, strictly associated to kitsch. It is camp rather in the sense that queens and drag queens are camp, incorporating associations to kitsch and queer. Much has been made of *Mamma Mia!*'s gay appeal, but I contend that its overt gay content, an uninspired and uninspiring subplot, provides little more than poorly (en)acted clichés and non-empowering antics. Yet the entire movie can be read as extremely gay, if not queer. The writer who reviewed it for *The Times* felt compelled to joke: 'They'll probably revoke my membership of the Straight Men's Sneering Association for this, but Mamma Mia! is actually rather wonderful.'[3]

Surprisingly, Colin Firth is undistinguished as a gay man in *Mamma Mia!*, and that is very regrettable, whereas he is stunningly good as a gay man in *A Single Man* (Ford, 2009). This may have everything to do with direction, of course. Firth is a good actor – that much was established long ago – but even good actors sometimes find it hard to play gay (whatever their own sexual orientation might be). In *Mamma Mia!* he is awkward, clumsy and occasionally queeny in an irredeemably unwelcome way. I suppose the idea might have been to show the character gradually coming to terms with his sexual orientation (and there is nothing intrinsically wrong with that), but if so, having him prance around at the very end, in the titles sequence, like a pre-Stonewall queen was an extremely bad idea. The other men are dressed in an equally camp way, their costumes no less flamboyant, but their dance moves are ordinarily 'manly', as opposed to Harry's. Is this supposed to mean that a gay man the minute he is reconciled with his homosexuality turns into a raving queen, mincing about with his bottom sticking out? Admittedly, the misunderstanding aboard the boat is amusing, when Harry's words on paternity are misinterpreted by Bill as a proclamation of gay pride, as it indicates that people around Harry are more aware of his sexual orientation than he is, but surely there was another way to suggest his more or less slow realisation. Don't they see how politically and epistemologically dubious the whole thing is? Indeed, how are we to understand this? Is he a repressed homosexual? Or a closeted one? Or both? Did he always refrain from mincing about, and now finally lets himself go? In which case are we supposed to assume that queeniness is innate – and if so, how monstrously essentialist and politically incorrect is that? Doesn't it tell us that all homosexuals are systematically 'effeminate', taking us back to nineteenth-century antiquated notions of 'inversion'? We didn't fight the Stonewall and Judith Butler wars for this.

One may also take exception to the way Harry deals with the securing-a-boyfriend situation – the engine of romcom. He is lucky enough to meet Petros, a local of course – you know those Greeks (actually played by Argentine Juan Pablo di Pace). Whereas Rosie actively pursues Bill, and clearly gets him in the end – for keeps (she sings 'Take a Chance on Me', she falls off a roof, and he catches her, knight-like, singing 'Take a Chance on Me' in his turn), whereas Donna not only gets Sam but actually gets married, gay Harry, having frolicked on the island with his dark handsome stranger, says to Donna inside the church during the wedding scene:

> I just wanted to say it's great to have even a third of Sophie. I never thought I'd get even that much of a child. Donna, you were the first girl I ever loved. Well, actually, you were the last girl I ever loved [*Harry looks at Petros, an old man makes the sign of the cross as he understands*]. Now, this gives me an excuse to come here much more often.

One wonders why he needs the excuse of one-third fatherhood to come to Greece and have sex with Petros. Hypothetically, Harry could take Petros to England or move to the island and set up house with him. But the film refuses this possibility, implying that 'gays don't do that', differentiating gay coupledom from straight by emphasising sexual desire over romantic commitment.

Obviously this harks back to the old debate about gays being less tempted by the comfort of a stable couple than straights, and whether this differentiation is a positive or negative thing. Should they ape straights, or on the contrary express their total liberation from the dictates of a heteronormative society and enjoy unrestrained sex? This debate was modified by the AIDS crisis but is still very relevant. There are assimilationist gays and revolutionary queers; there are even American Log Cabin Republicans who want to be conservative in every possible way, except that the person they wish to marry and with whom they want to raise right-wing children in a comfortable Christian suburb belongs to their own gender.

In that respect, Tanya can be read as a gay man (possibly a drag queen or even a transsexual): pre-diegetically she was a serial wife, which can stand not only for promiscuity but also for sugar daddying. Now she is a sort of cougar, and she disports herself with Pepper (who could be her grandson, if we are to believe Rosie), in an utterly liberated, carefree fashion. This young man won't be her last, and there are no wedding bells in the air this time, not for her. No one is taken in by her apparent rejection of Pepper, and when she ties a diaper-like towel around his loins to signify his extreme youth, it can evoke kinky games as much as anything else. Indeed that beach scene, 'Does Your Mother Know', is extremely camp and would not be disowned by any self-respecting drag queen. 'Yo, girls, we done good,' as Tanya says. Amusingly, reviewers did not see eye to eye on this. The *Times* reviewer, who must have slept through more than half the movie wrote: 'With the exception of Baranski's rather gruesome duet with a young barman on "Does Your Mother Know", the film is almost completely without campery. For a musical full of Abba songs, that is truly remarkable.'[4] Then he made his case worse, declaring:

> If you can resist a smile as 30 muscular chaps in tiny Speedos and huge Technicolor flippers bop away to

> 'Dancing Queen' [*sic* – it is actually 'Lay All Your Love on Me'] on a rickety Greek pier, then you are a straighter, even more sneering man than I ever was.[5]

Does he mean that it is gay but not camp? In contrast, the *New York Times* reviewer wrote: '[Ms. Baranski's] cougar-on-the-prowl rendition of "Does Your Mother Know" is the one genuinely, show-stoppingly sexy sequence in [the] film.'[6] In case the viewers failed to see that queer aspect in Tanya, she helps them with the phallic dry flower she uses as a penis sprouting from under her dress as she sings 'anybody can be that guy' in the 'Dancing Queen' number (reinforced by a butch back-to-front baseball cap and the aforementioned tampon).

But aren't the three girls basically raving drag queens? In the 'Super Trouper' number what's to differentiate them from cabaret queens in 1970s disco drag (observe the make-up and fake eyelashes)? Or in the even camper 'Dancing Queen' reprise and 'Waterloo' during the closing titles sequence? For a queer third-wave feminist and utter constructionist such as myself, most women are in female drag every day of their life – and of course even more so when they are *consciously* performing (a specific form or degree of) femininity. I never tire of quoting RuPaul's aphorism: 'We are born naked, everything else is drag.'

In 'Dancing Queen', Julie Walters/Rosie even turns drag king for a few seconds – better yet, she is abruptly in Elvis drag. Elvis drag is so recognisable that it notoriously transcends barriers of gender and race; there are infamous Japanese female Elvises, for example. It does not take her much more than a pair of glasses, a lowering of her voice and the couple of poses she strikes when she sings 'you come to look for a king', all of a sudden embodying the King of Rock with reasonable success.

So gay viewers might remain unconvinced by the gay Harry motif, but surely many of them rejoice at *Mamma Mia!*'s rewrite of the 1970s disco scene. The platform boots are particularly effective, it must be said. Platform shoes have carried many interesting connotations throughout the past seven or eight decades (olá Carmen Miranda), their wearers being often given to tongue-in-cheek statements. Any older gay man given to nostalgia will be transported, shivering, by some of the costumes. I say 'some', because the ludicrous anachronistic get-ups of the three men in the flashbacks are merely annoying. But the tremendous disco outfits hark back to an insouciant pre-AIDS age when you could sleep around without risking your life – the days of 'Dancing Queen', the days when you could go clubbing every night and unashamedly scream 'Gimme! Gimme! Gimme! A man after midnight'. Then you got one, and did it all over again the next day. On occasions you could even get two, or three, as Rosie and Tanya remind us: 'Rosie: What do you suggest we do with three men? Tanya: Now that takes me back.'

Another gay delight completes this treat: Dominic Cooper/Sky as 'eye candy', his male flesh displayed as sexual spectacle for the male gaze as well as for the female gaze. As one of the DVD bonus features indicates, one bed scene was making so much of that, half of Cooper's buttocks showing, that it was deleted. In the Making-of documentary on the DVD, Stellan Skarsgård reminds us of the fact that *Mamma Mia!* is very much a women's product – the men 'are the bimbos'. In the 'Lay All Your Love on Me' number Sky is made to show off his tanned fit body to maximum advantage, complete with seawater drops rippling down his abs. As if this were not homoerotic enough, his buddies the stags (preparing for his stag night) rise as one from the sea, emerging like Poseidon and an army of half-naked mermen, and they march on Sky in order to deprive him of female company – namely his fiancée's. As he is reclining over Sophie in his bathing trunks, every muscle in his body tensed, they lift him and tear him away from his heterosexual embrace. In a deleted scene included on the DVD Sky says to the boys: 'Why don't we just get drunk and drop our trousers?' No wonder this was dispensed with; perhaps it was deemed just a little too gay. Although most of the creative team of the movie seem to have been gay-friendly women, gay women (including director Phyllida Lloyd) and gay men, there might have been a co-producer or two who thought it excessive for a mainstream market. Drop their trousers indeed? To do what, one wonders.

Gays are famously fond of musicals (or so the cliché goes), ideally on the Broadway stage, otherwise adapted in Hollywood, or sometimes Hollywood originals, notably golden age musicals such as Gene Kelly vehicles *On the Town* (Donen and Kelly, 1949) or *Anchors Aweigh* (Sidney, 1945). These and other camp sailor musicals are amusingly referenced in the 'Money, Money, Money' number onboard a yacht. Sailors have always been a staple of erotic (gay) imagery, and Donna is certainly aware of the erotic potential of sailors, as she indicates by groaning whilst one massages her on deck. In many ways, *Mamma Mia!* rejects traditional heteronormative narratives. Young Sophie (Amanda Seyfried) does not get married to young Sky. Donna gets married to a divorced man two decades after they had a child (or not). She has never let a man dictate her conduct, and will never let a man come between her and her daughter. As she says, clearly a feminist: 'I won't be muscled out by an ejaculation.'

Meryl Streep is a gay icon. She might not be a 'traditional' gay icon, of the Cher variety, but a great many elements definitely qualify her, such as her camp performance in *Death Becomes Her* (Zemeckis, 1992). When she belts out 'The Winner Takes It All' she turns into a regular torch-singing diva. In 2009 showman Roy Cruz put on an all-male show in the US entitled *Streep Tease* that consisted exclusively of monologues from Meryl Streep vehicles. That says it all. In the ABC television series *Modern Family* (2009) the heterosexual mom does not like Meryl Streep in *Mamma Mia!*, whereas the gay dad does, pointedly. Meryl Streep and her fellow *Mamma Mia!* actresses can do camp. I disagree with the *New York Times* reviewer who wrote: 'It is safe to say that Ms. Streep gives the worst performance of her career – safe to say because it is clearly what she intends, and she is not an actress capable of failure.'[7] Precisely: one should not mistake tongue-in-cheek distance and camp for 'badness'. The movie offers a great many camp jokes, notably those jokes that revolve around the number of husbands Tanya has had and the amount of money she spends on cosmetics and plastic surgery – the best one, surely, being the lines 'We're the same age./Yeah, well, parts of us are.' If one is to believe Internet forums and blogs, hundreds of thousands of gays around the world share the *Modern Family* gay dad's affection for the movie – not thanks to the lacklustre overt gay subplot, but rather thanks to every other gay feature, including the numerous touches of camp humour. All this in no way means that *Mamma Mia!* cannot delight a mainstream cinema audience, evidently. La question, c'est 'Voulez-vous?'

Notes

1. 'The scene' also features in ABBA's disco hit and paean to no-strings sex 'Voulez-Vous'.
2. Andersson, Benny, Ulvaeus, Björn and Craymer, Judy, *Mamma Mia! How Can I Resist You? The Inside Story of Mamma Mia and the Songs of Abba*, London: Phoenix, 2008, p. 165.
3. Rifkind, Hugo, '*Mamma Mia! The Musical*: first review', *The Times*, 1 July 2008. http://www.timesonline.co.uk/tol/arts_and_entertainment/film/article4245117.ece (accessed 11 April 2011).
4. Ibid.
5. Ibid.
6. Scott, A. O., 'Does your mother know you sing ABBA tunes?', *New York Times*, 18 July 2008. http://movies.nytimes.com/2008/07/18/movies/18mamm.html (accessed 11 April 2011).
7. Ibid.

12

The hero of my dreams: framing fatherhood in *Mamma Mia!*

Sarah Godfrey

All three of *Mamma Mia!*'s major male stars were more than happy to acknowledge their peripheral status within its diegesis. Stellan Skarsgård suggested that, in a reversal of the customary sexual politics of contemporary cinema, he and his male peers were little more than 'the bimbos', with the women taking centre stage instead.[1] Pierce Brosnan was overheard murmuring, 'This is no place for a middle-aged man,'[2] during the shooting of the hen party scene, while Colin Firth drew on his previous experience as male eye candy in the BBC's celebrated serialisation *Pride and Prejudice* (Langton, 1995) and *Bridget Jones's Diary* (Maguire, 2001) in describing his place in this film: 'This is not unfamiliar to me ... they tend to wheel me in whenever they need someone to be the side salad.'[3] Certainly, in the characterisation of *Mamma Mia!* as a 'fun, cheesy, hugely tongue-in-cheek women's film', there has been far less attention paid to the role of men in the film, aside from recurring comments on their limited singing and dancing abilities.[4] However, it should be remembered that a search for an absent father propels the narrative: indeed, critic Dave Calhoun even suggested that the film could renamed *Paternity: The Musical*.[5] With that in mind, this chapter seeks to question the assumption that the male characters of the film are necessarily of lesser significance than the female characters, through detailed analysis of the film's presentation of its three potential fathers and the ways in which the very different star images of the three actors playing them relate to the representation of middle-aged masculinity and the narrative engagement with fatherhood that we see in *Mamma Mia!*

Ruminating on the resurgent cultural interest in fatherhood in the 1980s and 1990s, Tania Modleski was one of the first feminist critics who interrogated its celebratory tone. For whilst the new emphasis on active fatherhood offered an alternative to 'harsh notions of phallic paternity,'[6] Modleski suggested that it could equally be seen as a 'widening of the patriarchal sphere' that forcefully emphasised the importance of men as 'real fathers, "imaginary" fathers, godfathers, and, in the older sense of the term, surrogate mothers' at the expense of mothering carried out by women that was either marginalised, vilified or taken for granted.[7] One of the cultural texts Modleski had in mind was *Three Men and a Baby* (Nimoy, 1988), which interestingly bears a number of similarities to *Mamma Mia!* in its focus on a trio of joint fathers to a female child who are initially startled by having to assume the mantle of fatherhood but grow to love it. For Elizabeth Traube, *Three Men and a Baby* was 'the movie that showed us what fun mothering can be when it's done by the right men',[8] echoing Modleski's remarks about the film being an eloquent statement of 'men's desire to usurp women's procreative function'.[9] This chapter will examine whether these comments on an earlier film of tripartite fatherhood also ring true of this more recent film centred on a paternal trinity and whether, in spite of its maternally inclined title, *Mamma Mia!* really is *Paternity: The Musical*.[10]

A dream of fatherhood

While *Mamma Mia!* is, rightly, understood as offering an unusually positive rendering of the single-mother/daughter relationship (as Louise FitzGerald's chapter in this collection demonstrates), in its initial scenes the film certainly places much significance on fatherhood at both a literal and a symbolic level, seeming to coalesce with discourses within post-feminist culture that typically centre 'a male subject within emotional, familial narratives', as Yvonne Tasker suggests,[11] and/or revolve around a protagonist's 'father hunger'.[12] Sophie's desire to find her father in order that he perform the traditional patriarchal role of giving her away at her wedding is, after all, the dramatic premise upon which the whole film rests. Moreover, for Sophie it seems that finding her father means finding her true identity. The symbolic significance of the longed-for absent father is confirmed by the opening sequence of the film. The very first image we see is of an inky black nocturnal seascape, and the camera pans up to reveal Sophie in silhouette as she carries out her secret mission to send wedding invitations to her potential fathers, Bill (Skarsgård), Harry (Firth) and Sam (Brosnan), soundtracked by 'I Have a Dream'. Against the predominantly midnight blue *mise-en-scène*, the yellow letter box into which she posts her invitations appears hyperreal, like an illustration from a children's story. The romantic connotations of the imagery and music instantly imbue Sophie's search for her father with a starry-eyed idealism ('the wonder of a fairytale', to quote the accompanying song), which that will be sustained in each of the songs she sings with/about her fathers. Sophie's idealistic vision of paternity is further confirmed by her confident assertion to her friends that she will 'know' her father upon seeing him. In a perfect statement of 'father hunger' she says, 'I feel like there's a part of me missing and that when I meet my dad everything will fall into place,' as the camera moves in closer to her excited face. In a similar fashion, the first full musical number in the film, 'Honey Honey', closes with Sophie separated from her (slightly doubtful) friends, framed alone on a balcony like the iconic romantic heroine Juliet, an image of romantic expectancy as she sings, 'Now I'm about to see what you mean to me' to her imagined father.

However, the presentation of the three potential fathers in this opening part of the film both plays with and slightly denies the dimension of Freudian family romance suggested by Sophie's quest for her 'true identity' via confirmation of her paternal lineage. Each of the three men is an ideal father: handsome, apparently wealthy and accomplished in some sphere of expertise. They are also all carefully differentiated from each other – the 'lone wolf' biker guy in Marrakesh, the archetypal English gentleman, the distinguished-looking New York architect – and yet equalised by their passport pictures rolling up onto the screen like the result of a gamble on a fruit machine, a significantly less romantic image of potential fatherhood than that expressed by Sophie's wistful longing. Similarly, when the three men arrive on the island and meet Sophie for the first time, her expectations of instant recognition are confounded. Instead, the camera swish pans between them, each man made to look all the more inscrutable by the wearing of dark sunglasses. The soundtrack is momentarily muted as we adopt Sophie's point-of-view as she tries to work out which one of these strangers might be her father, not enjoying the revelatory moment she had hoped for.

Throughout the film, ABBA's songs of heterosexual love and desire are retooled as songs about the father/daughter relationship. So in the context of the film, 'Gimme, Gimme, Gimme (a Man after Midnight)' isn't a plea for sexual satisfaction but is used to accompany Sophie's summoning of her fathers, while the evocation of dizzying romantic enthralment in 'Honey Honey' is not sung in the first person but instead ventriloquised by a daughter pondering her origins via her mother's diary, anticipating a father who might 'look like a movie star' (and perhaps showing an undue fascination with her mother's sex life).[13] This tendency continues with the 'Our Last Summer' number, in which a love song is reworked for a sequence where Sophie gets to know each of her three dads better, and vice versa.

The song's narrative of Parisian romance is begun by Harry but becomes shared out by all three men, reminiscing about their youth ('the age of no regret') and their respective relationships with Sophie's mother. Paternity is still left tantalisingly uncertain as Sophie is shown to have qualities in common with all three men: she shares an artistic streak with Sam, she plays guitar with Harry and she steers the yacht with Bill. Although the tone is avowedly innocent, with the four of them sharing hearty platonic activities like campfire cooking and jumping into the sea, it still remains a sequence foregrounding the interaction between a nubile swimsuit-clad girl and three men who at this stage have no idea she may be their daughter, although they have already noted her resemblance to their former lover ('You are a little minx, just like your mother,' says Sam). This song ends on a by-now-familiar note of romantic expectation on Sophie's part as she silently asks Harry, 'Are you the hero of my dreams?' Sophie will eventually overcome her rather hyperbolic expectation of her father, but in order to understand fully the different forms of paternal heroism suggested by the film it is necessary to spend some time looking in more detail at the different modes of masculinity represented by the three potential fathers, inevitably informed by the star personae of the actors playing the roles.

From 007 to 'SOS'

Despite his illustrious and diverse film career, Pierce Brosnan's star persona is overwhelmingly dominated by his 1995–2002 tenure as James Bond. Indeed, the incongruity between his image as super suave secret agent and his unexpected new incarnation as croaky musical star was noted by many reviewers; as one suggested, 'For Bond purists, it must be like seeing your dad in a dress.'[14] But the resonance of that former role was obviously important for how *Mamma Mia!*'s Sam Carmichael would be understood, as Brosnan himself has implied: 'They could have got a better singer, but that wasn't the point. I was in on the joke of having James Bond play this part.'[15] Sometimes his suaveness is played fairly straight: our first glimpse of the character is through the window of a New York skyscraper; he stands, looking into the exterior middle distance while at the forefront of a bustling office. His natural authority is confirmed in his interactions with colleagues and clients; here is a man who is successful and self-assured but not constrained by the sartorial dictates of the corporate environment, with his wardrobe of jeans, shirt and loose tie in keeping with this professionalised artisan imagery. However, his outward display of confidence and control is revealed to be superficial. When bidding his clients and staff farewell, his cool exterior belies his excitement. The 'whoop!' of relief that he lets out as the taxi pulls off to go to the airport signifies his nervous anticipation at being reunited with the woman he loved 20 years ago.

One of the most explicit references to Brosnan's Bond comes in the lead-up to Sam's duet with Donna, 'SOS'. The camera follows Donna into an outbuilding, and although she is only in there momentarily, when she comes out Sam has appeared, as if out of nowhere, in archetypal secret agent style. When the camera zooms out to a wider shot it reveals Brosnan leaning against the wall in a typically 'Bond' stance, hands casually in pockets as he exudes an air of manly capability. In contrast, Donna is presented as stubborn and immature in rebuffing his offers of assistance with repairs, protesting against a 'middle-aged menopausal man' telling her 'how to run my life'. His wry smile suggests that he might understand Donna and her needs better than she understands herself, despite the 20-year hiatus in their relationship.

As the mature romantic hero of the film, Sam's function is as much to prove himself to be the 'right' partner for Donna as to be one of the possible fathers, and despite the cutting of his character's lament on his failed marriage, 'Knowing Me, Knowing You', in the translation from stage to screen, he still figures in far more musical numbers than either of the other two men, dueting with Donna on 'SOS', recipient of Donna's 'The Winner Takes It All' and lead singer on 'I Do I Do I Do' as well as 'When All Is Said and Done'. He is slightly privileged in his exchanges with daughter as well as mother; while the other two men are getting tied up and ravished by the hen party during 'Voulez Vous', Sophie and Sam share an affectionate joke on the terrace. It is interesting that he is also the only one of the triumvirate to already be a father, something used to further the aura of authority and experience surrounding him. As the only one of the men who has other children, Sam is positioned as the father figure who feels most able not only to offer Donna the benefit of his wisdom ('I have two grown up kids. ... I know a thing or two about letting go ...') but also to give Sophie advice about relationships and her life choices, even if she ultimately rejects his paternal intervention by reminding him that Donna 'knows me better than you do'.

In contrast with the scenes in which Sam is presented as gently authoritative, other scenes appear to adopt a more playful, tongue-in-cheek tone that mocks the notion of this 'middle-aged menopausal man' having been a global sex symbol and icon of suave masculinity. His limited singing abilities and the evidence of a little bit of middle-aged weight gain revealed beneath his open shirt help to humanise the previously unimpeachable suavity of Brosnan's image. His announcement of his undiminished love for Donna and impromptu marriage proposal at the wedding are sincere and heartfelt but not without their cheesy elements, including his winks and nods to the musicians to strike up their tune and his cocksure 'come and get it' gestures as he tells Donna, 'you love me and you know it!' With this in mind, it seems that accommodating Sam and his fellow fathers in 'the old goat house' earlier in the film may have been far from accidental, subtly sending up a masculinity that is late-middle-aged but still insists that it is 'not too old for sex'.

Darcy turned daddy

Harry Bright, played by Colin Firth, is another of the possible fathers. Our introduction to his character takes the form of a panning shot up his body that reveals an immaculately dressed man departing from his town house in a leafy, canal-facing street in the upmarket Maida Vale district of London. From his polished shoes to his three-piece suit and Windsor-knotted tie, Harry appears to represent the epitome of British establishment masculinity. The appearance of a housekeeper and chauffeur confirm his social status but, as with Sam, we intuit that all may not be as it seems, and as Harry makes his way to the airport he observes a young family playing in a park with a poignant melancholy that suggests some kind of loss or lack in his affluent life.

Harry's characterisation draws on Colin Firth's star persona at least as much as Sam's draws on Brosnan's. Firth's overriding image is that of the quintessential English gentleman, and Firth imbues Harry with the combination of aloofness and sensitivity that have characterised many of his roles in this mould, including his most celebrated role as the broodingly introspective Mr Darcy in the 1995 BBC series *Pride and Prejudice*. Not only does Firth brings a sense of actorly gravitas to the film, with five BAFTA awards already to his name (this predated his subsequent multi-award-winning role in *The King's Speech* (Hooper, 2010)) but his role as Harry also draws upon his recurrent casting as a gay man, notably in *A Single Man* (Ford, 2009) but also in *Where the Truth Lies* (Egoyan, 2005) and even his breakthrough role in *Another Country* (Kanievske, 1984) opposite Rupert Everett, a pairing reprised comically in *St Trinian's* (Parker, 2007). As such, *Mamma Mia!* appears to draw on an established cultural shorthand that posits a certain type of British masculinity as effete and invariably sexually repressed.

Repressed and fastidious Harry is the guy least at ease with roughing it on a Greek island, fussily concerned with locating a trouser press, and his lack of spontaneity is a source of humour in the film (particularly in juxtaposition with his rebellious youth as the guitar-smashing punk Harry Headbanger). Although he envies Bill's freewheeling lifestyle he admits that he is an armchair traveller who enjoys adventure vicariously: 'I may look like I'm pondering my securities but in reality I'm trekking across some remote corner of the planet.' The idea of Harry having a secret submerged self will prove important when the character recognises and accepts his hitherto latent homosexuality later in the film, but it's also the key to understanding the sweetness and sensitivity that lie beneath his apparently aloof and diffident exterior. It is not so much the case that Harry represents the kind of modern fathering that insists on a 'hands-on' approach but that his softness corresponds to a discourse of masculinity that is sensitive and emotionally supportive and that has to be read, retrospectively, in tandem with his emergent homosexuality. Of course the question of emotional articulacy is rather complicated by the fact that Harry is utterly inarticulate when it comes to expressing his own emotional needs. His stilted discomfort at being in such close proximity to his own past is particularly palpable when he comes face to face with Donna for the first time, and the connections between his sexuality and his awkwardness appear to be intrinsic to his characterisation as a gentle sugar daddy to Sophie, the daughter whom he longs to indulge regardless of biological connection.

The emotional opening-up initiated by Harry's journey into fatherhood finally precipitates his being able to come out as gay. This culminates in a joyous shirtless embrace of his new lover in the orgiastic scenes following the (highly symbolic) eruption of Aphrodite's fountain. Harry dancing, his soon-to-be-discarded wet white shirt clinging to his chest, cannot help recall the scene in *Pride and Prejudice* that first propelled Firth into the spotlight. But here the nineteenth-century man of property, the ultimate repressed romantic hero, has become the newly liberated twenty-first-century gay dad.

The Scandinavian lone wolf

Bill Anderson (Stellan Skarsgård) appears first of all three of the film's fathers, cruising through a bustling exotic marketplace on his Harley Davidson. His khaki shorts and gilet, 'Erasure' tour T-shirt (an intriguing hint of queerness in the otherwise ultra-blokeish façade) and Australian outback hat instantly construct him as a rugged free spirit, unfettered by the confines of convention.[16] The 'evil eye' tattoos that adorn his knees (and buttocks, we later discover) consolidate this impression, and also hint at an interest in non-Western spiritual traditions. His wild, unreconstructed masculinity is further confirmed when he swings pirate-style onto his yacht from the quayside. Perhaps in keeping with his 'lone wolf' identity, Bill is also the father who is, if not exactly reluctant, then at least wary about the possibility of taking on a daughter. He is the first of the men to be suspicious about the 'serendipitous' events that are taking place, and when he realises that Sophie might be named after his aunt, who has also provided the legacy enabling Donna to buy the hotel, he is clearly unsettled. Indeed, his jokily panicked response to Sophie's suggestion that he is her father is to ask, 'You're not going to tell me that you have a twin sister, are you?' He is the last of the three men to react to the news that Donna does not know for certain which of the men is Sophie's dad, and when he does it is to pronounce that he will also 'take a third!', as if the prospect of shared fatherly responsibility is easier for him to take on. Or it could be that Bill does not want to miss out on this new adventure of paternity, especially when his two less outwardly adventurous paternal peers are so eager to embrace their new role. He needs to grasp the nettle of fatherhood in order to live up to his self-image as a man afraid of nothing – even fatherhood.

Bill's role in the paternal triptych may appear somewhat ambiguous, failing to offer either the financial or emotional support proffered by the other dads. But perhaps he plays his part in inspiring Sophie to make the break from the island and sail off round the world with Sky. As a man who lives his life on the sea, Bill can be likened to the Odysseus of Greek mythology, and his role in bringing the men to the island (in answer to a 'siren call' perhaps?) is both symbolically and literally central to the narrative. As a traveller and a writer he provides other men with a fantasised version of his life; Harry proclaims that his 'books are a godsend on dull business trips', realising his wanderlust vicariously through Bill's work. Indeed, that Bill is termed 'Bloke on a Boat' clearly delineates his form of masculinity from that of Sam and Harry; where Harry's characterisation owes much to Firth's star image as 'perfect Englishman' and Sam's is defined through an emphasis on quiet authority, paternal experience and (hetero)sexual attractiveness, Bill is 'a bloke'.

Of the three actors, Stellan Skarsgård is arguably the one with the least developed star image, and while he is better known in Sweden, the homeland he shares with ABBA, he is less established as a global star than either of his male co-stars. Among his most significant roles is that of the paralysed oil rig worker, Jan, in *Breaking the Waves* (von Trier, 1996), but he has also had a large number of supporting roles in films, including *Good Will Hunting* (Van Sant, 1997). Nonetheless he is probably best known to British and American audiences for another shipmate role, as 'Bootstrap Bill' in the *Pirates of the Caribbean* franchise. While the characters of Sam and Harry owe much to the defining characteristics of the respective star images of Brosnan and Firth, Skarsgård's image is less fixed and quirkier and this seems entirely in keeping with Bill's narrative function as a less conventional paradigm of masculinity.

An inconclusive conclusion

From feeling the lack of a father in her life, Sophie soon moves into having a surfeit of fathers wanting to give her away at her wedding, a situation that takes on nightmarish and claustrophobic dimensions during the 'Voulez Vous' sequence, with Sophie surrounded by whirling concentric circles of dancers, rendered expressionistic via distorted sound and cold blue lighting. Although this paternal surplus is sometimes played as tragedy, more often it comes across as farce, as when the three men skirt around the edges of the hen party, overhearing the Dynamos perform 'Super Trouper', with each man claiming it as 'his' song. This comedic approach is repeated during the wedding ceremony when they all stand up in the church at the mention of Sophie's dad being present before clocking each other and rather sheepishly resuming their seats.

However, the long-awaited moment of paternal revelation fails to materialise. No angry, jealous outbursts between Donna's former lovers but instead a tacit agreement to remain uncertain tripartite fathers rather than submit to paternity testing, with Harry saying,'It's great to have even a third', and Sam agreeing, 'We can find out if you want but I'm with Harry.' The very fact that the men agree to each take a third of a daughter can be seen as much as offering a comment on cultural discourses of fatherhood as it does on the commodification of young women. It could be that *Mamma Mia!* acknowledges the complexity and contradictions of post-feminist discourses of fatherhood and suggests that no one man will ever be able to fulfil the gamut of requirements in its current hegemonic form: spontaneous, reliable, new man, unreconstructed bloke, breadwinner, adventurer. On the one hand, the refusal to resolve the issue of paternity means the symbolically powerful paternal triptych remains intact. If no one man is confirmed as the father, all three remain fathers. As Louise FitzGerald suggests, it barely matters that neither the characters nor the audience discover which man is the biological father because the fact of paternity is far less important than the symbolic power that the possibility of being a father bestows upon the men. Fatherhood functions to facilitate a recuperative or restorative process for all three of the men.[17] In responding to Rosie's flirtation, Bill appears to get over his antipathy to commitment, while Sam regains his lost love, and Harry is able not only to admit his sexual orientation but to act on his desires. Despite the fact that, according to Colin Firth, *Mamma Mia!* expresses 'a real tenderness about the notion of these three grizzled, middle-aged men who find out there's more to their lives than they thought',[18] there could be a problem with the emphasis placed on fatherhood as magical panacea for all forms of male identity crisis at the expense of the daughter's experience or the mother/daughter bond. Is the film enacting a return to the 'Restoration of the Father ... symbolic, literal, potential' that Robin Wood saw as the 'dominant project, ad infinitum and post nauseum' of Hollywood cinema in the 1980s?[19]

On other hand, the men have not been the only beneficiaries of this unresolved paternal quest. Sophie makes it clear at the aborted wedding ceremony that her previous anxieties and anger over her uncertain origins have now evaporated: 'I have no clue which one of you is my dad but I don't mind.' Indeed, *Mamma Mia!* is a film that ultimately rejects the widespread cultural fixation on father hunger. The successful endpoint of Sophie's investigations is not her correct identification of her father but her final recognition that it doesn't matter who her father is. She reconnects with her mother and asks her to give her away at her wedding instead, but then abandons the marriage in favour of a reconceived future of mobility and adventure with a boyfriend rather than a husband.

This is a cinematic vision of fatherhood that doesn't centre on 'usurp[ing] rather than complement[ing] the female position by taking over the mother's role', as Stella Bruzzi suggests of films such as *Kramer vs. Kramer* (Benton, 1979) or *Ordinary People* (Redford, 1980).[20] Nor does it seem to express a serious sense of 'the lack of a strong, conventional father' like a number of ostensibly rebellious nineties visions of fatherhood, such as *Fathers' Day* (Reitman, 1997), *The Birdcage* (Nichols, 1996) or *Big Daddy* (Duganr, 1999).[21] Instead, *Mamma Mia!*'s final vision of parenthood emphasises pluralism and balances the different elements in the new configuration of Sophie's family. It doesn't quite tally with Sky's earlier assertion that 'you don't need a father, you have a family' but neither does it privilege paternal input over maternal in the manner identified by Tania Modleski. In the film's penultimate scene, Sky and Sophie leave the island to embark on their journey, and the pier, which has been the backdrop to some of the key moments in the film, is once more the setting for this final silhouetted *au revoir*. The reprise of 'I Have a Dream' underlines the satisfactory resolution of Sophie's initial endeavours. Sophie embraces each of her fathers in turn, although the indistinct nature of the three silhouettes renders absolute identification of the three men almost impossible. However, Sophie's final and most sustained embrace before her departure from the island is with her mother. Sophie and Donna are positioned in the middle of the frame in what can be read as a celebration of the exclusive bond shared by mother and daughter. However, the presence of the three men in the foreground of the shot appears to complicate this reading, possibly suggesting the omniscience of the paternal triptych. In one way, the construction of this image can be understood as confirming the paternal authority that in turn suggests that the mother/daughter bond is no longer exclusive and will, in future, be mediated by the presence of the three men in their lives. But at the same time the men are held at a distance, hanging back from the end of the pier, precluded from the physicality of Donna and Sophie's bond. As such they are rendered impotent onlookers; they are present but peripheral and possibly destined to remain satellite figures in Sophie's life, never able to compete with the depth of the revived mother/daughter relationship.

That *Mamma Mia!* might offer a slightly different take on its father figures than its predecessors and contemporaries is demonstrated by its post-narrative musical coda. Rather than upholding due reverence towards a longed-for patriarch, or even adhering to the 'hot dads' syndrome of eroticised paternity that Hannah Hamad identifies in recent media representations of fatherhood, Sophie's three fathers are brought back on stage for their curtain call, but trussed up in slightly ridiculous multicoloured ABBA-esque jumpsuits and platforms, tottering around and giving their all to 'Waterloo'.[22] Although the film initially seems to be another narrative of father hunger, with its daughter longing for a quasi-romantic 'hero of my dreams' incarnated by a heart-throb film star, paternal heroism in *Mamma Mia!* seems ultimately to be more about mucking in, strutting your stuff and realising that actually you win (a new sense of identity and belonging) when you lose (your patriarchal dignity).

Notes

1. Skarsgård interview on DVD documentary 'The making of *Mamma Mia!*'
2. Spencer, Charles, 'A mamma of a movie', *Daily Telegraph*, 28 December 2007, p. 33.
3. Andersson, Benny, Ulvaeus, Björn and Craymer, Judy, *Mamma Mia! How Can I Resist You? The Inside Story of Mamma Mia! and the Songs of Abba*, London: Phoenix, 2008, p. 248.
4. Reid, Melanie, 'These dancing queens can be high art too', *The Times*, 14 July 2008.
5. Calhoun, Dave, '*Mamma Mia!*', *Time Out*, 14 July 2008, p. 84.
6. Modleski, Tania, *Feminism without Women: Culture and Criticism in a 'Postfeminist' Age*, London: Routledge, 1991, p. 79.
7. Ibid., p. 80.
8. Traube, Elizabeth G., *Dreaming Identities: Class, Gender and Generation in 1980s Hollywood Movies*, San Francisco: Westview, 1992, p. 145.
9. Modleski, *Feminism without Womem*, p. 70.

10. Calhoun, 'Mamma Mia!'
11. Tasker, Yvonne, 'Practically perfect people: postfeminism, masculinity and male parenting in contemporary cinema', in Murray Pomerance (Ed.), *A Family Affair: Cinema Calls Home*, London: Wallflower, 2008, p. 176.
12. Modleski, *Feminism without Women*, pp. 88–9.
13. It's also true of the deleted song between Sophie and Bill, 'The Name of the Game', which converts a rather oedipal love song (about a young woman who sees herself as 'a bashful child beginning to grow') into a straightforward narrative of father/daughter bonding. The number employs familiar romantic iconography, with the pair depicted silhouetted against a dramatic clifftop landscape with waves crashing below.
14. Calhoun, 'Mamma Mia!'
15. Hattersley, Giles, 'Mamma mia, there's a fire within Judy Craymer's soul', *Sunday Times*, 23 November 2008, p. 2.
16. The band featured on Bill's T-Shirt are gay British electro-pop duo Erasure, who released an EP of ABBA covers called *ABBA-esque* in 1992.
17. Fitzgerald, Louise, 'Negotiating lone motherhood: gender, politics and family values in contemporary popular cinema', University of East Anglia PhD thesis, 2009, p. 254. http://ueaeprints.uea ac.uk/10577/1/Thesis_fitzgerald_L_2009.pdf (accessed 30 April 2011).
18. *Mamma Mia!* production notes, BFI Library.
19. Wood, Robin, *Hollywood from Reagan to Vietnam and Beyond*, New York: Columbia University Press, 1986, p. 172
20. Bruzzi, Stella, *Bringing Up Daddy: Fatherhood and Masculinity in Post-War Hollywood*, London: BFI, 2005, p. 110.
21. Ibid., p. 191.
22. Hamad Hannah, 'Hollywood's hot dads: tabloid, reality and scandal discourses of celebrity postfeminist fatherhood', *Celebrity Studies*, Vol. 1, No. 2, 2010, pp. 151–69.

13

What does your mother know? *Mamma Mia!*'s mediation of lone motherhood

Louise FitzGerald

In a 2008 interview with MSN News, Ann Wood, who played Donna Sheridan in the Australian production of the *Mamma Mia!* stage show, recounted how the recent birth of her child inspired her portrayal of the show's maternal figure. Describing how motherhood had made her feel 'more connected to scenes like "Slipping through My Fingers"', Wood explained that when she sang the lyrics she felt the pain 'in a way I didn't before'.[1] Wood's admission that as a mother this scene had a deeper resonance for her was reflected in many responses on Internet forums and websites discussing the merits of the film's version of ABBA's 'Slipping through My Fingers', which was described variously as 'heart warming', 'deeply emotional' and 'the best bit of the film'.[2] The same scene was described by IMDb reviewers as the 'money shot', and comments left on the YouTube clip of the song publicly attested to its emotionality, describing the importance of the song in giving public voice to the respondents' deep love for their mothers and/or daughters.[3] Such sentiments might suggest that some of the success of the film could be credited to its tender and heart-warming treatment of a female relationship that has traditionally been so scrutinised and pathologised within popular cinema.

More significant for the purpose of this chapter is the way in which so many of the responses to the 'Slipping through My Fingers' scene were couched in terms of empowerment. The scene might have made 'me and mum cry so hard', notes one respondent, but it also reminded her that 'we always did it together; who needs a father!'[4] Such open appreciation for a mother raising her child single-handedly, evident in the latter quote, is not so unusual; recently public figures from all walks of life have openly declared respect for their mother's fortitude in raising children in fatherless homes.[5] These public testimonials appear to contradict the cultural, political and social emphasis on fatherhood and subsequent circulating discourse correlating all social ills to 'father hunger'. Indeed, rather than regurgitating cultural anxieties about the lone mother/daughter dyad that underpins derogatory discourses about the detrimental female cycle – a discourse so regularly associated with this female paradigm – *Mamma Mia!* seems to accord agency to, and respect for, its lone mother. More notably, *Mamma Mia!* appears to challenge and resist a cinematic tradition whereby the voice and image of the lone mother are regularly filtered through a male and persistently patriarchal lens. In sharp contrast to classic lone mother/daughter narratives in films such as *Stella Dallas* (Vidor, 1937), *Mildred Pierce* (Curtiz, 1945) and *Mommie Dearest* (Perry, 1981), and more contemporary films like *P.S. I Love You* (LaGravense, 2007), *Because I Said So* (Lehmann, 2007) and *Something's Gotta Give* (Meyers, 2003), *Mamma Mia!* allows the daughter to fully express her desire to be more like her mother.

Of course, this apparently positive presentation of a relationship that has so often been coded as deeply problematic might be a result of screenwriter Catherine Johnson's social identity as a lone mother herself; it is well documented that she had tenacious negotiations with Universal to resist a more traditional rendering of lone motherhood.[6] Nonetheless, it is with these issues in mind that this chapter is structured to explore the potential for *Mamma Mia!* to work, borrowing Kathleen

Karlyn Rowe's phrase, as the 'cultural antidote' to the persistent cinematic practice of constructing lone motherhood in relation to patriarchy and as always in need of strict regulation.[7]

'I won't be muscled out by an ejaculation!'

Mamma Mia! is noteworthy because it appears to offer a more feminist-inflected film (a discourse that positively surrounds this film) that challenges the hegemony of psychoanalysis, disrupts the primacy of fatherhood and offers points of refusal for its female protagonists and for the female audience.[8] The film offers a narrative in which women find solace with one another – a presentation of women seldom seen in a cultural environment that is so suspicious of female camaraderie and that relies on forms of female misogyny for the success of deeply troubling cultural texts.[9] *Mamma Mia!*'s more positive rendering of older women has been commented on as one of the main indicators of a feminist underpinning, a point reiterated on feminist websites, where it is noted that the film unusually foregrounds 'women of all ages and body shapes' and celebrates older women's sexual desire.[10] Moreover, the narrative trope of the older woman and younger man relationship that has become such a regular feature of post-feminist cinema in films such as *Prime* (Younger, 2005) and *In the Land of Women* (Kasdan, 2007) and television shows like *Cougar Town* (ABC, 2009 is wholly renounced by Tanya (Christine Baranski) in her performance of 'Does Your Mother Know?' This scene, wherein Tanya ridicules Pepper's (Philip Michael's) unfettered desire for her, reframes the lyrics of a song originally sung as a castigation of female rebellion by an older man as words that undermine the posturing of a prepubescent boy.

However, I suggest it is the film's apparently unconventional rendering of the lone-mother/daughter dyad where there is potential for a feminist reading. Despite psychoanalytic theory and cultural wisdom that warns of the dangers posed to the lone-mothered daughter (these include promiscuity, early and unwed pregnancy, self-esteem and commitment issues, engaging in self-harm, poor academic achievement and so on), *Mamma Mia!* presents Sophie as an intelligent, well-balanced and healthy young woman. Donna is adventurous and markedly independent; she runs her own business and works hard to ensure her subjectivity according to a backstory – a move that legitimates Donna as a woman as well as a mother. Donna's subject position means that she is individualised; in other words, she does not become an exemplar of a certain set of derogated female characteristics that are so often associated with the figure of the lone mother. Rather, her experience of motherhood is absolutely validated in the musical number 'Slipping through My Fingers'. The 'money shot' scene takes place just after Sky (Dominic Cooper) tells Sophie that she does not need to know who her father is in order to know herself, which is followed by Sophie telling Sam (Pierce Brosnan) that her mother knows her better than he does. These two brief scenes explicitly undercut ideological dogma that persistently undermines the agency of the lone mother in the reification of the father as the essential element in the psychological development of the female self and remind the audience of the value (a word seldom associated with lone motherhood) of this mother's influence on her daughter's inner well-being. Having rejected Sam's demand to speak with her about giving her away at the wedding and highlighted his limited knowledge of her, Sophie runs to her mother to ask for her help to get ready for the wedding. The first strains of 'Slipping through My Fingers' take place as Donna and Sophie enter Sophie's bedroom, a space usually framed as the private place into which daughters escape from their mothers. Donna, leaning against a large, free-standing mirrors sings not to her daughter but to herself. Although we see Sophie in this shot, she is sitting in front of another mirror with her back towards her mother. By framing

Sophie within the two mirrors we get only a blurred image of her. This absence or blurring of Sophie within the frame is significant because Donna is positioned as the central focus: it is her experience of the process of rupture and separation that is being emphasised, not her daughter's. Marianne Hirsch suggests that maintaining focus on the maternal experience from the persceptive of the mother is a trope seldom visible within popular cinema because priority is always given to the daughter's perspective. This is probably because the process of separation is so central to ideas about the identification process of daughters.[11] In fact, Sophie rarely shares screen time with her mother when Donna is singing; when the two women are together the emphasis of Donna's singing shifts; the music becomes extra-diegetic rather than diegetic. The shift from diegetic to extra-diegetic mediates some of the more problematic lyrics of 'Slipping through My Fingers'; rather than focusing on the persistent expression of maternal guilt in the words of the song as sung by the maternal figure, viewers are instead treated to a montage of images of Donna taking care of her daughter's bloodied leg, painting her daughter's toenails, sharing moments of laughter and sitting together on a rocking chair – an iconic image of 'good' maternalism – set to music. The only time that Donna and Sophie share the screen throughout the duration of the song is when they sing the last verse together. This scenario takes place after a brief break in the music during which Sophie expresses her fear that she has failed because she has not achieved the things her mother has, including raising a child alone. Donna explains that she 'wouldn't have had it any other way' and adds, 'Look what we have had.' These words have a particular resonance within a political and cultural environment that always casts the lone-mothered family as lacking and might account somewhat for the rhetoric of empowerment used by respondents highlighted earlier. In recognition of her mother's role in her life, Sophie asks Donna to give her away at the wedding. After Donna agrees to her daughter's request, both women turn to face the mirror (although we don't see the reflected image) and consolidate their bond singing the lyrics 'sometimes I wish I could freeze the picture and save it from the funny tricks of time'. It is no longer a song about maternal dislocation but one that highlights the emotional pain of separation for mother and daughter: a shared experience of longing for time to stand still rather than a pathologised narrative of symbolic matricide that has so regularly permeated mother/daughter narratives.[12]

Perhaps most noticeably, *Mamma Mia!* challenges the traditional role of the father in the wedding ritual by allowing the mother to give her daughter away in marriage. Of course, the film still abides by the premise that the daughter has to be 'given away', but that the mother is sanctioned to replace the father figure suggests a challenge to the systematic undermining of the primacy of the lone mother in the prioritisation of the narrative of 'father hunger' that pervades contemporary mainstream cinema. While the narrative centralises the father figure in the guise of Sam Carmichael, Harry Bright (Colin Firth) and Bill Anderson (Stellan Skarsgård), director Phyllida Lloyd and screenwriter Catherine Johnson seem all too aware of the traditional narrative plots that centralise the 'healing' power of fatherhood. Clearly Sam, Harry and Bill are important figures for Sophie, but it is her mother that she turns to for emotional support. In fact, *Mamma Mia!* suggests that it takes more than one man to provide a fully rounded paternal role in Sophie's life, and that Donna has been, and remains, the singularly most reliable and nurturing agent in her daughter's world.

That Sophie should later choose to delay her wedding also indicates an ambivalence towards the wedding culture that has become so centralised within post-feminist consumer culture. The film does give us a wedding, but it is not the lavish affair that has been celebrated in recent films such as *Because I Said So*, *My Big Fat Greek Wedding* (Zwick, 2002), *27 Dresses* (Fletcher, 2008), *The Wedding Date* (Kilner, 2005), *Made of*

Honour (Weiland, 2008), *Bride Wars* (Winick, 2009) and *A Royal Engagement: Princess Diaries 2* (Marshall, 2004) and as such could be read as a backlash against what Cele C. Otnes and Elizabeth H. Pleck describe as the 'spectacle and celebration of romantic consumer culture'.[13] More importantly, in deciding to not get married (just like her mother) but to travel the world to broaden her own horizons, Sophie contradicts prevailing 'commonsense' ideology that daughters who reject highly patriarchal Freudian principles of socialisation have a 'particularly difficult time ... because they inevitably modelled themselves on their mothers, only to later realise that this is not how they want to be, or how they want to live'.[14] This is not to suggest that Sophie is the mirror image of her mother, only that her mother's advice is given more dominance than that of the father figures despite an initial narratological focus on the rhetoric of 'father hunger'. In this sense, *Mamma Mia!* might serve to dispute Lacanian theory about the mutual dependence of the mother and her daughter and ostensibly function as a text that turns its back on what Lucy Fischer describes as the established trope of 'replicating the role of psychoanalysis in the construction of motherhood'.[15]

The idea posited here that the wedding narrative, or more precisely the rejection of the central wedding narrative, is influenced by a feminist perspective is reinforced in Catherine Johnson's recollections of the changes she made to the script during workshop sessions. Johnson recalls that in the initial draft of the script, Sophie did not want to get married; rather, Donna was active in pushing her daughter into marriage. The dynamics created in the original script by the characterisation of an overbearing mother and a daughter who sees the impending wedding as 'frightening' made Johnson re-evaluate the politics of the narrative:

> I thought, Jesus Christ, when is this play set? Is it set now or in the Victorian age? Why on earth is this girl doing

what her mother tells her? My age group grew up in the 1970s, it was the generation who had been saying 'You don't need a man to have a fulfilling life'. So why was I writing a mother from the dark ages saying 'Oh darling, it's a dream for you to have a white wedding'?[16]

Johnson's evocation of the seventies as a time when women were demanding an end to prescriptive ideas about marriage as the zenith of their life serves to highlight her own investment in a form of feminist politics. It is perhaps interesting to note here that ABBA songs, which, as Malcolm Womack's chapter suggests, are problematic in terms of gender representations, are being used to frame a narrative that is ostensibly more politically progressive in its treatment of women in general, and lone mothers in particular. For instance, 'Waterloo' tells the story of a woman who finally surrenders to the unwelcome attention of a pursuing male – a narrative that is not noteworthy as readily endorsing female emancipation. Nonetheless, that Johnson appears to recognise the influence of feminism on her creative process is indicative of the more progressive politics of this film and made manifest nowhere more clearly than in the wedding scene, in which Sophie (in the presence of a vicar, the congregation and God, one supposes) declares that she does not care how many men Donna has had sex with.[17] Ostensibly, this scene offers one of the more subversive representations of a lone mother on screen. Accounts of promiscuous lone mothers who have multiple sexual partners proliferate in the social and political world, where the rhetoric of immoral and predatory unmarried mothers serves to differentiate and consolidate the requisites of 'good' maternalism (married, white and middle class) from 'bad' (single, poor, working class and often marked by race). Donna might be embarrassed by her daughter's public renunciation of female sexual morality, but it is a moment in which the lone mother can 'own' sexual agency without fear of causing damage to her daughter's inner psychology.

And yet, even as the film offers these moments of feminist potential, the more progressive presentation of a lone mother/daughter formation can be undermined by the film's setting on a Greek island, a liminal space where discourse and actions not normally sanctioned in the 'real' world can be legitimated in a spatial and temporal nirvana. *Mamma Mia!* is still a film about a girl's desire to find her father, one that showcases the girlish behaviour of older women (a central theme of post-feminist culture). It presents troubling representations of Greek men and women, marginal at best and figures of ridicule at worst, and closes with a heterosexual marriage. And it is a man, Sky, who sanctions this lone mother/daughter unit as a 'family'; in fact Donna and Sophie never refer to themselves as such. The film's central tension is exactly the conflict between mother and daughter, and the voice of reason, once held by the woman, is given over to the male characters who function as symbolic patriarchs of the narrative. Indeed the final scene of the film in which Donna and Sophie say their farewells, is overseen by the three men. Although Harry, Sam and Bill stand at a distance from mother and daughter, the scene still suggests that the relationship between Donna and Sophie is no longer exclusive, that Donna has indeed been muscled out by an ejaculation.

Despite the film's challenge to 'father hunger', reliance on the fantasy of fatherhood provides the central narrative thrust of *Mamma Mia!*, thus reinforcing the cultural overdetermination of traditional power dynamics of masculinity and fatherhood. Whilst neither Sophie nor the audience discovers which of the men is her biological father, it is not really significant to the ideological schema of the film, because fatherhood is offered as a space for transformation for the men rather than their duty of care for Sophie. Sam marries Donna and in so doing redeems himself from the accusations of abandonment she articulates so forcefully in 'The Winner Takes It All'. Bill, a man known for his impulsive, adventurous spirit and lack of roots, gains a surrogate family and a space in which he might form some long-lasting attachment now that age has caught up with this 'lone wolf'. And Harry finally finds the strength to act on his impulses, an action that results in him 'coming out of the closet'. Interestingly it is his desire to act as Sophie's father that enables his tentative avowal of his sexuality (albeit done for comedic affect), a process that surely highlights the deep cultural investment in fatherhood as the primary factor in the construction of masculinity regardless of, or despite, sexual proclivities.[18] Thus the ideological role of the lone mother/daughter dyad in this film is to facilitate the reconstitution of masculinity, an act that especially negotiates the lone mother's subject position because she functions as a filter for the anxieties of white middle-class masculinity rather than as an individual. Just like the lone mothers in *Jerry Maguire* (Crowe, 1996), *Pay It Forward* (Leder, 2000), *Erin Brockovich* (Soderbergh, 2000), *Chocolat* (Hallström, 2000), *In the Valley of Elah* (Haggis, 2007), *Gone Baby Gone* (Affleck, 2007), *Monster's Ball* (Forster, 2001) and *The Sixth Sense* (Shyamalan, 1999), amongst others, Donna reconstructs the unfettered masculinity of not just one but three men, and provides them with a ready-made family in which to consolidate and act out their new-found paternalism and reconfigured masculinity.

In addition, even as the film attempts to support its lone mother by highlighting traditional and punitive ideas about lone motherhood, maternalism is still under scrutiny because the film ridicules Donna's mother by framing her as a detrimental force in Donna's life – a woman whom Donna had to reject in order to protect her 'self'. That Tanya should berate Donna for 'sounding like her mother' suggests that whilst the film might be offering a more liberal worldview, it still sanctions the long-held tradition of 'mother blame' that underpins western psychoanalysis and traditional ideas about gender socialisation. Indeed by framing Donna's mother as the gatekeeper of more traditional ideas of femininity and motherhood, *Mamma Mia!* suggests that it is women who are to blame for more regressive attitudes towards lone motherhood. That *Mamma Mia!* uses another woman to articulate such rhetoric surely undermines the idea that this film celebrates female relationships and motherhood. Ironically, for a film that has been embraced as a tender presentation of the mother/daughter bond, *Mamma Mia!* actually reinforces the maternal binary in positioning one mother in direct opposition to another and uses female sexual morality as the lightning rod.

These contradictions implicit in *Mamma Mia!* make for a complex analysis of the film's lone mother/daughter relationship and its feminist-inflected narrative; on the one hand *Mamma Mia!* clearly presents highly sentimentalised images of a lone mother and her daughter and tenders a more liberal feminist perspective on the social and cultural construction of lone motherhood. For example, although Sophie is sanctioned to draw attention to her mother's competence in having raised a child alone while single-handedly running a business, the film mediates the possibility of a more progressive presentation of lone motherhood through a narrative that highlights Donna's inability to maintain the family home and business, her ignorance of technology and her reliance on Sky to make the business more profitable. Indeed, the ramshackle state of their house is indicative of Donna's inability to provide a home for her daughter, a theme reinforced in another lone mother/daughter pairing in *The Princess Dairies*, where Mia (Anne Hathaway) and her mother, Helen (Caroline Goodall), live in an old fire station. In imaging Sophie's and Mia's houses as a having a previous function other than living accommodation, *Mamma Mia!* and *The Princess Diaries* reinforce the cultural imaging of the lone-mothered house as not a 'proper' home, not the home of a real woman and a proper mother – a fact that is reinforced by the absence of any scene in *Mamma Mia!* other than 'Slipping through My Fingers' in which Sophie and Donna are located together within the home. Moreover, the idea that Donna is an independent woman is undermined through the narrative of their inheritance of the island and hotel from another maternal figure, who, although absent from the film, functions as Donna's benevolent surrogate mother and serves to reinforce the good/bad mother binary as the antithesis to Donna's mother. More significantly, *Mamma Mia!* re-places Donna into a traditional familial role as wife by the end of the film, thus rescuing her from the 'potential threat' of remaining a single woman and lone mother. And *Mamma Mia!* also maintains the long-held idea that the construction of femininity requires Sophie to position herself simultaneously in accordance with and at a distance from her mother in order to maintain a viable and healthy relationship with her self and her mother.

It is this push-and-pull dichotomy that provides the narrative conflict in many films showcasing the lone mother/daughter dyad that have emerged over the last decade. However, rather than regurgitating cultural anxieties about inept lone motherhood that correlate promiscuity, drug taking and unmarried teenage motherhood with fatherlessness, the high visibility of older lone-mothered daughters within mainstream popular film is affirmed by her ability to differentiate what Rosi Bradotti might describe as the difference 'within women'.[19] Put more simply, age serves to delineate women from other women, creating a generational dynamic that produces conflict within women. Catherine Driscoll has argued that this form of delineation has had a profound effect on the politics of feminism by excluding female adolescents. Stating that feminism is reliant upon the adolescent female (in that feminism is always looking forward towards what the next generation might become), Driscoll maintains that feminism simultaneously separates itself from female adolescence through discourses that reify female 'maturity, autonomy and individuality'.[20] However, I suggest that films such as *Mamma Mia*, *The Princess Diaries*, *Because I Said So* and *Ice Princess* (Fywell, 2005, a film that explicitly codes its lone mother as a feminist in her role as a women's studies professor) actually reverse the generational dynamic as described by Driscoll. By implicitly casting their lone mother figures as women having 'childish' politics, films such as *Mamma Mia!*

cast the lone mother figure as requiring re-education from her post-feminist daughter, whose social concerns distance her from her mother's potentially threatening politics. With these issues in mind I argue that *Mamma Mia!* represents a wider trend within mainstream cinema that sees the negotiation of the lone mother figure through its inception of popular feminism as the politics of childish, immature and threatening women – a belief system that women must relinquish if their daughter's needs and desires are to be 'properly' facilitated. Indeed, the dual meaning of the term *Mamma Mia!* – 'my mother' and a colloquialism for shock and dismay – might indicate that a more cautious approach should be taken in the cultural celebration of this lone mother figure.

The lone mother as a 'potential threat'

The reference I make here to the lone mother as a threatening figure is not a provocative one; lone mothers are, on account of their single status, seen as holders of excessive female power and autonomy (even though they rarely have it), and it is these 'uncharacteristically' female attributes that are highlighted in discursive practices that correlate lone motherhood with feminism. In fact, much anti-feminist rhetoric points to lone mothers as indicative of the 'ills' of feminism, as the end product of feminism gone too far; her independence and distance from traditional notions of motherhood and femininity render the lone mother as a symbol of inappropriate matriarchy.[21] Even as the film does not explicitly code Donna as a feminist mother, the description of her as a feisty woman, her wearing of dungarees (iconic of second-wave feminism) and her refusal to be 'muscled out by an ejaculation' surely draw attention to the rejection or subversion of patriarchal authority. Her fierce refusal of Sam's and Harry's offers of financial and practical help codes Donna as a woman who can 'do it all', a discourse that is so vigorously disputed and employed to ratify anti- and post-feminist claims that feminism has deceived women in their quest for equality. And it is difficult not to see how the phallic symbolism of the glue gun and drill draws attention to Donna as an emasculating figure, a woman who openly challenges male proprietorship of the phallus. Indeed, a symbolic reading of the scene in which Donna is using a glue gun to close up a fissure to prevent water gushing from it might suggest an allegorical rejection or sealing up of her femininity entirely.

The examples given here are indicative of the ways in which *Mamma Mia!*'s lone mother could be read as an embodiment of feminist sensibilities, but it is Donna's objections to Sophie's plans to marry that consolidate her feminist position. This is most evident in the scene that follows the 'night before the wedding celebrations', where Donna expresses her concerns about her daughter's well-being:

> Donna: Last night, you and Sky, what's wrong?
> Sophie: I don't know what to do?
> Donna: You don't have to do anything, it's not too late to call off the wedding. People will understand. Isn't that what you want?
> Sophie: That's what you want!
> Donna: No.
> Sophie: You have no idea, you never had a wedding, you never did the marriage thing. You just did the baby thing – well good for you.
> Donna: I know, I don't know why you are going off on one.
> Sophie: I love Sky and I want to be with him. I don't want my children growing up not knowing who their father is – it's crap!

I suggest the fissure between Donna and Sophie evident in this argument reflects the alleged conflict between feminist and post-feminist attitudes towards marriage and fatherhood. Donna embodies the ideologies of a politics that supposedly encouraged women to renounce marriage and to raise children alone (a reading reinforced by an earlier scene in which Donna says if Sophie were more like her she 'would not be married at the age of 20 – or at all!'). In contrast, Sophie's dialogue consolidates post-feminist, neoconservative family values and ideology that elevate the institution of marriage and proffer fatherhood as the panacea for the psychological and social disruption allegedly caused by lone mothers and feminism. According to *Mamma Mia!* Donna's regressive and oppressive (read feminist) attitude towards marriage denies Sophie her 'birth' right to become a wife; indeed, her feminist-inflected maternalism is as problematically oppressive for Donna as it is for her post-feminist daughter. For, once Sophie has drawn attention to the result of her mother's decision to raise her in a fatherless environment, Donna renounces her cynicism towards the marriage and says that Sophie 'is going to have a beautiful wedding'. It is the preparations for the wedding that bond the two women, and, whilst Sophie's request for her mother to give her away might seem like a subversive moment that undermines the primacy of fatherhood, I would suggest that by accepting a key role in her daughter's wedding, Donna is making clear that she has renounced her 'childish' anti-marriage attitudes. Thus, Sophie has succeeded in the re-education of her mother's misdirected beliefs. Moreover, by casting off the 'burden' of feminism, Sophie's desire to know her father is sanctioned by Donna, who intervenes in the vicar's welcoming speech (which explicitly casts Donna and Sophie as an incomplete family when the vicar refers to Donna as the representative of Sophie's family) to introduce Harry, Sam and Bill as the candidates for the role of Sophie's father. Having played a central part in the wedding and stepping aside to allow the 'fathers' to share the stage, Donna proves to her daughter that she has turned her back on her old, immature and oppressive ways – a mutual process that enables Sophie to cancel her wedding, not because she doesn't want to get married but rather because Donna has relinquished her old ways and allowed Sophie to form a relationship with her fathers, whose earlier words of encouragement to her to seek adventure before marrying Sky are given narratological prominence. Sky might have been right when he suggested that she didn't need a father in order to find herself, but the closing scenes of *Mamma Mia!* suggest that in finding her fathers, Sophie feels complete. And anyway, Sky really didn't want to get married! The final consolidation of Donna's new-found emancipation from feminism comes when Sam declares his everlasting love for her, and in his rendition of 'I Do, I Do, I Do, I Do', Sam asks Donna to marry him. Donna's acceptance of his proposal and subsequent marriage to Sam complete Sophie's family, a process that absolutely strengthens the negotiation of lone motherhood and systematically reinforces the post-feminist, neo-liberal project of ratifying the social and political significance of marriage and fatherhood.

That the lone mother and her daughter are being employed to disavow feminism in this manner is ironic given that both female social identities are often discussed under the rubric of female rebellion. But it is also highly apt that this dyad should be employed in the role of disavowing feminism because in so doing they are both recuperated into the post-feminist ideological repudiation of feminism. By casting Donna as immature through implication of her feminist belief system, *Mamma Mia!* challenges the conceptualisation of feminism as a politics of mature independent women who have rejected a hedonistic lifestyle for one that is more politically and socially engaged. That the post-feminist daughter is teaching her mother to step away, or distance herself, from her politics in order to allow her daughter to become the woman she has the (birth) right to be demonstrates that the older fatherless daughter is not a passive figure rather she successfully positions feminism as limiting. The task then for the daughters of cinematic lone mothers like Donna is to negotiate the minefield of the mother's psychology in order to free themselves from the burden of care, enhance their own chances of happiness and remind us of what their mother doesn't know.

Notes

1. Field, Katherine, 'Motherhood inspires *Mamma Mia!* star', *MSN News*, 28 October 2009. http://news.ninemsn.com.au/entertainment/920981/motherhood-inspires-mamma-mia-star (accessed 17 February 2011).
2. See http://www.sing365.com/music/lyrics.nsf/slipping-through-my-fingers-lyrics-abba/d76035766dc4d18548256, where reviewers of the song discuss their emotional responses to 'Slipping through My Fingers' (accessed 9 March 2011).
3. Holman, Curt, 'Mamma mia: who's your daddy?', Comment board for *Mamma Mia!*, 16 July 2008. http://www.imdb.com (accessed 9 March 2011).
4. One of many postings relating to the various versions of *Mamma Mia!*'s 'Slipping through My Fingers' scene available via http://www.youtube.com (accessed 6 March 2011).
5. The most public praise given to a lone mother came from President Barack Obama in his inauguration speech on 20 January 2009.
6. In much the same vein as *Mamma Mia!*, films such as *Thirteen* (Hardwick, 2003), *The Princess Diaries* (Marshall, 2001), *A Royal Engagement: The Princess Dairies 2* (Marshall, 2004), *The Heartbreakers* (Mirkin, 2001), *The Perfect Man* (Rosman, 2005), *Aquamarine* (Allen, 2006), *Spanglish* (Brooks, 2004), *Anywhere but Here* (Wang, 1999), *Where the Heart Is* (Williams, 2000), and *Gas, Food, Lodging* (Anders, 1992) also hinge on the figures of the lone mother and her daughter in narratives that potentially resist social and psychoanalytical discourses that suggest that the mutuality of the lone mother/daughter relationship is one that is dangerously symbiotic.
7. Karlyn Rowe, Kathleen, 'Film as cultural antidote: *Thirteen* and the maternal melodrama', *Feminist Media Studies*, Vol. 6, No. 2, 2006, pp. 453–68.
8. Hirsch, Marianne, *The Mother/Daughter Plot: Narrative, Psychoanalysis, Feminism*, Bloomington: Indiana University Press, 1998, p. 117.
9. Diane English's film *The Women* (2008) and the British television show *Four Brides* (Living TV, 2009–) are just two prime examples of this trend.
10. http://www.feminsite.com and http://www.thefeministspectatorblogspot.com are two of the feminist-based websites that foregrounded the feminist overtones of *Mamma Mia!* (accessed 26 January 2011).
11. Hirsch, *The Mother/Daughter Plot*.

12. See Hirsch, *The Mother/Daughter Plot*; Jay, Betty, *Weird Lullabies: Mothers and Daughters in Contemporary Film*, Bern: Peter Lang, 2008.
13. Otnes, Cele C. and Pleck, Elizabeth H., *Cinderella Dreams: The Allure of the Lavish Wedding*, Berkeley: University of California Press, 2003, p. 5.
14. Kaplan, Ann E., *Women and Film: Both Sides of the Camera*, London: Routledge, 1993, p. 85.
15. Fischer, Lucy, *Cinematernity: Film, Motherhood and Genre*, Princeton NJ: Princeton University Press, 1996, p. 87.
16. Andersson, Benny, Ulvaeus, Björn, and Craymer, Judy, *Mamma Mia! How Can I Resist You? The Inside Story of Mamma Mia! and the Songs of ABBA*, London: Phoenix, 2008, p. 159.
17. The often somewhat misogynistic undertones of ABBA's songs might be made more complex by Andersson's large financial donation to the Feminist Initiative, a Swedish political party that ran for election in 2006 fighting to challenge the Swedish marriage laws. See the following website for more information: http://www.thelocal.se/19906/20090606/ (accessed 4 March 2011).
18. This is not to suggest that homosexuality and fatherhood are mutually exclusive but rather that fatherhood has become a 'magical' solution to any sort of 'crisis in masculinity' within popular culture. That *Mamma Mia!* frames Harry's sexuality as a 'bit of a joke' suggests that homosexuality, whilst perhaps not coded as a 'crisis', is still regarded as something to laugh at.
19. Rosi Bradotti cited in Driscoll, Catherine, *Girls: Feminine Adolescence in Popular Culture and Cultural Theory*, New York: Columbia University Press, 1993, p. 13.
20. Ibid, p. 132
21. See Doyle, Laura, *The Surrendered Wife: A Woman's Spiritual Guide to True Intimacy with a Man*, New York: Simon and Schuster, 2001, and Coulter, Ann, *Guilty Liberal Victims and Their Assault on America*, New York: Crown, 2008, for their staunch anti-feminist approach to gender politics. These two texts are regularly referred to by fathers' rights groups and men's groups in their continued assault on lone motherhood and feminists, who are seen as the central factor in the obsolescence of masculinity. See http://www.angryharry.com as an example of the rhetoric employed by men's groups.

14

Afterword: when all is said and done

Sue Harper

This collection of essays demonstrates that the film version of *Mamma Mia!* is an incredibly rich cultural text. It can carry a wide range of interpretations, and can be discussed in terms of female agency and authorship, feminism, queer theory, stardom and performance style. Works of popular art that elicit and carry such a wide variety of readings, and which perform such a wide range of cultural tasks, have major social significance. But the richness of such works should not lead us into thinking that they are polysemic. *Mamma Mia!*, like other works of its type, is not an 'open text'. That category tends to be populated by works with high-art aspirations, cultural status and textual difficulty, and the intellectual labour required to decode them confers distinction on their consumers.

Rather, *Mamma Mia!* cannot really be understood without recourse to the concepts of low status, gender difference and textual incoherence. In these regards, it is precisely analogous to *The Wicked Lady* (Arliss, 1945). I have argued elsewhere that the latter film was characterised by critical hostility, an exclusively female audience and a texture that was incoherent, but through which viewers could pick their way with aplomb. I want to argue that this very textual incoherence in performance and cinematic style is also part of the meaning of *Mamma Mia!* It certainly enraged the critics, who expended much bile on the singing abilities of Pierce Brosnan and the dancing skills of Colin Firth. But a work like this attains the status of Grand Myth by its confident handling of the dominant explanatory narratives of the culture. The casual and sometimes clumsy performances are part of its meaning.

There are some instructive differences between *The Wicked Lady* and *Mamma Mia!*, though. The former overstimulates the eye by a layered and contradictory *mise-en-scène*, and by asymmetrical compositions. The latter presents much less ambiguous settings and clothes (the heart in the sleeve of Donna's Dynamo outfit), and virtually every composition is centrally balanced, encouraging a sense of security. The heroine of *The Wicked Lady* permits the female audience to experience, in a vicarious way, those pleasures it had been denied by historical circumstance and by official propaganda about the necessity of feminine modesty and restraint. *Mamma Mia!*, on the other hand, encourages older female viewers to recuperate their own past, and to imagine themselves as free once more. Such a group is too large, and too visible, to permit us to ascribe the film with 'cult' qualities, since cult films celebrate a private world on the boundaries of hegemony. *Mamma Mia!* audiences may dress up in the gear, and sing along with the tunes, but that is a distinct kind of cultural phenomenon.

Of course, the film draws its energy from the Utopian impulse, and purveys a certainty that love can never be broken, that pity can be consoled, that desire can never die and that all manner of things shall be well – in short, the triumph of hope over experience. Its power depends on the willing suspension of rational disbelief. Older women like myself who have colourful pasts and uncertain futures find this particularly potent, and I suppose I ought to say that the film is very high in my own personal pantheon, alongside *The Scarlet Empress* (Sternberg, 1934) and *I Know Where I'm Going!* (Powell and Pressburger, 1945). Those films show the process of women taking uncertain steps towards their chosen futures. *Mamma Mia!* allows me to walk towards my younger self, and overlay that with a patina of pleasure and power. It is commonly termed a 'feelgood' movie, but I'd want to think about it as a 'can-do' one.

Afterword: when all is said and done

What makes *Mamma Mia!* unique, and perhaps accounts for its outstanding popularity, is the way it combines a range of mythic references, some more deep-rooted than others. It thus attains a level of *mythic saturation*. There are quotations from classical mythology, which anchor it firmly in western civilisation. Consider the hen night sequence, in which the intoxicated female dancers capture the male interlopers, in a style redolent of the Bacchanalian revels. In these, women are the bearer of the Dionysian principle – passionate, disorderly, orgiastic, *dangerous* – and the film touches on their predatory nature. But in a volte-face typical of the film, the 'capture' is followed by the incursion of masked males, who vault into the sacrificial arena and mete out a pleasurable (if firm) return to order. It is like the rape of the Sabine women. And in an earlier scene, the hero, significantly named Sky, summons his entourage of young *kouroi*, who arise from the sea like Poseidon or Neptune. But the power implicit in that image is comically defused by the flippers that they wear, which make them appear clumsy. And so the film gives with one hand and takes away with the other, thus providing a tension that can be slaked and a desire that can be satiated.

Mamma Mia! also deploys the stuff of fairy tales. There is a marked tripling structure in its narrative – the three fathers, the three 'mothers', the three young girls. This is combined with the familiar topoi of the lost father, the bride who is not a bride and the "crone" who is magically transformed. Such well-worn routines are revitalised in the film, but the rehearsal of them is pleasurable rather than stale. In addition, the film implicitly refers to the 'magical island' in *The Tempest*; Phyllida Lloyd noted in the film's production notes that the island is, like Shakespeare's, a place of search and transformation. All popular art combines well-worn motifs with a modicum of novelty, but *Mamma Mia!* is particularly conservative in the way it combines culturally residual elements. It makes the act of partaking in the experience of the film rather like enacting a ritual. Everyone knows the roles that are on display (especially as the film has the familiarity of the stage play and the ABBA songs) and this enforces a tolerance of, and perhaps a preference for, a casual style of enactment. We forgive those celebrants in a pageant who may muff their lines or drop their candles.

But more is at issue. Where *Mamma Mia!* innovates is in the intense nature of its historical anchorage. Virtually the first conversation in the film gives a date: July 1970. We are told repeatedly that Sophie is 20, so the diegesis takes place in 1990. But the whole film is suffused by the desire to validate the 1970s: to see the young Donna not as a 'silly little slut' but as a young woman experimenting, albeit clumsily, with her own sexuality. The film presents a very *long* 1970s though. Bill is presented as a hippy, suffused with the spirit of 1968, whereas Harry is shown in flashback as a punk who sold his Johnny Rotten T-shirt to buy Donna a guitar. But the whole complex period, with its shifts and conflicts, is presented as a period of liberation. This is entirely at odds with the commonsensical version of the 1970s, which is that it was a decade of strikes, social insecurity and global crisis. Rather, *Mamma Mia!* implicitly argues that the radical destabilisation of the systems of meaning that took place in the 1970s was extremely positive in its effects, and that the sexual revolution did not result in women's further repression (as is often argued by radical feminists) but in their autonomy and transformation.

The final scene is particularly important from this point of view. Gorgeously arrayed in 1970s gear – silver lamé, thigh boots, platforms, flares, medallions – the cast march, with varying degrees of co-ordination, towards the camera. It is an intensely self-reflexive scene, which argues that looking silly does not matter at all; walking towards your own choice, and casting off your customary inhibitions, do matter a lot. Streep says directly to the audience: 'Do you want another one?' The answer, of course, is 'yes', because an element of repetition and familiarity is crucial to the pleasure provided by the film. But at the same time, *Mamma Mia!* is doing something quite revolutionary, in that it is actively reforming and reconstructing popular memory, and making us see the recent past in a fresh and positive light.

Bibliography

Adams, Guy, 'There's a new genre in Tinseltown, and it's all about female friendship', *Independent*, 8 June 2008. http://www.independent.co.uk/arts-entertainment/films/news/theres-a-new-genre-in-tinseltown-and-its-all-about-female-friendship-842485.html (accessed 29 April 2011).

Adnum, Mark, 'Meryl Streep: our lady of the accents', *Spiked*, 11 February 2009. http://www.spiked-online.com/index.php/site/article/6204 (accessed 13 April 2011).

Akers, Anne, '*Mamma Mia!* An analysis of the UK's most popular film of all time', University of York MA dissertation, 2009. http://www.stripeyanne.org/MammaMiaDissertation.pdf.

Altman, Rick, *The American Film Musical*, Bloomington: Indiana University Press, 1987.

——, 'A semantic/syntactic/pragmatic approach', in Barry Keith Grant (Ed.), *Film Genre Reader*, 3rd edition, Austin: University of Texas Press, 2003.

Andersson, Benny, Ulvaeus, Björn and Craymer, Judy, *Mamma Mia! How Can I Resist You? The Inside Story of Mamma Mia! and the Songs of ABBA*, London: Phoenix, 2008.

Ang, Ien, *Watching Dallas: Soap Opera and the Melodramatic Imagination*, London: Methuen, 1985.

Anon., 'It's a rich gal's world', *Mirror*, 9 July 2008, p. 23.

——, 'Review of reviews', *Guardian*, 14 July 2008, p. 29.

——, '*Mamma Mia!* saves Welsh cinema', *Cinema Business*, October 2008, p. 7.

——, '*Mamma Mia!* rules UK', *Screen International*, 19 December 2008, p. 5.

——, 'Cineworld revenues up by 4.4%', *Cinema Business*, January 2009, p. 4.

——, '*Mamma Mia!* becomes the biggest selling DVD ever!', *What DVD.net*, 1 January 2009. http://www.whatdvd.net/mamma-mia-becomes-the-biggest-selling-dvd-ever-dvd-review-296.html (accessed 11 April 2011).

——, 'How *Mamma Mia*'s Judy Craymer became the £90m dancing queen', *Daily Mail* (Femail), 3 April 2009, p. 11.

——, 'Maggi Hambling and Phyllida Lloyd honoured', *Pink News*, 5 January 2010. http://www.pinknews.co.uk/2010/01/05/maggi-hambling-and-phyllida-lloyd-honoured (accessed 11 April 2011).

Anthony, Andrew, 'A super trouper for the silver screen', *Observer*, 29 June 2008, p. 41.

Arthurs, Jane, 'Revolting women: the body in comic performance', in Jane Arthurs and Jean Grimshaw (Eds), *Women's Bodies: Discipline and Transgression*, London: Cassell, 1999.
Bainbridge, Caroline, and Yates, Candida, 'Feminine enunciation in the cinema', *Paragraph: A Journal of Modern Critical Theory*, Vol. 25, No. 3, 2002, pp. 129–42.
——, 'Cinematic symptoms of masculinity in transition: memory, history and mythology in contemporary film', *Psychoanalysis, Culture and Society*, Vol. 10, No. 3, 2005, pp. 299–318.
——, 'Everything to play for: masculinity, trauma and the pleasures of DVD technologies', in Caroline Bainbridge, Susannah Radstone, Michael Rustin and Candida Yates (Eds), *Culture and the Unconscious*, Basingstoke: Palgrave Macmillan, 2007, pp. 107–22.
——, *A Feminine Cinematics: Luce Irigaray, Women and Film*, Basingstoke: Palgrave Macmillan, 2008.
——, 'They've taken her: psychoanalytical perspectives on mediating maternity, feeling and loss', *Studies in the Maternal*, Vol. 2, No. 1, 2009. http://www.mamsie.bbk.ac.uk.
——, 'On not being a fan: masculine identity, DVD culture and the accidental collector', *Wide Screen*, Vol. 2, No. 1, 2010. http://widescreenjournal.org/index.php/journal/article/view/39/48.
Barker, Martin and Brooks, Kate, *Knowing Audiences: Judge Dredd, Its Friends, Fans and Foes*, Luton, UK: Luton University Press, 1998.
Barkham, Patrick, 'Oh, what a beautiful life in cinema', *Guardian* (G2), 16 February 2011, pp. 2–3.
Basinger, Jeanine, *A Woman's View: How Hollywood Spoke to Women, 1930–1960*, New York: Knopf, 1993.
Benedict, David, 'Phyllida Lloyd has best of both worlds', *Variety*, 6 April 2009, p. 4.
Bennet, Catherine, 'My, my, how can I resist you?', *Observer*, 7 December 2008, p. 17.
Bergen, Ronald, 'Obituary: Pete Postlethwaite', *Guardian*, 3 January 2011, p. 32.
Bidisha, 'Why the *Sex and the City 2* reviews were misogynistic', *Guardian* (G2), 4 June 2010, p. 18.
Billen, Andrew, 'Catherine Johnson on *Mamma Mia!* and new play *Suspension*', *The Times*, 21 February 2009, p. 20.
Boase, Tessa, 'Every night 10,000 people around the world sing along to the ABBA musical', *Daily Express*, 1 June 2002, p. 45.
Bollas, Christopher, *Being a Character: Psychoanalysis and Self-expression*, London: Routledge, 1987.

Bradshaw, Peter, 'Super pooper', *Guardian* (Film and Music), 11 July 2008, p. 7.
Broman, Per F., '"When all is said and done": Swedish ABBA reception during the 1970s and the ideology of pop', *Journal of Popular Music Studies*, Vol. 17, No. 1, 2005, pp. 45–66.
Brook, Danae, '*Mamma Mia!* I'm a £6M single mother', *Mail on Sunday*, 12 September 1999, p. 37.
Brown, Mick, '*Mamma Mia!* movie spells money, money, money', *Guardian*, 30 October 2008, p. 12.
——, 'Meryl Streep: mother superior', *Telegraph*, 4 December 2008. http://www.telegraph.co.uk/culture/film/3563965/Meryl-Streep-mother-superior.html (accessed 11 April 2011).
Bruzzi, Stella, *Bringing Up Daddy: Fatherhood and Masculinity in Post-War Hollywood*, London: BFI, 2005.
Bryant-Bertail, Sarah, *Space and Time in Epic Theater: The Brechtian Legacy*, Rochester, NY: Camden House, 2000.
Buckley, Michael, 'Stage to screen: Phyllida Lloyd and Dominic Cooper talk about *Mamma Mia!* movie', *Playbill*, 29 June 2008. http://www.playbill.com/features/article/119022-STAGE-TO-SCREENS-Phyllida-Lloyd-and-Dominic-Cooper-Talk-About-Mamma-Mia-Movie (accessed 11 April 2011).
Burnetts, Charles, 'Steven Spielberg's "feelgood" endings and sentimentality', *New Review of Film and Television Studies*, Vol. 7, No. 1, 2009, pp. 79–92.
Calhoun, Dave, '*Mamma Mia!*', *Time Out*, 14 July 2008, p. 84.
Campbell, Matthew. 'The *Mamma Mia!* weddings in Greece', *Sunday Times*, 9 August 2009, p. 13.
Cavell, Stanley, *Pursuits of Happiness: Hollywood Comedy of Re-Marriage*, Cambridge, MA: Harvard University Press, 1981.
Chang, Justin, 'A "Knight" to remember', *Variety*, 14 July 2008, p. 36.
Christiansen, Rupert, 'Meltdown', *Harpers and Queen*, July 1990. Available from *Simply Streep*. http://www.simplystreep.com/site/magazines/199007harpersandqueen (accessed 17 April 2011).
Christopher, James, 'Here we go again', *The Times* (T2), 10 July 2008, p. 16.
Church, David, 'Notes toward a masochizing of cult cinema: the painful pleasures of the cult film fan', *Offscreen*, Vol. 11, No. 4, 2007. http://www.offscreen.com/index.php/pages/essays/masochizing_of_cult_cinema (accessed 15 March 2011).
Cliquet, Robert, 'Major trends affecting families in the new millennium: Western Europe and North America', *Major Trends Affecting Families:*

A Background Document Prepared by the Programme on the Family, New York: United Nations, 2003.

Coates, Norma, '(R)evolution now: rock and the political potential of gender', in Shelia Whitely (Ed.), *Sexing the Groove: Popular Music and Gender*, London: Routledge, 1997.

Cochrane, Kira, 'The mother of all musicals', *Guardian* (G2), 27 November 2008, pp. 7–8.

Conrich, Ian, 'Musical performance and the cult film experience', in Ian Conrich and Estella Tincknell (Eds), *Film's Musical Moments*, Edinburgh: Edinburgh University Press, 2006, pp. 115–31.

Cook, Pam, 'Border crossings: women and film in context', in Pam Cook and Philip Dodd (Eds), *Women and Film: A Sight and Sound Reader*, Philadelphia: Temple University Press, 1993.

——, *Screening the Past: Memory and Nostalgia in Cinema*, London: Routledge, 2005.

Coulter, Ann, *Guilty: Liberal Victims and Their Assault on America*, New York: Crown, 2008.

de Hart, Jeffrey, 'Interview with Bosse Carlgren', *Agnetha Fältskog Worldwide Fan Club*, 12 February 1998. http://www.carlgrens.info/htmlfiles/lyricsfiles/jeffey4th.html (accessed 5 January 2011).

Deleyto, Celestino, 'Between friends: love and friendship in contemporary romantic comedy', *Screen*, Vol. 44, No. 2, 2003.

Dick, Bernard F., *Anatomy of Film* (trans. Ioanna Davarinou), Athens: Patakis, 2005.

Donoghue, Courtney Brannon, 'Rebooting Meryl Streep: from icon to boffo', *Celebrity Gossip, Academic Style*, 23 August 2009. http://www.annehelenpetersen.com/?p=352 (accessed 11 April 2011).

Doyle, Laura, *The Surrendered Wife: A Woman's Spiritual Guide to True Intimacy with a Man*, New York: Simon and Schuster, 2001.

Driscoll, Catherine, *Girls: Feminine Adolescence in Popular Culture and Cultural Theory*, New York: Columbia University Press, 1993.

Dyer, Richard, *Stars*, London: BFI, 1986.

——, *Only Entertainment*, London: Routledge, 1987.

——, *Only Entertainment*, 2nd edition, London: Routledge, 2002.

Ebert, Roger, '*Mamma Mia!*', *Chicago Sun Times*, 17 July 2008. http://rogerebert.suntimes.com (accessed 20 April 2011).

Eco, Umberto, '*Casablanca*: cult movies and intertextual collage', *Faith in Fakes: Essays* (trans. William Weaver), London: Secker & Warburg, 1987.

Elsaesser, Thomas, 'Vincente Minnelli', in Rick Altman (Ed.), *Genre: The Musical: A Reader*, London: Routledge, 1986.

Feltz, Vanessa, 'Give us girls the feelgood films we want', *Express*, 20 January 2009, p. 11.

Feuer, Jane, 'The self-reflective musical and the myth of entertainment', in Steven Cohan (Ed.), *Hollywood Musicals: The Film Reader*, London: Routledge, 2002.

Field, Katherine, 'Motherhood inspires *Mamma Mia* star', *MSN News*, 28 October 2009. http://news.ninemsn.com.au/entertainment/920981/motherhood-inspires-mamma-mia-star (accessed 17 February 2011).

Fischer, Lucy, *Cinematernity: Film, Motherhood and Genre*, Princeton, NJ: Princeton University Press, 1996.

Fitzgerald, Louise, 'Negotiating lone motherhood: gender, politics and family values in contemporary popular cinema,' University of East Anglia PhD thesis, 2009. http://ueaeprints.uea.ac.uk/10577/1/Thesis_fitzgerald_l_2009.pdf (accessed 30 April 2011).

Francke, Lizzie, *Script Girls: Women Screenwriters in Hollywood*, London: BFI, 1994.

French, Karl, *ABBA Unplugged*, London: Portrait, 2004.

Frith, Simon, *Performing Rites: On the Value of Popular Music*, Cambridge, MA: Harvard University Press, 1996.

Frye, Northrop, *Anatomy of Criticism: Four Essays*, London: Penguin, 1990.

Fryer, Jane, 'Mamma mania!', *Daily Mail*, 26 December 2008, p. 12. http://www.dailymail.co.uk/femail/article-1101958/Mamma-mania-We-join-chorus-line-phenomenally-popular-film.html#ixzz1MG2dAGRT (accessed 13 April 2011).

Gant, Charles, 'ABBA hit top note', *Sight and Sound*, September 2008, p. 9.

Gardner, Lynn, 'Arts reviews, theatre: *Mamma Mia!*', *Guardian*, 8 April 1999, p. 11.

——, 'Here I go again: Catherine Johnson on life after *Mamma Mia!*', *Guardian* (G2), 26 February 2009, p. 24.

Gledhill, Christine (Ed.), *Home Is Where the Heart Is: Studies in Melodrama and the Woman's Film*, London: BFI, 1987.

Glieberman, Owen, '*Mamma Mia!*', *Entertainment Weekly*, 19 July 2008. http://edition.cnn.com/2008/SHOWBIZ/Movies/07/18/ew.review.mammamia/index.html (accessed 8 January 2011).

Glitre, Katrina, *Hollywood Romantic Comedy: States of the Union, 1934–1965*, Manchester: Manchester University Press, 2006.

Goffman, Erving, *The Presentation of Self in Everyday Life*, London: Penguin, 1959.

——, *Frame Analysis: An Essay on the Organisation of Experience*, Cambridge, MA: Harvard University Press, 1974.

Goodridge, Mike, '*Mamma Mia! The Movie*', *Screen International*, 4 July 2008, p. 21.

Grant, Catherine, 'Secret agents: feminist theories of women's film authorship', *Feminist Theory*, Vol. 2, No. 1, 2001, pp. 113–30.

——, 'Auteur machines? Auteurism and the DVD', in James Bennett and Tom Brown (Eds), *Film and Television after DVD*, London: Routledge, 2008.

Gray, Johnathan, 'New audiences, new textualities: anti-fans and non-fans', *International Journal of Cultural Studies*, Vol. 6, No. 1, 2003, pp. 64–81.

Hamad, Hannah, 'Hollywood's hot dads: tabloid, reality and scandal discourses of celebrity postfeminist fatherhood', *Celebrity Studies*, Vol. 1, No. 2, 2010, pp. 151–69.

Hanks, Robert, 'Streep meets her Waterloo', *Independent* (Arts and Books Review), 11 July 2008, pp. 8–9.

Haskell, Molly, *From Reverence to Rape: The Treatment of Women in the Movies*, Chicago, IL: University of Chicago Press, 1973.

——, 'Finding herself: the prime of Meryl Streep', *Film Comment*, May/June 2008. Available from *Simply Streep*. http://www.simplystreep.com/site/magazines/200805filmcomment (accessed 17 April 2011).

Hattersley, Giles, 'Mamma mia, there's a fire within Judy Craymer's soul', *Sunday Times* (News Review), 23 November 2008, p. 2.

Hesmondhalgh, Damian, 'Cultural imperialism', in John Shepherd and David Horn (Eds), *Continuum Encyclopedia of Popular Music of the World, Volume 1: Media, Industry and Society*, New York: Continuum, 2003.

Heuring, David, '*Mamma Mia!* makes the leap to the big screen', *British Cinematographer*, July 2008, p. 24.

Hills, Matt, *Fan Cultures*, London: Routledge, 2002.

——, '*Star Wars* in fandom, film theory and the museum: the cultural status of the cult blockbuster', in Julian Stringer (Ed.), *Movie Blockbusters*, London: Routledge, 2003, pp. 178–89.

——, 'Realising the cult blockbuster: *The Lord of the Rings*, fandom and residual/emergent cult status in "the mainstream"', in Ernest Mathijs (Ed.), *The Lord of the Rings: Popular Culture in Global Context*, London: Wallflower, 2006, pp. 160–71.

——, 'The question of genre in cult film and fandom: between contract and discourse', in James Donald and Michael Renov (Eds), *The Sage Handbook of Film Studies*, London: Sage, 2007.

Hirsch, Marianne, *The Mother/Daughter Plot: Narrative, Psychoanalysis, Feminism*, Bloomington: Indiana University Press, 1998.

Hiscock, John, 'Meryl Streep, the singing and dancing queen', *Telegraph*, 4 July 2008. http://www.telegraph.co.uk/culture/film/3555667/Meryl-Streep-the-singing-and-dancing-queen.html (accessed 31 January 2011).

Hollinger, Karen, *In the Company of Women: Contemporary Female Friendship Films*, Minneapolis: University of Minnesota Press, 1998.

Hollows, Joanne, 'The masculinity of cult', in Mark Jancovich, Antonio Lazaro Reboll, Julian Stringer and Andy Willis (Eds), *Defining Cult Movies: The Cultural Politics of Oppositional Taste*, Manchester: Manchester University Press, 2003, pp. 35–53.

Horowitz, Jay, 'That madcap Meryl, really!', *New York Times*, 17 March 1991. http://www.nytimes.com/1991/03/17/movies/that-madcap-meryl-really.html (accessed 15 April 2011).

Hunter, Allan, 'So thank you for the music', *Express*, 11 July 2008, p. 48.

Hunter, I. Q., 'Beaver Las Vegas! A fan-boy's defence of *Showgirls*', in Xavier Mendik and Graeme Harper (Eds), *Unruly Pleasures: The Cult Film and Its Critics*, Guildford: FAB Press, 2000, pp. 187–201.

——, 'From adaptation to cinephilia: an intertextual odyssey', in Thomas Van Parys and I. Q. Hunter, (Eds), *Science Fiction across Media: Adaptation/Novelisation*, London: Glyphi, 2013.

Ide, Wendy, 'ABBA get drabber', *The Times*, 12 July 2008, p. 10.

Irigaray, Luce, *This Sex Which Is Not One* (trans. Catherine Porter), Ithaca, NY: Columbia University Press, 1977.

——, *Je, Tu, Nous: Towards a Culture of Difference* (trans. Alison Martin), London: Routledge, 1993.

Jakobson, Roman, *Selected Writings III: Poetry of Grammar and Grammar of Poetry*, The Hague: Mouton, 1981.

Jay, Betty, *Weird Lullabies: Mothers and Daughters in Contemporary Film*, Bern: Peter Lang, 2008.

Jeffries, Stuart, 'A legend lightens up', *Guardian* (G2), 2 July 2008, p. 10.

Jermyn, Deborah, and Redmond, Sean (Eds), *The Cinema of Kathryn Bigelow: Hollywood Transgressor*, London: Wallflower, 2003.

Johannson, Ola, 'Beyond ABBA: the globalization of Swedish popular music', *Focus on Geography*, Vol. 53, No. 4, 2010, pp. 134–41.

Johnston, Claire, 'Women's cinema as counter-cinema', in Barry Keith Grant (Ed.), *Auteurs and Authorship: A Film Reader*, Oxford: Blackwell, 2008.

Johnstone, Iain, *Streep: A Life in Film*, London: Psychology News, 2009.

Kaplan, Ann E., *Women and Film: Both Sides of the Camera*, London: Routledge, 1993.

Kaplan, James, 'Nobody does it better', *Premiere*, November 2002. Available from *Simply Streep*. http://www.simplystreep.com/site/magazines/200211premiere/ (accessed 11 April 2011).

Karlyn Rowe, Kathleen, 'Film as cultural antidote: *Thirteen* and the maternal melodrama', *Feminist Media Studies*, Vol. 6, No. 2, 2006, pp. 453–68.

Kermode, Mark, *It's Only a Movie: Reel Life Adventures of a Film Obsessive*, London: Random House, 2010.

Klein, Melanie, *Envy and Gratitude and Other Works 1946–63*, London: Hogarth Press, 1975.

Klinger, Barbara, *Beyond the Mutliplex: Cinema, Technologies, and the Home*, Berkeley: University of California Press, 2006.

Knapp, Raymond, *The American Film Musical and the Performance of Personal Identity*, Princeton, NJ: Princeton University Press, 2006.

Kuhn, Annette, 'Women's genres: melodrama, soap opera and theory', *Screen*, Vol. 25, No. 1, 1984.

——, *An Everyday Magic: Cinema and Cultural Memory*, London: I.B.Tauris, 2002.

——, '*Screen* and screen theorizing today', *Screen*, Vol. 50, No. 1, 2009, pp. 1–12.

Landesman, Cosmo, 'Mamma Mia! – The Sunday Times review', *Sunday Times*, 13 July 2008. http://entertainment.timesonline.co.uk/tol/arts_and_entertainment/film/film_reviews/article4304527.ece (accessed 18 March 2011).

Lane, Anthony, 'Euro visions: *Mamma Mia!* and *Journey to the Centre of the Earth*', *New Yorker*, 28 July 2008. http://www.newyorker.com/arts/critics/cinema/2008/07/28/080728crci_cinema_lane (accessed 18 April 2011).

La Sale, Mick, 'Mamma Mia!, a musical vacation', *San Francisco Chronicle*, 18 July 2008. http://www.articles.sfgate.com/2008-07-18/entertainment/17172633_1_mamma-mia-phyllida-lloyd-amanda-seyfried (accessed 18 April 2011).

Lebeau, Vicki, 'The arts of looking: D. W. Winnicott and Michael Haneke', *Screen*, Vol. 50, No. 1, 2009, pp. 35–44.

Leder, Kerstin, 'Audiences talking "fear": a qualitative investigation', Aberystwyth University doctoral thesis, 2009. http://cadair.aber.ac.uk/dspace/handle/2160/2738 (accessed 21 May 2012).

Lehman, Peter, *Running Scared: Masculinity and the Representation of the Male Body*, Philadelphia, PA: Temple University Press, 1993.

Leibovitz, Annie, *At Work*, New York: Random House, 2008.

Leigh, Danny, 'About a girl', *Guardian* (Weekend), 5 October 2002, p. 26.

Lodderhose, Diana, 'Hitting the high notes', *Screen International*, 4 January 2008, pp. 22–3.

Luzón-Aguado, Virginia, 'Star studies today: from the picture personality to the media celebrity', *BELLS: Film Studies Now*, Vol. 13, 2008.

McCarthy, Jenny, 'Thank god for the music', *Sunday Telegraph* (Seven), 13 July 2008, p. 30.

McQuail, Denis, 'With the benefits of hindsight: reflections on the uses and gratifications paradigm', in Roger Dickinson, Ramaswami Harindranath and Olga Linne (Eds), *Approaches to Audiences*, London: Arnold, 1998, pp. 151–65.

McRobbie, Angela, 'Postfeminism and popular culture', *Feminist Media Studies*, Vol. 4, No. 3, 2004.
——, 'Postfeminism and popular culture: Bridget Jones and the new gender regime', in Yvonne Tasker and Diane Negra (Eds), *Interrogating Postfeminism: Gender and the Politics of Popular Culture*, Durham, NC: Duke University Press, 2007.
Malcolm, Derek, 'My, my, how can you resist?', *Evening Standard*, 10 July 2008, p. 41.
Mathijs, Ernest, and Mendik, Xavier, 'Editorial introduction: what is cult film?', in Ernest Mathijs and Xavier Mendik (Eds), *The Cult Film Reader*, Maidenhead, UK: Open University Press, 2008, pp. 1–12.
Maychick, Diana, *Meryl Streep: The Reluctant Superstar*, London: New English Library, 1984.
Mayne, Judith, 'Female authorship reconsidered (the case of Dorothy Arzner)', in Barry Keith Grant (Ed.), *Auteurs and Authorship: A Film Reader*, Oxford: Blackwell, 2008.
Meier, Leslie M., 'In excess? Body genres, "bad" music, and the judgment of audiences', *Journal of Popular Music Studies*, Vol. 20, No. 3, 2008.
Mintzer, Jordan, '*Mamma Mia!*', *Variety*, 14 July 2008, p. 36.
Mitchell, Wendy, 'Making a mega-hit: the key ingredients', *Screen International*, 7 November 2008, pp. 6–7.
Mittell, Jason, 'Smoke gets in my eyes: on disliking *Mad Men*', *Just TV*, 29 July 2010. http://justtv.wordpress.com/2010/07/29/on-disliking-mad-men/ (accessed 15 March 2011).
Modleski, Tania, *Feminism without Women: Culture and Criticism in a 'Postfeminist' Age*, London: Routledge, 1991.
Mueller, John, 'Fred Astaire and the integrated musical', *Cinema Journal*, Vol. 24, No. 1, Autumn 1984, pp. 28–40.
Neale, Steve, *Genre and Hollywood*, London: Routledge, 1999.
Negra, Diane, *What a Girl Wants: Fantasizing the Reclamation of Self in Postfeminism*, London: Routledge, 2009.
Nochimson, Martha P., 'Kathryn Bigelow: feminist pioneer or tough guy in drag?', *Salon.com*, 24 February 2010. http://www.salon.com/entertainment/movies/film_salon/2010/02/24/bigelow (accessed 25 March 2011).
O'Hara, Helen, '*Mamma Mia!*', *Empire*, December 2008, p. 32.
Otnes, Cele C., and Pleck, Elizabeth H., *Cinderella Dreams: The Allure of the Lavish Wedding*, Berkeley: University of California Press, 2003.
Paphides, Pete, and Foster, Patrick, 'The way old friends do?', *The Times*, 26 March 2009. http://entertainment.timesonline.co.uk/tol/arts_and_entertainment/music/article7076415.ece (accessed 11 April 2011).

Pavia, Will, 'Actors' singing experience? Mostly in the bath', *The Times*, 1 July 2008, p. 4.

Peary, Danny, *Cult Movies: A Hundred Ways to Find the Reel Thing*, London: Vermilion, 1982.

Plantinga, Carl, 'The scene of empathy and the human face on film', in Carl Plantinga and Greg M. Smith (Eds), *Passionate Views: Film, Cognition and Emotion*, Baltimore, MD: Johns Hopkins University Press, 1999.

——, 'Disgusted at the movies', *Film Studies*, No. 8, Summer 2006, pp. 81–92.

Plaskin, Glenn, 'Meryl Streep's focus is work: private life is not for sale', *Seattle Times*, 21 September 1990. http://www.community.seattletimes.nwsource.com/archive/?date=19900921&slug=1094375 (accessed 17 April 2011).

Potiez, Jean-Marie, *ABBA: The Book*, London: Aurum Press, 2003.

Potter, Cherry, 'Sex and the older woman', *Guardian*, 23 February 2004. http://www.guardian.co.uk/world/2004/feb/23/gender.film.html (accessed 20 March 2011).

Ramanathan, Geetha, *Feminist Auteurs: Reading Women's Film*, London: Wallflower, 2006.

Read, Jacinda, 'The cult of masculinity: from fan-boys to academic bad-boys', in Mark Jancovich, Antonio Lazaro Reboll, Julian Stringer and Andy Willis (Eds), *Defining Cult Movies: The Cultural Politics of Oppositional Taste*, Manchester: Manchester University Press, 2003, pp. 54–70.

Reid, Melanie, 'These dancing queens can be high art too', *The Times*, 14 July 2008, p. 22.

Rifkind, Hugo, '*Mamma Mia!* The musical: first review', *The Times*, 1 July 2008. http://entertainment.timesonline.co.uk/tol/arts_and_entertainment/film/article4245117.ece (accessed 6 January 2011).

Robey, Tim, 'Film reviews: *Mamma Mia!* and more', *Telegraph*, 11 July 2008. http://www.telegraph.co.uk/culture/film/filmreviews/3556138/Film-reviews-Mamma-Mia-and-more.html (accessed 6 January 2011).

Roll, Jack, 'A star born for the 80s', *Newsweek*, January 1980. Available from *Simply Streep*. http://www.simplystreep.com/site/magazines/198001newsweek (accessed 17 April 2011).

Rose, Hilary, 'How *Mamma Mia!* producer Judy Craymer cracked Hollywood', *The Times*, 28 June 2008, p. 5.

Rutsky, R. L., and Wyatt, Justin, 'Serious pleasures: cinematic pleasure and the notion of fun', *Cinema Journal*, Vol. 30, No. 1, 1990.

Schatz, Thomas, 'New Hollywood, new millennium', in Warren Buckland (Ed.), *Film Theory and Contemporary Hollywood Movies*, London: Routledge, 2009.

Scott, A. O., 'Does your mother know you sing ABBA tunes?', *New York Times*, 18 July 2008. http://movies.nytimes.com/2008/07/18/movies/18mamm.html (accessed 11 April 2011).
——, 'That unmistakeable Streepness', *New York Times* (Arts), 18 February 2010, p. 1.
Shumway, David, 'Rock 'n' roll sound tracks and the production of nostalgia', *Cinema Journal*, Vol. 38, No. 2, 1999.
Silverstein, Melissa, 'Guess what? Women buy more movie tickets than men', *Women and Hollywood*, 11 March 2010. http://www.womenandhollywood.com (accessed 30 April 2011).
Smith, Alistair, '*Mamma Mia!* strikes big screen deal', *The Stage*, 21 April 2006. http://www.thestage.co.uk/news/newsstory.php/12334/mamma-mia-strikes-big-screen-deal (accessed 11 April 2011).
Smith, Helena, 'Money, money, money for Greek island as *Mamma Mia!* draws tourist hordes', *Guardian*, 20 December 2008, p. 3.
Spencer, Charles. '*Mamma Mia!*', *Daily Telegraph*, 27 March 2004, p. 17.
——, 'A mamma of a movie', *Daily Telegraph*, 28 December 2007, p. 33.
Tally, Margaret, 'Something's gotta give: Hollywood, female sexuality and the "older bird" chick flick', in Susan Ferris and Mallory Young (Eds), *Chick Flicks: Contemporary Women at the Movies*, London: Routledge, 2008.
Tarr, Carrie, *Diane Kurys*, Manchester: Manchester University Press, 1999.
Tasker, Yvonne, *Working Girls. Gender and Sexuality in Popular Cinema*, London: Routledge, 1998.
——, 'Practically perfect people: postfeminism, masculinity and male parenting in contemporary cinema', in Murray Pomerance (Ed.), *A Family Affair: Cinema Calls Home*, London: Wallflower, 2008.
——, 'Vision and visibility: women filmmakers, contemporary authorship and feminist film studies', in Vicki Callahan (Ed.), *Reclaiming the Archive: Feminism and Film History*, Detroit, MI: Wayne State University Press, 2010.
——, and Negra, Diane (Eds), *Interrogating Postfeminism: Gender and the Politics of Popular Culture*, Durham, NC: Duke University Press, 2007.
Taylor, Greg, 'Pure *quidditas* or geek chic? Cultism as discernment', in Jeffrey Sconce (Ed.), *Sleaze Artists: Cinema at the Margins of Taste, Style and Politics*, Durham, NC: Duke University Press, 2007.
Telotte, J. P., 'Beyond all reason: the nature of cult', in J. P. Telotte (Ed.), *The Cult Film Experience: Beyond All Reason*, Austin: University of Texas Press, 1991.
Thomas, Deborah, *Beyond Genre: Melodrama, Comedy and Romance in Hollywood Films*, Moffat, Scotland: Cameron and Hollis, 2000.

———, '"Knowing one's place": frame-breaking, embarrassment and irony in *La Cérémonie* (Claude Chabrol, 1995)', in John Gibbs and Douglas Pye (Eds), *Style and Meaning: Studies in the Detailed Analysis of Film*, Manchester: Manchester University Press, 2005.

Tincknell, Estella, 'The soundtrack movie, nostalgia and consumption', in Ian Conrich and Estella Tincknell (Eds), *Film's Musical Moments*, Edinburgh: Edinburgh University Press, 2006.

Tookey, Chris, '*Mamma Mia!* Thank you for the musical! Now for the money! money! money!, '*Mail Online*, 10 July 2008. http://www.dailymail.co.uk/tvshowbiz/reviews/article-1034188/Mamma-Mia-Thank-musical-Now-Money-Money.html (accessed 13 March 2011).

Traube, Elizabeth G., *Dreaming Identities: Class, Gender and Generation in 1980s Hollywood Movies*, San Francisco: Westview, 1992.

Ulvaeus, Björn, 'Filesharing is defended by gigging performers, but who pays the songwriter?', *Sunday Times*, 12 September 2009, p. 12.

Vincentelli, Elisabeth, *ABBA Gold*, New York: Continuum, 2004.

———, 'Meryl Streep: the great pretender', *Independent*, 8 May 2005. Available from *Simply Streep*. http://www.simplystreep.com/site/magazines/200505theindependent (accessed 17 April 2011).

Ward, Audrey, '*Mamma Mia!* overtakes *Titanic* as UK's highest grossing movie', *Screen International*, 16 December 2008, p. 5.

Wearing, Sadie, 'Subjects of rejuvenation: aging in postfeminist culture', in Yvonne Tasker and Diane Negra (Eds), *Interrogating Postfeminism: Gender and the Politics of Popular Culture*, Durham, NC: Duke University Press, 2007, pp. 277–310.

West, Kevin, 'Two queens', *W Magazine*, May 2006. http://www.wmagazine.com/celebrities/archive/lindsay_lohan_meryl_streep (accessed 16 April 2011).

Whelehan, Imelda, 'Not to be looked at: older women in recent British cinema', in Melanie Bell and Melanie Williams (Eds), *British Women's Cinema*, London: Routledge, 2010.

Whitford, Margaret, *Luce Irigaray: Philosophy in the Feminine*, London: Routledge, 1991.

Williams, Linda, 'Film bodies: gender, genre, and excess', *Film Quarterly*, Vol. 44, No. 4, 1991, pp. 2–13.

Williams, Rachel, '"It's like painting toys blue and pink": marketing and the female-directed Hollywood film', *Scope: An Online Journal of Film Studies*, December 2000. http://www.scope.nottingham.ac.uk/article.php?issue=dec2000&id=291&section=article (accessed 11 April 2011).

Winnicott, Donald W., 'Transitional objects and transitional phenomena: a study of the first not-me possession', *International Journal of Psychoanalysis*, Vol. 34, 1957, pp. 89–97.

Wloszczyna, Susan, 'Streep relishes *Mamma Mia!* role', *USA Today*, July 2008. http://www.airforcetimes.com/entertainment/movies/gns_streep_071508 (accessed 15 April 2011).

Wood, Karen, 'An investigation into audiences' televisual experience of *Strictly Come Dancing*', *Participations*, Vol. 7, No. 2, 2010, pp. 262–91.

Wood, Robin, *Hollywood from Reagan to Vietnam and Beyond*, New York: Columbia University Press, 1986.

Woodward, Kathleen, *Aging and Its Discontents: Freud and Other Fictions*, Bloomington: Indiana University Press, 1991.

York, Ashley Elaine, 'From chick flicks to millennial blockbusters: spinning female-driven narratives into franchises', *Journal of Popular Culture*, Vol. 43, No. 1, 2010, pp. 3–25.

Young, Robert M., 'Transitional phenomena: production and consumption', in B. Richards (Ed.), *Crises of the Self*, London: Free Association Books, 1989, pp. 57–72.

Index

20th Century Fox, 94
27 Dresses, 39, 150, 210
2001: A Space Odyssey, 157
10,000 BC, 2

A

ABBA, 2–5, 11–13, 20–9,
    30–34, 41, 42, 47, 72,
    80, 84–86, 110, 120, 123,
    130–134, 137, 138, 145,
    147, 152, 153, 158, 169,
    178, 180, 181, 192, 198,
    203, 205, 212, 226, 227
ABBA-esque, 24
ABBA Gold, 45
*ABBA: The Lovers Whose Music
    Conquered the World*, 24
ABBA: The Movie, 11, 20, 23
*The Adventures of Priscilla,
    Queen of the Desert*,
    11, 145, 181
Alderman, Naomi, 50
All About Eve, 165
Altman, Rick, 98
Amazing Grace, 69
American Graffiti, 131
Anchors Aweigh, 187
Anders, Allison, 45
Andersson, Bill, 96, 102, 103,
    105, 112, 119–121, 173,
    182, 191, 193, 197–9,
    201, 210, 213, 219, 226
Andersson, Benny, 12, 20–4,
    26–29, 31, 32, 34, 41,
    42, 52, 117, 181
Ang, Ien, 132
Anka, Paul, 23
Arthurs, Jane, 171

Arzner, Dorothy, 51, 53, 97
At Work, 60
Australia, 2, 11
'auteur machines', 40

B

Baldwin, Alex, 172
Bale, Christian, 4
The Banger Sisters, 164
The Bangles, 170
Baranski, Christine, 6, 34, 72, 96,
    102, 103, 110, 111, 114,
    117–120, 122, 169, 178, 184
Barmania, Noorjehan, 50
Barrymore, Drew, 97
Basinger, Jeanine, 98
The Beatles, 35, 181
Because I Said So, 165, 206,
    210
Big Daddy, 202
Bigelow, Kathryn, 37–40, 50, 54
The Big Lebowski, 155
Bindel, Julie, 6, 87
The Birdcage, 202
Birthing Mamma Mia!, 45
Björn Again, 11
Blade Runner, 155
Bollas, Christopher, 85
Bourdieu, Pierre, 132
Bradotti, Rosi, 216
Breaking the Waves, 198
Bride Wars, 105, 210
Bridget Jones's Diary, 3,
    46, 146, 189
Bright, Harry, 96, 102, 112,
    182, 183, 191, 193,
    196, 197, 199, 210, 213,
    214, 217, 219, 226

Britten's *Gloriana*, 48
Brosnan, Pierce, 10, 13, 34, 110–1, 120, 122, 123, 140, 147, 148, 151, 158, 189, 193–5, 199, 223
Bruzzi, Stella, 201
Bryant-Bertail, Sarah, 31
Burnetts, Charles, 136
Bush, George, 66
Butler, Judith, 183

C

Calendar Girls, 164
Cameron, James, 39
Carlgren, Bosse, 25
Carmichael, Sam, 134, 96, 100, 102, 105, 110, 112, 113, 121–3, 173, 183, 191, 193, 195, 199, 201, 208, 210, 213, 217, 219, 220
Carousel, 1, 138
Cazale, John, 64
Cervenka, Exene, 26
Chamberlain, Lindy, 65
Charlie's Angels, 94, 99
Charlie's Angels: Full Throttle, 94
Cher, 187
Chess, 41
Chicago, 5
chick flick, 4
'Chiquitita', 9, 102
Chocolat, 214
Christiansen, Rupert, 62
The Chronicles of Narnia: Prince Caspian, 3
Church, David, 158
Cineworld, 2
A Clockwork Orange, 146, 155
Coates, Norma, 85
Columbia, 94

Coogan, Steve, 13
Cook, Pam, 38, 39, 106
Cooper, Dominic, 9, 33, 47, 112, 186
Costello, Elvis, 12
Cougar Town, 207
Countryfile, 163
Coward, Noel, 13
A Cry in the Dark, 65

D

Dance Girl Dance, 53
Dancing at Lughnasa, 68
'Dancing Queen', 7, 9, 10, 12, 34–35, 52, 72, 73, 88, 103, 158, 168, 169, 178, 180, 181, 185, 186
The Dark Knight, 2–5
Davis, Bette, 62, 165
Death Becomes Her, 187
The Deer Hunter, 63, 68, 69
Deleyto, Celestino, 104
De Niro, Robert, 64
Desperately Seeking Susan, 99
The Devil Wears Prada, 67, 68, 165
Dick, Bernard F., 105
Dirty Dancing, 154
Disillusion, 25
Disney, 94
Dixon, Alesha, 163
Djurkovic, Maria, 49
'Does Your Mother Know', 24, 34, 48, 117, 171, 173, 184, 185, 207
Donna and the Dynamos, 30, 47–8, 53, 72, 100, 103, 105, 114, 116, 169, 170, 179, 198, 224
Dreamgirls, 5
Driscoll, Catherine, 216
Dyer, Richard, 61, 121, 151, 155

E

Eat Pray Love, 150
Eco, Umberto, 152
Elsaesser, Thomas, 71
Elva Kvinnor I et Hus ('Eleven Women in One House'), 25
Ephron, Nora, 38
Erasure, 24, 198
Erin Brockovich, 214
Europop, 3
Eurovision Song Contest, 32, 131

F

Failure to Launch, 97
Fältskog, Agnetha, 20–8, 31, 32, 35, 178
Fame, 158
Fathers' Day, 202
female-centered blockbuster, 4
feminism, 6–8, 22, 49–51, 53, 54, 78, 79, 84, 87, 90, 106, 179, 207–9
Fifty Shades of Grey, 150
Fight Club, 146, 155
Firth, Colin, 10, 41, 112, 140, 147, 151, 153, 156, 182, 189, 196, 198, 201, 223
Fischer, Lucy, 211
Fleetwood Mac, 25
Four Weddings and a Funeral, 139
Freaky Friday, 164
French and Saunders, 24
The French Lieutenant's Woman, 60, 69
The Fugees, 12
The Full Monty, 3, 140, 157

G

'Gimme, Gimme, Gimme', 27, 186, 192

Get Carter, 155
'girl-friend flick', 95
'Girls Just Wanna Have Fun', 179
Glee, 5
God Bless America, 69
Gone Baby Gone, 214
Gone with the Wind, 153
Good Will Hunting, 198
Grant, Catherine, 40, 50, 51
Gray, Jonathon, 146
Guaspan-Tzavaras, Roberta, 66

H

Hairspray, 5
Hallström, Lasse, 20
Hamad, Hannah, 203
Hancock, 2
Hardwick, Catherine, 39
Harold and Maude, 155
Harry Potter, 53, 94
Harry Potter and the Philosopher's Stone, 3
Haskell, Molly, 62, 65, 69, 97
Hathaway, Anne, 67, 215
Hepburn, Katharine, 62, 64
High School Musical, 5
Hills, Matt, 87, 141, 153
Hirsch, Marianne, 209
Hoffman, Dustin, 64
Hollinger, Karen, 97–99
Hollows, Joanne, 154, 158
Holocaust, 63
'Honey, Honey', 34, 103, 146, 191, 192
The Hurt Locker, 37

I

I Am Legend, 95
Ice Princess, 216

Mamma Mia!

'I Do, I Do, I Do, I Do, I Do',
    11, 27, 100, 195, 220
If, 155
'I Have a Dream', 27, 28, 191
I Know Where I'm Going, 224
*I Now Pronounce You Chuck
    and Larry*, 12
In the Land of Women, 207
In the Valley of Elah, 214
Irigaray, Luce, 80, 81, 87, 88
Iron Man, 95
It's Complicated, 67, 96, 151,
    172

J

Jackson, Michael, 35, 119, 181
Jakobson, Roman, 100
James Bond, 152, 193, 194
Jameson, Fredric, 131
Jermyn, Deborah, 37
Jerry Maguire, 146, 214
Johansson, Scarlett, 163
Johnny Rotten, 226
Johnson, Catherine, 21, 22, 29,
    30, 39, 40, 44–6, 49, 52,
    77, 78, 206, 211, 212
Johnston, Claire, 53, 54, 97
juke-box musical, 5, 22, 28, 133
Julia, 63, 99
Julie and Julia, 67

K

Kael, Pauline, 64, 72, 73
Kaplan, James, 61
Karlyn Rowe, Kathleen, 207
Keaton, Diane, 167
Kelly, Gene, 187
Kermode, Mark, 14, 15
Khun, Annette, 97, 131
The King's Speech, 149, 196

Kitsch, 12, 181
Klein, Melanie, 90
Klinger, Barbara, 151, 154
'Knowing Me, Knowing You',
    12, 32, 73, 89
*Knowing Me, Knowing You
    with Alan Partridge*, 13
Kramer vs. Kramer, 63, 65,
    201

L

La Cérémonie, 111
Lady Gaga, 179
'Lay All Your Love on Me', 9,
    32, 33, 49, 100, 186
Ledger, Heath, 4
Leibovitz, Annie, 60
Lingstad, Frida (Anna-Frid),
    20–4, 26–8, 31, 32,
    35, 178
Little Britain, 24
Lloyd, Catherine, 42
Lloyd, Phyllida, 5, 15, 16, 33,
    39, 40, 46–52, 69, 77–8,
    102–3, 187, 210, 225
Lord of the Rings, 53, 153
Love Actually, 3
Lupino, Ida, 97
Luzón-Aguado, Virginia, 66
Lynn, Vera, 29

M

'Macarena', 119
Made of Honour, 210
Mad Men, 148, 149
Mad Money, 99
Madonna, 12, 120, 179, 180
Maychick, Diana, 65
Mayne, Judith, 41, 51
Mayo, Simon, 15

McConaughey, Matthew, 97
McRobbie, Angela, 78
Meier, Leslie M., 134
Men United Against *Mamma Mia!*, 150
Meryl Streep: The Reluctant Superstar, 65
Meyers, Nancy, 38
'mia effect', 10
Mildred Pierce, 206
Mills & Boon, 150
Miranda, Carmen, 186
Mirren, Helen, 163
Mittell, Jason, 148
Modern Family, 187, 188
Modleski, Tania, 190, 202
Mommie Dearest, 206
'Money, Money, Money', 29, 44, 187
Monroe, Marilyn, 62
Monster-in-Law, 165
Monster's Ball, 214
Moodyson, Lukas, 12
Morton, Samantha, 50
Morvern Callar, 50
The Mother, 164
Moulin Rouge, 5
Muriel's Wedding, 11, 12, 158, 181
Music & Lyrics, 97
Music of My Heart, 66
My Big Fat Greek Wedding, 210
Mystic Pizza, 98
'My Way', 22

N

The Nanny, 165
Negra, Diane, 78, 79
News Corp, 94
Nicholson, Jack, 167
Nicks, Stevie, 26

Nine to Five, 99
Nochimson, Martha P., 37, 38

O

O'Connor, Sinead, 12
O'Hara, Maureen, 53
Oklahoma, 1
One Fine Day, 173
On the Town, 187
Opera North, 48
Ordinary People, 201
O'Reilly, Miriam, 163
Otnes, Cele C., 211
'Our Last Summer', 192
The Outlaw Josey Wales, 140

P

Papp, Joseph, 62
Paramount, 94
Parker, Sarah Jessica, 101
Partridge, Alan, 13
Pay It Forward, 214
Peary, Danny, 153
Peet, Amanda, 171
Pepper, 34, 117, 118, 184, 207
Petros, 183
Phantom of the Opera, 5
Philip, Michael, 34, 117, 118
Philips, Arlene, 163
Pink Flamingos, 155
Pirates of the Caribbean, 94
Plan Nine From Outer Space, 149
Plantinga, Carl, 134
Playbill Magazine, 51
Pleck, Elizabeth H., 211
Postcards from the Edge, 68
post-feminism, 8, 43, 52, 53, 77–9, 84, 88, 89, 164, 198

Postlethwaite, Pete, 10
A Prairie Home Companion, 68
Pride and Prejudice, 152, 189, 196
Priestly, Miranda, 67, 68
Prime, 207
The Princess Diaries, 215
The Producers, 5
The Proposal, 166
P.S. I Love You, 206
Pulp Fiction, 131

R

Raise the Red Lantern, 137
Ramanathan, Geetha, 54
Ramsay, Lynne, 50
Read, Jacinda, 154, 158
Redmond, Sean, 37
Reeves, Keanu, 171
Repo Man, 155
Rock Me, 34
The Rocky Horror Picture Show, 127, 153, 155, 158
Rolling Stone Magazine, 60
The Room, 149
Rosie, 29, 52–53, 72–3, 96–7, 100–5, 113, 114, 117, 119–121, 170, 171, 173, 183–5, 201
Roth, Ann, 49
A Royal Engagement: Princess Diairies 2, 211
RuPaul, 185
Rutsky and Wyatt, 136, 138

S

Sachs, Andrea, 67
Saturday Night, 119
The Scarlett Empress, 224
Schatz, Thomas, 94
Schindler's List, 137

Screen International, 2, 3
Seven Brides for Seven Brothers, 1
Sex and the City (HBO), 84, 101
Sex and the City: The Movie, 4, 94, 95, 105, 166, 167
Sex and the City 2: The Movie, 94, 150
Seyfried, Amanda, 9, 33, 49, 50, 112, 117
Shakespeare, William, 225
Sheridan, Donna, 6, 9, 29, 34, 35, 44, 46, 47, 51–4, 69–73, 96, 97, 100–5, 110, 112–7, 121, 122, 168–171, 173, 174, 179, 180, 183, 194, 195, 197, 198, 200, 202, 205, 208, 211–224, 226
Shirley Valentine, 156
Showgirls, 146, 152, 153
Shumway, David, 131
Sid Vicious, 23
Silkwood, 6, 63, 66, 68
Sinatra, Frank, 22
Sing-a-Long-a Sound of Music, 127
A Single Man, 182, 196
Single White Female, 99
Sirk, Douglas, 155
The Sixth Sense, 214
Skarsgård, Stellan, 14, 15, 47, 112, 140, 152, 186, 189, 198
Sky, 9, 28, 32–3, 100, 103, 105, 112, 186, 187, 202, 208, 213, 214, 217, 220, 225
Sleepless in Seattle, 173
'Slipping through My Fingers', 9, 50, 152, 205, 206, 208, 215
Slumdog Millionaire, 140
Something's Gotta Give, 151, 164, 166, 171, 173, 206
Sony, 94
Sophie, 9, 28, 29, 30, 33–5, 50, 96, 97, 100–1, 103–5, 112, 122, 167, 168, 180,

183, 186, 187, 191–3, 195, 197–200, 201–3, 209, 211–9, 225
Sophie's Choice, 63, 68
'SOS', 12, 25, 27, 32, 121, 122, 194, 195
The Sound of Music, 138, 153, 155
Star Wars, 153
Steel Magnolias, 98, 99
Stella Dallas, 206
Stevenson, Juliet, 163
Stonewall, 182, 183
Streep, Meryl, 5, 6, 9, 15, 34, 45, 47, 53, 60–73, 96, 110, 111, 113–117, 120, 122, 146, 152, 156, 163, 165, 169, 172, 187, 188
Strictly Come Dancing, 135, 148, 163
St Trinian's, 196
Sunset Boulevard, 165
'Super Trouper', 29, 30, 72, 169, 185, 198
Swanson, Gloria, 165
The Sweetest Thing, 105
The Switch, 166

T

'Take a Chance on Me', 9, 100, 119–121, 173, 183
Tally, Margaret, 164, 171
Tanya, 6, 30, 34, 35, 52, 53, 72, 73, 96, 97, 100–4, 110, 113, 114, 117, 118, 167, 168, 170–172, 174, 179, 180, 184–186, 188, 207, 214
Tasker, Yvonne, 38–40, 45, 78, 98, 191
Taxi Driver, 155
Taylor, Greg, 154
Telotte, J. P., 153

The Tempest, 225
Thank You For The Music, 27, 28, 29, 33
That's Me, 25
Thelma and Louise, 99
The Thing, 155
Thomas, Deborah, 109, 111, 112
Three Men and a Baby, 190
Tillsammans/Together, 12
Time Warner, 94
Tincknell, Estella, 131
Titanic, 4, 154
Traube, Elizabeth G., 190
tribe of women, 39, 42, 46, 54
The Trip, 13
Twilight, 39, 150

U

Ulvaeus, Björn, 11, 12, 20–4, 26–29, 31, 32, 34, 41, 42, 117, 152, 181
Under the Tuscan Sun, 165
Universal, 2, 3, 34

V

Valkyrie, 3
Van Laast, Anthony, 49, 118
Variety, 4
Verfremdungseffekt, 31, 33
Viacom, 94
Vincentelli, Elizabeth, 31, 62
Von Trier, Lars, 47
'Voulez-Vous', 48, 195, 198

W

Waissel, Katie, 164
Walken, Christopher, 69
Walker, Lesley, 49

Walters, Julie, 14, 72, 96, 103, 110, 111, 114, 119, 120, 121, 123, 148, 169, 185
Watching Dallas, 132
'Waterloo', 12, 15, 16, 32, 169, 185, 203, 212
Wayne, John, 62
Wearing, Sadie, 52, 164, 166, 167
The Wedding Date, 210
Westlife, 12
Whatever Happened to Baby Jane, 165
Whelehan, Imelda, 164–6
'When All Is Said and Done', 34, 173, 195
When I Kissed the Teacher, 27
Where the Truth Lies, 196
The Wicked Lady, 223, 224
Williams, Linda, 134, 148
'The Winner Takes It All', 13, 29, 71, 100, 105, 121, 122, 187, 195, 213

Winnicott, Donald Woods, 82, 83, 85
Winterson, Jeanette, 6, 54, 87
Withnail and I, 155
Wood, Karen, 135
Wood, Robin, 201
Woodward, Kathleen, 168

X

X, 25
X Factor, 164

Y

York, Ashley Elaine, 95, 127

Z

Zambarloukos, Haris, 49
Zawiskowski, Sophie, 64

www.ingramcontent.com/pod-product-compliance
Lightning Source LLC
Chambersburg PA
CBHW051519230426
43668CB00012B/1665